THE SHOW

Mark Aarons was an investigative reporter on ABC Radio National for twenty years, and was the founding executive producer of *Background Briefing*. He is the author or co-author of six books, including investigations of war criminals in Australia and the Vatican's role in smuggling mass killers, and works on Israel, Western intelligence, and East Timor. His most recent book was *The Family File*, an account of four generations of the Aarons family who were members of the Communist Party of Australia over seven decades, based on the largest single collection of ASIO files in history.

John Grenville joined the National Civic Council (NCC, also known as The Movement and The Show) in 1957, and operated as an influential but secret NCC member in the trade union movement for a decade. A committed Catholic, he was a senior official of the Victorian Trades Hall Council in the 1960s and 1970s, and federal secretary of the Federated Clerks' Union from 1973 to 1975. He resigned from the NCC and his union position in 1975 in the midst of a bitter faction fight that ultimately tore the organisation apart in the early 1980s. He continued to work for the labour movement, as a freelance industrial advocate for many small and medium-sized unions.

THE SHOW

ANOTHER SIDE OF SANTAMARIA'S MOVEMENT

Mark Aarons
with John Grenville

SCRIBE
Melbourne • London

Scribe Publications
18–20 Edward St, Brunswick, Victoria 3056, Australia
2 John St, Clerkenwell, London, WC1N 2ES, United Kingdom

First published by Scribe 2017

Typeset by the publishers in 12/17 pt Fairfield
Printed and bound in Australia by Griffin Press

 The paper this book is printed on is certified against the Forest
Stewardship Council® Standards. Griffin Press holds FSC chain
of custody certification SGS-COC-005088. FSC promotes
environmentally responsible, socially beneficial and economically
viable management of the world's forests.

Scribe Publications is committed to the sustainable use of natural resources
and the use of paper products made responsibly from those resources.

9781925322316 (Australian edition)
9781925548440 (e-book)

A CiP entry for this title is available from the National Library of Australia.

scribepublications.com.au
scribepublications.co.uk

In memory of Mary Grenville

Contents

Abbreviations

ACTU	Australian Council of Trade Unions
AFL–CIO	American Federation of Labor–Congress of Industrial Organisations
ALP	Australian Labor Party
ASIA	Australian Stevedoring Industry Authority
ASIO	Australian Security Intelligence Organisation
CIA	US Central Intelligence Agency
CDC	Central Disputes Committee (CPA body responsible for internal security)
CIS	Commonwealth Investigation Service
CPA	Communist Party of Australia
DLP	Democratic Labor Party
FIA	Federated Ironworkers' Association
FIET	International Federation of Commercial, Clerical, Professional and Technical Employees
IAF	Industrial Action Fund
ICF	International Chemical Workers' Federation
IFPCW	International Federation of Petroleum and Chemical Workers
ISO	Institute of Social Order (Jesuit organisation in Melbourne)

NCC	National Civic Council
WWF	Waterside Workers' Federation
YCW	Young Christian Workers

In key aspects the Movement was the 'mirror image' of the Communist Party: in terms of passionate social concern, disenchantment with 'unjust' capitalism, organisational structure and 'democratic centralism', conspiratorial methods and secrecy, a sense of apocalyptic struggle, messianism, and a conviction about the historical role of the 'party' and its leader.

BRUCE DUNCAN,
Crusade or Conspiracy?
Catholics and the anti-communist struggle in Australia

Preface

I began work on this book in 1991. The original idea was that it would be a parallel history of the Communist Party of Australia (CPA) and the Catholic Social Studies Movement, known most commonly as The Movement and, after 1957, as the National Civic Council (NCC). An officially endorsed body of the Australian Catholic bishops from 1945 to 1957, its inner-sanctum members among the clergy and laity affectionately called it 'The Show'—a term that I use interchangeably with 'The Movement' in this account.

The titanic struggle between the CPA and The Show for control of the trade union movement and influence in the Australian Labor Party is well documented. So, too, is the biography of Bartholomew Augustine (Bob) Santamaria, the driving force behind The Movement's formation, and its outstanding intellectual and organising director from its humble beginnings in 1942 until his death in 1998.

Although now swept away by modernity and the end of the Cold War, in the middle decades of the 20th century the CPA and The Show were two of the most powerful and influential organisations in Australian politics. They were opposed in a relentless pursuit of their ideals, which, in many ways, mirrored each other. Their members were passionate—even fanatical—in propounding their causes, and were prepared to make considerable personal sacrifices to achieve their political and social goals. While mutually antagonistic, there were many common threads in the ideologies of the two organisations—especially a shared, trenchant critique of modern capitalism and an optimism for the future of humanity springing from their deeply held beliefs.[1]

The differences between the two organisations were, however, also profound. At the time they joined battle in the midst of World War II, the CPA was an integral part of the international communist movement, tightly tied to Josef Stalin's Soviet Union in ideology, practice, and organisational methods. Despite abundant evidence of Stalin's crimes—perpetrated against all 'opponents', real and manufactured—the CPA embraced his Soviet model, lock, stock, and barrel, justifying mass repression as necessary to impose the 'dictatorship of the proletariat', defeat the enemies of the working class, and build socialism.

The Movement was concerned by communism's atheism and, especially, Stalin's brutal repression of organised religion. It understandably feared that a victorious CPA revolution would be the end of Christian—and more particularly, Catholic—civilisation in Australia. Yet many of the CPA's leaders and committed activists were lapsed Catholics who—like their counterparts in The Movement—had first learned social-justice principles from the church's teachings. This helps to explain many of the common threads in their otherwise diametrically opposed worldviews. But whereas communists looked forward to the dramatic and 'inevitable' evolution of human society from 'monopoly capitalism' through the transitional stage of 'scientific socialism' and finally to the 'highest stage' of human development—communism—Show members were more inclined to be backward looking. While rejecting capitalism's gross exploitation of ordinary people, under Santamaria's leadership The Movement embraced a kind of feudal Catholicism that nostalgically saw small landholding agrarianism as central to a simple life based around a fundamental, traditional Christian society founded on the family unit, turning its face against the powerful secularising forces that became predominant in the decades after World War II.

Many events intervened in the more than twenty-five years since research for this book began, not least a serious horse-riding accident that befell my close collaborator and advisor, John Grenville, which left me without a compass to guide me through the maze of the Catholic side of the story. I knew the communist part well, having been brought up in a prominent CPA family, and our plan was to use our inside knowledge of the two political movements to track some of the most significant Australian political developments of the 20th century in as close to a 'real time' history as could be constructed from hitherto inaccessible historical records.

This book is a more modest but, I hope, still worthwhile enterprise. It is not a history of The Movement, nor a biography of Santamaria. There are comprehensive works covering both of those already available—notably, Bruce Duncan's forensic account of the organisation, and Gerard Henderson's life story of Bob Santamaria.[2] The latter, in particular, contains important material reflecting the views of rank-and-file Show members who, by and large, remained loyal to their leader throughout his 45-year stewardship until his death in 1998, although a significant number became disillusioned and resigned in the midst of the Labor Split, especially in New South Wales. The attitudes and motivations at the rank-and-file level of the organisation are, however, beyond the scope of this book.

So, too, is a detailed account of the numerous union struggles that occurred between The Movement and their supporters, and the communists and their allies. For almost forty years, these two forces waged an unrelenting battle for control of many unions—large and small, industrial and craft—and implemented very different styles of industrial policy in improving members' wages and conditions, as well as adopting radically opposed union political-campaigning techniques. There are many histories of individual unions that recount such matters, and therefore they are not included here.

The primary purpose of this work is to provide an analysis of the impact of Santamaria's decision to model his Movement (for it was *his* from the beginning) completely on the Communist Party. This book's major theme, therefore, is the impact that importing the CPA's chief characteristic of the early 1940s—Stalinism—had upon The Show's development, operations, and virtual demise upon Santamaria's passing.

Another central theme explores The Movement's character as an effective clandestine intelligence agency. While others have skimmed the surface of this aspect of its history, this book deals with the subject in a way no others have attempted before, utilising the only Movement archive disclosing its *modus operandi* known to be in the public domain. It also delves into its close relationship with official intelligence agencies—especially the Australian Security Intelligence Organisation—at a depth not achieved in other studies, including by the official historians of ASIO.[3]

It deals with major examples of the protagonists' clandestine operations against each other, using once top-secret archives, revealing both The Movement and the CPA's methods in what have hitherto been deeply buried secrets contained in internal organisational files.

To add a sense of financial perspective, wherever I have cited the currency units of pounds and shillings used at the time, I have inserted their roughly equivalent current-day values.

Modelled completely on the Communist Party

A senior member of Australia's Catholic hierarchy made a momentous decision in late 1942. On the recommendation of Bob Santamaria, a 26-year-old scion of an Italian migrant family running a greengrocer's shop in working-class suburban Melbourne, Archbishop Daniel Mannix took the first steps towards establishing what evolved into an official, secret national organisation, controlled and financed by the Australian bishops—to fight communism in the trade union movement and the Australian Labor Party (ALP).[1] By the time the bishops as a whole officially endorsed this initiative three years later, it had adopted an innocuous-sounding name: the Catholic Social Studies Movement. After it finally emerged from the shadows in 1954, it became widely known as simply 'The Movement'.

It became central to the tumultuous Labor Split of the

mid-1950s, in turn causing bitter divisions among Australian Catholics at all levels, from the hierarchy to the local parish. As a consequence, its operations were referred to the Vatican, which ultimately ruled that a church-controlled body could not engage in the kinds of political activities in which it was involved. It soon re-surfaced as a strictly lay operation—still strongly supported by Mannix and, initially, by the majority of the church hierarchy—renaming itself the National Civic Council (NCC).

Its youthful leader only fully emerged from obscurity in the midst of the Labor Split, but then quickly became one of Australia's best known, most powerful, and influential political voices. In late 1942, Bob Santamaria presented his embryonic plan to Mannix: to build a national movement to match and, over time, better the communists at their extraordinarily effective union organising.[2] Secrecy was at the core of Santamaria's plan: not just keeping his organisation secret from the outside world, but running its far-reaching operations clandestinely.

Appropriately, one of the first outsiders to learn in detail about The Show's aims and organisation was himself well practised in secrecy. A rising star in the Australian intelligence community, he would, like Santamaria, later become well known, despite both men's natural proclivity to operate behind the scenes.

The church's secret was disclosed at a clandestine rendezvous in mid-1944 in faraway, sleepy wartime Perth. By then, all the Victorian-based bishops had given their official endorsement to this work; on Mannix's initiative, Santamaria presented them with a detailed plan in late 1943 (as recorded a few months later in his first annual report of the Movement's work, headed 'Report on Anti-Communist Campaign'). It was still a closely held secret, known only to the chosen faithful. Reporting to his superiors, the security officer described his newly acquired informant as a 'militant Roman Catholic priest' who had established contact through a fellow Catholic working in the Commonwealth Security Service's Perth headquarters. The priest had his own agenda, hoping to obtain information and practical assistance to enable his recently established Movement to more effectively fight the 'Red Menace'.[3]

As these two unlikely representatives of church and state discussed their common anti-communist struggle, the anti-Nazi coalition in Europe was beginning the massive military operations that would ultimately destroy Hitler's war machine. Stalin's Red Army, then widely admired as our 'gallant ally', was slowly but surely fighting its way out of the Soviet Union, moving relentlessly westwards towards Warsaw and Central Europe and, eventually, onwards to Berlin. The Western allies were desperately extending the toe-hold they had grabbed in France after D-Day, and feverishly preparing for the dash to liberate Paris, opening the way for their eastwards thrust into Germany.

At this decisive moment in world history, the church was preparing for another battle—a quiet, subterranean war against communism. On its outcome, Australia's bishops believed, rested the very future of Christian civilisation.

The man who established contact with Australian intelligence was 32-year-old Father Harold Lalor, a diocesan priest in Perth who, a few years later, was to become a leading Jesuit in Melbourne. Over the following years, Lalor emerged as an indefatigable Movement advocate, preaching that the church's fight against communism was a life-and-death struggle. Lalor became a principal organiser of the struggle against 'an existing peril to the things we hold most dear', personifying The Show to many of the flock.[4] His fiery oratory 'at confidential Church meetings' on themes such as '"Ten Minutes to Midnight"—the threat from communist Asia' galvanised frightened Catholics into contributing hundreds of thousands of dollars for this 'eleventh hour, fifty-ninth minute' fight.[5]

It was Lalor who first drew the Security Service's attention to the existence of the bishops' secret Movement, which, he explained, was dedicated to 'a planned anti-Communist campaign'. With a flair for the melodramatic, Lalor made his mark on the intelligence officer. An experienced radio broadcaster, Lalor had been sent to Rome by the Perth archdiocese in 1933 to study for the priesthood, and, after being ordained in 1939, returned home, where he became well versed in the propaganda techniques used to convey to the faithful the imminent danger that communism posed to their church.

Lalor soon emerged as one of The Show's public faces, while its increasingly authoritarian leader remained behind the scenes until forced into the glare of publicity in 1954. A central plank of Santamaria's conception was that Show members had to be carefully screened and handpicked for this clandestine crusade, pledging never to reveal its existence to anyone outside the ranks, let alone to speak publicly of its work.[6]

Lalor and Santamaria formed a close bond. By 1950, Lalor had been admitted to the Society of Jesus (the Jesuits), had relocated to Melbourne, and had been appointed director of the Institute of Social Order (ISO), a newly formed Jesuit social-studies unit. In 1953, the ISO shifted operations to Belloc House in Kew, which became something of a second Show headquarters, supplying the theological basis of the organisation's mission to the faithful, who were guided by the clerical leadership it provided. This was spread through the institute's periodical, Social Survey, which, under Lalor's editorship, 'was virtually a theoretical journal for The Movement', as one historian has described it.[7] Another historian credits Lalor with developing The Show's 'doctrinal basis', in which he declared that members were *instruments* in the Hands of Christ', who 'should treat a note from headquarters "as if it were signed *not* by a Movement executive, but by Our Lord Himself".'[8]

But in mid-1944 Father Lalor's mission was to forge what soon became a pervasive relationship between Australian intelligence and The Movement. It is not clear whether Lalor established this contact on his own initiative or at Santamaria's direction; but, as important initiatives were rarely taken without the leader's assent, it is possible that the order originated from Show headquarters in Melbourne.

At this top-secret meeting, Lalor wasted little time in revealing his own role in 'directing the necessary action' in Western Australia.[9] The man to whom he disclosed the bishops' closely guarded secret was G.R. (Ron) Richards, an experienced intelligence officer who, like Lalor, specialised in communism. Known in local Perth circles as the 'Black Snake' or 'Ron the Con', Richards had been a tough and canny Western Australian Police Special Branch officer who had made a name for himself in the early years of the war, conducting effective anti-communist operations during the period when the CPA was declared an illegal organisation by the federal government.[10] He later rose to one of the most senior positions in the Australian Security Intelligence Organisation (ASIO) after it was formed in 1949 in the wake of British and American warnings that a Soviet espionage ring was operating in Australia.

In a somewhat ironic twist, the naturally ultra-secretive Richards found himself in the public spotlight in the mid-1950s during the royal commission on Soviet espionage, as the man who supervised Vladimir Petrov's defection. By then he was a trusted lieutenant of ASIO's director-general, Brigadier Charles Spry, who later developed a mysterious and politically controversial relationship with Santamaria.

Declassified Security Service files contain fascinating insights into the genesis of The Show. Richards' boss, Lieutenant-Colonel Henry Moseley, deputy director of security for Western Australia, had little doubt that:

> [T]he original approach was made by Father Lalor with the idea of sounding out Mr. Richards as to his and this Service's knowledge of Communist activities and further to ascertain whether this Service would assist Lalor's organisation in fighting Communism.[11]

In his report to Moseley, Richards noted that the priest was 'well known here for his outspoken attacks on the Communist Party per medium of his radio session "The Catholic Answer"', and that Lalor had attempted to obtain information on the following areas:

1. (a) In which specific manner is the Communist Party directing, or likely to direct, its policy towards immediate post-war conditions with relation to:
    (1) Trade Unions
    (2) Youth
    (3) Demobilised service personnel

   (b) What is the real degree of influence possessed by the Communist Party in vital Trade Unions?

   (c) Is the planned control of great industrial unions a political move to secure advantages in the event of the development of a revolutionary situation following on a chaotic post-war state of affairs, through the medium of mass strikes or a general strike?

(d) Would it be possible to successfully curb the present trend towards Communism by the waging of an intensive offensive against Communism by all anti-Communist forces acting in concert, such offensive to be directed against the Communist Party control of industrial trade unions by vigorously opposing Communist Party members or supporters whenever they attempt to attain executive positions and also by attacking their ideology and political theories by means of oral and printed propaganda?

(e) In what manner could an anti-Communist campaign be most successfully undertaken?[12]

Stressing that he had not divulged any official intelligence on such matters, Richards emphatically concluded that the priest's information was 'of important security interest'. In Canberra, the director-general of security, Brigadier William Simpson, was excited by Richards' intelligence coup. A former deputy judge advocate of the Australian army, Simpson ordered an operation to penetrate The Movement because it had 'possibilities which may become of definite Security interest ... Will you please examine the possibility of getting someone into the organisation.'[13]

There is no evidence in the intelligence files that this was done. However, within a few years Simpson's order had been stood on its head: ASIO feared that The Movement had effectively penetrated Australian intelligence. But a relationship was underway between what was, in effect,

the church's own secret intelligence service and Australia's
official intelligence community. In one form or another, this
relationship persisted for the following thirty years.

Brigadier Simpson's enthusiastic response to Richards'
report prompted Colonel Moseley to dispatch a further memo
to Canberra, reporting that membership of The Movement
'set up by Father Lalor ... is confined to followers of the
Roman Catholic faith'; the militant priest 'would welcome the
assistance of non-Catholics in fighting Communism but not as
members of his organisation.'[14]

In this simple sentence, Moseley was prophetic about what
later became a bitter sectarian religious feud, culminating in
its political sequel—the Labor Split of the mid-1950s.

Attached to the colonel's memo was a particularly sensitive
document that Lalor had provided to Richards. It was a top-
secret report on the 'imminent Communist danger' that 'was
handed to Mr. Richards by Father Lalor with a statement that
it contain[ed] a summary of the proceedings of a [special]
conference of Roman Catholic Bishops which was held in
Melbourne towards the end of 1943'.[15] This was, in fact, a
meeting of all the Victorian bishops (from Melbourne, Sale,
Ballarat, and Sandhurst)—convened by Mannix—after which
The Show assumed the *official* status of a state-wide operation.
The document handed to Richards was Santamaria's first
annual report of this incipient organisation.[16] His report noted
that 'an earlier memorandum'—prepared for Mannix by 'a
small group of Catholic laymen'[17]—had outlined 'the reasons
for the special action which has been taken since in this
sphere':

1. At the time there was a landslide in the number of unions
   which were falling into Communist hands.

2. Thousands of pounds of trade union money were obviously being devoted to revolutionary causes.

3. A definite beginning had been made on the policy of bringing the social and economic pressure which a union can exert on its members, to compel them to support Communist policies in the political, educational and religious spheres.

4. The amalgamation of trade unions had begun. It was pointed out that this was the crux of the development of trade unions, from the stage in which they were industrial weapons to the stage where they were intended to become political weapons in the hands of the Communist Party.

5. The probabilities that this development would facilitate general strike policies, especially dangerous in what the Communists term 'a revolutionary situation' were emphasised.[18]

Noting 'the urgency of the situation', Santamaria's 1944 report stated that the 'organisation was accordingly brought into being to deal with the whole problem', just as he had recommended in late 1942. His report noted that 1943 had been a crisis year, 'vitally important' in the communists' plans to amalgamate many key unions under their control. This was to be followed by 'a series of mass strikes' in 'general preparation for the post-war period.'[19] The crisis confronting The Show's leaders in 1943 had forced them:

... to act far more hurriedly than we would have wished ... It would clearly have been better for us had we been able to prepare a strong industrial organisation and to weld it together completely before we were compelled to throw it into action. The rapid development of the move towards amalgamation made this impossible. We were compelled to use whatever forces were ready to hand, without using all the precautions which we would have wished as to the reliability of the people we were compelled to use.

As a result of this, some people were brought into the ad hoc organisation which was established who should not have been introduced, but no serious damage has resulted—to date at least.[20]

Santamaria then spent six pages detailing The Show's partially successful battles against union amalgamations, outlining their increasingly effective opposition to communist leaders in individual unions, and recounting the 'barrage of propaganda' distributed over the recent past. In looking to the future, he promised to rectify past organisational weaknesses in 1944:

In place of the loosely organised federation of active groups (which is all that we had time to develop in the past year owing to the urgency of direct action) we intend to found a disciplined national organisation which *will be modelled completely on the Communist Party* and which will *work on the same principles of organisation*. [Emphasis added.][21]

It was a truly breathtaking aim, for at that moment the CPA was at its peak of political and industrial influence. Steeled by three years of clandestine existence after having been banned by Robert Menzies' conservative government in 1940, the CPA's membership rose from 4,000 to its high point of around 20,000 in late 1944. In keeping with the rigid ideological and organisational orthodoxy then gripping the international communist movement, the CPA was itself modelled on Moscow's ideal structure for a revolutionary party—dedicated to the overthrow of capitalism and the suppression of all opposition through the imposition of the 'dictatorship of the proletariat'. This required a highly disciplined organisation and authoritarian direction by the central leadership, labelled 'democratic centralism' in communism's lexicon. The CPA, like all communist parties, slavishly followed Stalin's every policy directive, and frequently used ruthless political and organisational tactics.

In short, the CPA was a formidable opponent on which to model the fledgling Movement. It is an intriguing commentary on the outlook of the bishops, priests, and laymen who founded and developed the organisation that they chose the communist model as their own. They believed clandestine operations were the only effective means to beat their highly organised opponents, whose outward face masked secret cells dedicated to the domination of the union movement and, eventually, the country.

They also adopted a ruthless approach modelled on the CPA's own, and were prepared to demand—and exercise—an equally rigorous discipline on their members. Logically, ruthless tactics had to be adopted, Santamaria maintained, for this was not a fight to be conducted using even the usual 'rough and tumble' tactics that characterised union politics. As the CPA was using the full panoply of Stalinist 'dirty tricks', The Movement had to follow suit.

Having chosen the enemy's organisational structure and methods of work, from its inception The Show laid itself open to the charge of adopting the enemy's essential characteristics. This would come back to haunt the Catholic

Church and its Movement, as more and more evidence of its own ruthless and secretive tactics leaked out. But when the Victorian bishops considered Santamaria's plan in late 1943, they apparently raised no objection to their Movement being 'modelled completely on the Communist Party'; nor did the other Australian bishops when they endorsed it as an official national organisation in September 1945.

Santamaria's report explained what this intended:

> That is to say we will make our qualifications for admittance very high, admitting only people who are ready to do active work for the movement and to pay a membership fee of 26/- [$89] a year.
>
> The provisional constitution of this organisation has been drawn up. Those two features have been given a great deal of emphasis since we are ready to manage with very small numbers of active members in preference to large numbers of members whose membership would only be nominal.
>
> The organisation will be on a national basis. Its executive will be *subject to democratic checks*. But while it is in power it will have extensive powers of discipline and direction over its members.
>
> We are not unaware of the fact that the existence of such an organisation makes us open to dangers, especially if unreliable members should be included who at a later date would reveal its existence to others. However, we believe that this danger already exists, that the opposition firmly believes that such an organisation already exists, and that *if the existence of such an organisation were later broadcast through sectarian channels it would not even be news*. [Emphasis added.][22]

Apparently, none among the bishops found this last statement contradictory, even self-defeating. Why adopt a secret approach if public exposure was inevitable? Furthermore, if exposure would have no effect on The Show, why not announce its existence from its inception? The bishops' acceptance of this approach was an error of judgement that many in the hierarchy later came to regret, although it has been misleadingly claimed that they strongly advocated keeping their organisation secret while Santamaria felt a certain uneasiness with this approach.[23] A decade later, it resulted in a very public, sectarian brawl that brought the church little credit in many decidedly anti-communist circles. The Movement's secrecy also came to be a distinctly important factor in undermining its effectiveness, as it ultimately became for the communists.

Santamaria's claim that The Show's executive would be 'subject to democratic checks' proved, in practice, illusory. As he rapidly imposed himself upon the organisation, the executive became Santamaria's personal plaything, and the rank and file had no effective say in who exercised power or how it was wielded. He only shared power with those he *selected* to run the organisation's national office, exercising 'discipline and direction' with all the authoritarian traits of the communist enemy, and using their 'democratic centralist' model to wield unchallenged power.[24]

The decision to use the CPA's own methods inexorably assured that the fate of the two organisations became inextricably linked. Perversely, as The Show achieved spectacular successes over the following decade in reducing its enemy's influence in the union movement, the more it assumed its characteristics; and the weaker the CPA became in the 1950s and 1960s, the more The Show's propaganda stressed the imminent dangers it posed—in concert with Chinese and Soviet communism—in order to reinforce the commitment of the faithful who provided the grunt work and financial support that underpinned its success. On the other hand, the smaller the CPA grew and the less control it exercised over trade unions, the more its propaganda stressed the evil role of the church's Movement. The two forces increasingly needed each other to justify their own existence to their followers—and the world in general.

The bishops could hardly say that they were not exposed to the inherent dangers of Santamaria's approach, for his 1944 report explicitly recommended that Show members make the same sacrifices as the CPA's:

> The membership fee is purposely being fixed on a high scale, since we want our members to make the same financial sacrifices for their movement that members of the Communist Party make for theirs. Even on this fee they will be far short of this objective, but for a beginning it will be a good test for them.[25]

Just as the communists intended such financial sacrifice to engender a strong—even fanatical—sense of loyalty, commitment, and discipline to their cause, Santamaria wanted to create a similar atmosphere among Show members. The policy also had its practical side:

> We are hoping that the organisation will be able to pay for itself on this basis. Our budget for the first year is £1665 [$114,000]. When this is compared with the annual income of £25,000 [$1.7 million] which the Communist Party obtains from membership fees alone, it will be seen that our

resources in the financial sphere are pitifully small compared with the task which we face.[26]

Santamaria's assessment of The Movement's annual income proved to be a considerable under-estimate. Before long, special financing drives among ordinary Catholics, businessmen, and other vested interests raised far in excess of these sums and quickly overwhelmed the CPA's financial capacity, which dramatically declined as its membership plummeted between 1945 and 1955 and it lost many unions to The Show's anti-communist campaign. In addition, Archbishop Mannix—the Melbourne church leader with the closest ties to Santamaria—had already given generously, making 'a personal grant of £3000 [$203,000]' at The Movement's inception.[27] Mannix rapidly became one of its greatest advocates, defenders, and financiers; his initial grant ensured that its early propaganda and organising work met with considerable success. As discussed in the next chapter, in 1945 the bishops budgeted £10,000 [$685,000] a year for the work—which increased over the following years—further strengthening its financial base.[28]

Santamaria's 1944 report was firmly rooted in the successful relationship he shared with Mannix. Melbourne was the model to be used nationally, so he recommended that The Show's work be subject to 'the Authority of the Ordinary' (that is, each bishop should exercise control over its work in his diocese):

While there is general agreement among all persons concerned, ecclesiastical and lay, about the desirability of our general objective, there is naturally a wide diversity of views on the methods to be adopted.

Our view, given with respectful submission, is that whatever method is approved by the Ordinary, his authority is essential if that method is to be generally accepted. The success of the movement in Melbourne originates in this fact and this fact alone.

In addition, interstate co-ordination is indispensable. Our fight is with organisations which have a national basis and whose central leadership is able to guide the smallest local branch. If we attempt to fight this with a variety of organisations, without national unity, working without a national plan, unco-ordinated, and acting on a purely diocesan basis, we would be much better occupied in doing nothing.[29]

From the beginning, Santamaria advocated that the church—through the bishops—should be seen to officially control The Movement's policies and finances. The bishops' involvement, however, gave a layman (Santamaria) almost unprecedented power in the world of ordinary Catholics. As one of the leading historians of the Australian church has observed:

[I]t is difficult to recapture the awe in which they [bishops] were once held by Catholics ... In the Catholic imaginative world the authority of bishops was underpinned by Christ; to deny one was to deny the other; to disobey one was to disobey the other. Thus obedience to the authority of the bishops was not a mere notional assent, but bit deep into the emotions. Those who spoke with the authority of the bishops could count on a flow-on from this psychology of obedience. Catholic critics of the organisation were told that their criticism made them disloyal to the Church, at odds with 'the mind of the hierarchy'—almost like traitors in wartime.[30]

There was, however, an inherent contradiction in the notion of the local bishop *approving* the method of work to be used in his diocese while the national executive *co-ordinated* the work from its headquarters in Melbourne. In practice, what Santamaria wanted was the imprimatur of the local bishop to ensure the faithful supported the cause, which, imitating the communists, he personally directed throughout the farthest reaches of the land, effectively usurping 'the Authority of the Ordinary'.

Santamaria's 1944 report to the bishops conceded that a healthy plurality of opinion existed about the methods to be employed in the anti-communist fight. Such notions were soon abandoned in favour of a single, centrally controlled 'master plan', devised by Santamaria and directed by the selected few in The Show's national leadership. In this manner it reflected the CPA, as inevitably it would, having modelled itself so thoroughly on the enemy. In true Stalinist style, The Show's national executive—supposedly 'subject to democratic checks'—virtually came to possess the wisdom of the church itself, issuing instructions from on high to loyal members pledged to carry out their directions without demur. Indeed, by 1956 this had become such a poisonous issue that, in the midst of the bitter divisions inside the hierarchy caused by the Labor Split, one bishop contended that 'a National Executive meeting resembles a Soviet Parliament in which the dictator's measures receive more or less unanimous approval'.[31]

Furthermore, there was a not inconsiderable problem with Santamaria's policy of the bishops officially controlling his Movement: it involved strictly *political* activity in unions and, more particularly as members gained control of major unions, in the ALP. The layman who recommended this approach—and the bishops who approved it—believed that such involvement by the church in the secular world was compatible with official Vatican teachings. Unfortunately, in this they were ultimately disappointed; in 1957, the Vatican ruled that The Show's work could not be done either by the church or even in its name. This edict followed bitter recriminations among the bishops about the consequences of the Labor Split that created hostile factions within both the hierarchy and the laity.[32]

These divisions within the church highlighted another aspect of Santamaria's decision to base The Show upon the CPA: like the Stalinists, he regularly found that events forced him to twist the facts to suit the particular circumstances in which he found himself. The communists regularly had to alter their domestic policies at Moscow's dictate—for example, reversing their early support for the war effort in 1939 (which they had initially declared to be an 'anti-fascist war') when Stalin subsequently decreed it was an 'imperialist war'. Similarly, when Santamaria disagreed with the policies adopted by many of the bishops in the 1950s after his covert plan to control the ALP was publicly exposed—causing bitter divisions in political and church circles—he falsely maintained that The Movement had always been a strictly *lay* organisation, not an official church body.[33] Such dishonesty became part and parcel of his *modus operandi*, just as it had long been for the communists.

In the mid-1940s, the immediate problem for Santamaria, however, was that there were 'traitors' in his midst. As he had prophesied in his 1944 report, there were, indeed, 'unreliable members' prepared to reveal The Movement's 'existence to others'. This was the catalyst for his first great deceit.

2

Truth will out

Sydney's Town Hall was packed with official delegates, members, and sympathisers. There was standing room only, and the atmosphere was electric as the huge crowd waited for the commencement of the Communist Party of Australia's fourteenth congress. It was Thursday 9 August 1945, the day the United States dropped its second atomic bomb, on Nagasaki, Japan, forcing that country's unconditional surrender and bringing to a close the era of what communists termed 'Fascist Imperialism'. The faithful gathered at this mass rally believed that a new day was dawning, ushering in the last stages on the triumphant road to socialism.

It was a time of great rejoicing for Australian communists. Their once-tiny party had developed into a powerful force from the mid-1930s, when it started to capture control of many key industrial, white-collar, and transport trade unions. Its membership had grown fivefold during World War II and, as their congress would demonstrate over the following few days, its influence was felt throughout the length and breadth of the country. From the rural backblocks and country towns, through the industrial and working-class suburbs of the major cities and in all the armed forces, the CPA exercised unprecedented power. Few amongst the crowd doubted that it would grow even mightier and soon replace the 'bourgeois reformists' of the Australian Labor Party as the major force in the labour movement.

Two months earlier, the CPA's power had been demonstrated with an awesome display of organisation and tactics at the Australian Council of Trade Unions' (ACTU) congress, unionism's national policy forum. In alliance with other militant union leaders, the communists exercised a majority of ninety delegates on the floor.[1] Of the five ACTU executive members directly elected by congress, three openly carried CPA cards. All the major policies adopted gave communist unionists great satisfaction, and they looked forward to expanding their influence in the coming period.

The massive public meeting at the Sydney Town Hall that Thursday evening was a 'pageant' for the party's 25th anniversary, celebrated at the zenith of its power. 'The program commenced with music and community singing.'[2] Speakers included the parsimonious Scottish-born general secretary, J. B. (Jack) Miles, an egotistical Stalinist who exercised power ruthlessly and was widely known as the 'old man' or simply as JBM; Fred Paterson, a distinguished and charismatic Queensland barrister who was the first (and only) communist member of parliament; Alan Finger, a medical doctor and graduate of Melbourne University who had been dispatched to Adelaide in the mid-1930s to revive the CPA's flagging fortunes; and Tom Wright, another methodical Scotsman who had been a long-time communist cadre in the union movement, rising to the position of federal secretary of the Sheet Metal Workers' Union.

The real business began the following day when CPA national president Lance Sharkey—the cunning former lift operator who would be elevated to general secretary in 1948—declared the congress open, and proposed the election of honorary presidium members. To sustained applause, his first nomination was Generalissimo Stalin, followed by a who's who of international communism: former Soviet foreign minister Vyacheslav Molotov; Georgi Dimitrov, the legendary Bulgarian who had faced down Hitler during the Reichstag fire trial in Berlin; China's Mao Tse Tung (Mao Zedong) and General Chu The (Zhu De), still four years away from seizing power from the Kuomintang; Marshall Tito, the former anti-Nazi partisan commander who ruled Yugoslavia; Maurice Thorez, leader of the powerful French party; Palmiro Togliatti, head of the even more powerful Italian party; Dolores Ibárruri, known worldwide as *La Passionara* for her defiant stance during the Spanish civil war; and British party leader Harry Pollitt.[3]

Although physically absent, the cream of international communist leaders symbolically shared the stage with the Australian presiding committee. The most powerful members were the triumvirate of Sharkey, Miles, and Richard Dixon, the warm-hearted and intellectually gifted assistant general secretary who had learned his politics in the rugged school of Lithgow's coal mines. This group had run the CPA since a Moscow-inspired purge in the early 1930s, which had begun the process of turning it into a disciplined, effective force, modelled completely on Stalinist principles of 'democratic centralism'. This allowed the national leadership to enforce an iron discipline, right down to the tiniest branch in the most far-flung rural region, while the membership had a notional ability to exercise democracy over the centre.

Their work had transformed the CPA from a tiny left-wing sect with some influence in the union movement into a party that could rightly challenge the ALP for leadership of the labour movement. One historian has estimated that by 1945, communists 'held controlling positions in unions with a membership of 275,000 and influence in unions with a membership of 480,000, or 40 per cent of all unionists'.[4] Communists controlled powerful unions in major industries, including transport, the waterfront, shipping, iron and steel manufacturing, mining, retail, and clerical, and had far-reaching influence in manufacturing and engineering, as well as in many smaller unions.

Operating through highly disciplined, secret 'union fractions', a relatively small but very dedicated cadre of CPA members exercised a decisive influence, not only on the policies and tactics of individual unions, but on the powerful ACTU that established national industrial policy at its biennial congresses. Furthermore, CPA influence was strong in the ALP, the traditional party of Australian workers, and it had well-developed branches in universities, literary and cultural groups, the scientific community, and locality areas nationwide.

Nevertheless, in the previous couple of years, communist unionists had noticed a marked increase in organised resistance to their expanding base of influence. In this, Santamaria had been intuitively correct in declaring in his 1944 report to the Victorian bishops that the communists already knew that a secret Catholic organisation was active in the unions, although he was wrong in declaring that public exposure would not be major news. Communists labelled this organisation 'Catholic Action'. Ironically, so did Australian intelligence. Both the CPA and various intelligence services may have confused the church's official, publicly declared National Secretariat for

Catholic Action with The Movement—an entirely separate and secret organisation with an almost exclusively political and industrial purpose. There was further confusion because Santamaria also held senior posts in both organisations, although few outsiders knew this, or about his unprecedented influence on the church hierarchy.

Santamaria was also intuitively correct when he hinted at the possibility that an unreliable Catholic might lift the veil of secrecy surrounding The Show. The bishops certainly made a major error of judgement when they accepted some of the bland assertions in his 1944 report. Santamaria had assured them that almost no consequences would follow exposure of its secretive operations. Less than two years later, his self-deception was revealed when another of Santamaria's top-secret reports to the bishops found its way into outside hands. Unlike the document handed to Ron Richards by Father Lalor—which remained classified in Security's vaults for almost fifty years—this one went straight to the enemy, who gleefully published it, embroiling the church in the first of several embarrassing public controversies surrounding The Show.

SIX WEEKS AFTER the CPA's fourteenth congress, another significant event occurred in Sydney. Australia's bishops convened on 19 and 20 September 1945 for an extraordinary meeting, held—among other reasons—to give their official imprimatur to The Movement and to vote it £10,000 [$685,000] per annum to fund its operations.[5] Soon after the meeting concluded, Santamaria's 'Second Annual Report' to the bishops 'on the anti-Communist Campaign' fell into the CPA's hands. By year's end, large extracts had been published in a polemical pamphlet ominously titled *Catholic Action At Work*.[6]

In his 1981 autobiography, Santamaria falsely blamed the leaking of his report on an unnamed bishop who, he alleged, had inadvertently left his copy under the pillow in his railway sleeping compartment on the way to the meeting. The document was supposedly one of only thirty that Santamaria had arranged to have printed professionally. It was headed 'Completely Confidential', rendering the security breach even more dangerous, as he noted, although by 1981 he claimed to see the humorous side of the incident.[7]

This story was not new, and had floated around Show circles for many years, long before Santamaria published his autobiography. The culprit's name—Brisbane's Archbishop James Duhig—became an integral part of Santamaria's tale.[8] Duhig's identity finally emerged publicly in 1986 when one-time Santamaria protégé Gerard Henderson—later a critic and his biographer—published Santamaria's account. According to Henderson, the church's secret had been compromised when Duhig travelled by train from Brisbane to Sydney for the conference. When he retired to his sleeping compartment, he apparently studied Santamaria's report, and as he went to sleep, allegedly tucked the document under his pillow. Conveniently for this version of history, there it remained the next morning when, in Henderson's words, the 'ageing archbishop' disembarked.[9] In his 2015 biography of Santamaria, Henderson repeated this version, despite the fact that he had been informed in 2011 that it was false.[10]

Duhig's alleged security lapse became the official—and enduring—account of how the communists learned of the church's secret Movement. Versions of this cover story were widely disseminated among the rank and file who, trusting their leader's much-revered word, believed that the report had been compromised by Duhig when it was discovered in his sleeping compartment by a communist sympathiser in the Australian Railways' Union, who conveyed it to CPA headquarters in Sydney.

In 1996, Santamaria confirmed this fictional account in writing to Catholic historian Bruce Duncan who, innocently enough, cited it in his comprehensive history; it has also made its way into other reputable histories.[11] This version suited Santamaria's purposes, deflecting as it did from the simple truth: either treachery in his own ranks or, at the very least, a disgraceful lapse of security for which he could have been held personally responsible as The Show official in charge of writing and circulating the report.

The truth emerged during an interview I conducted with former senior communist union leader Jack Hughes—whose responsibilities as a senior CPA member had included combating The Movement. Hughes was well placed to know the provenance of Santamaria's report, insisting it 'came from Victoria ... to Jack Blake and then to Sydney.'[12] Blake was a legendary CPA leader who, like Dixon, had been toughened by the brutal working conditions digging coal underground in Lithgow. He was originally from Newcastle, England, where his Geordie name was Fred Airey. After immigrating to Australia in the early 1920s he joined the CPA, which dispatched him to the International Lenin School in Moscow in the early 1930s, where he was steeped in communist ideology, organisational methods, strategy, and tactics. On his return, Airey adopted the cover name 'Jack Blake', a conspiratorial practice then common among senior CPA members in their largely fruitless efforts to confuse the Commonwealth's security apparatus.[13]

The problem for Santamaria's cover story was that Blake was secretary of the CPA's *Victorian* branch at the time he obtained the document in 1945. When the Duhig story was recounted to Blake, he rejected completely the archbishop's alleged role. The truth was more prosaic. According to Blake, the report had been brought into the CPA's office in Melbourne, having been procured from someone inside The Movement.[14] It had not been obtained in Sydney by a communist sympathiser in the railways' union, but had been simply handed over the counter at CPA headquarters, 700 kilometres away, in Santamaria's hometown. Blake was adamant that the source of the document was Melbourne, not Sydney, and that it was passed to him by an anonymous *Catholic* source.

One possible explanation is that someone in the inner circle—a senior cleric, or one of the tiny group of laity with access to the report—disagreed so vehemently with the bishops' policy of establishing a secret, church-endorsed Movement that he thought it best to deliver the news directly to the enemy. This seems highly unlikely.

Another possibility is that it leaked from the print shop where Santamaria had arranged for it to be typeset and printed. The decision to print the report raises interesting questions. If, as Santamaria maintained in his autobiography, the number of copies required was only thirty, why give the job to a printer with the attendant security risk of providing access to people who might be hostile to the church's (and The Show's) interests?[15] Why have the report typeset at all, which was expensive in those days, and required expert proof-reading by possibly unreliable print-shop staff? Why not follow the course adopted for the 1944 report, which was an internal print job, using an old-fashioned roneo machine?

So another intriguing possibility arises: having typeset and printed his report (at considerable expense), did Santamaria order more than the thirty copies he claimed in his autobiography, intending a much broader distribution once the bishops had approved his proposals? He was supremely confident that they would support his recommendations, with good cause. In expectation of receiving their imprimatur, did Santamaria plan to selectively distribute it to the apparatus that he had built since late 1942–early 1943, when Mannix had first provided in-principle endorsement of The Movement?

In support of this possible explanation, it is pertinent that Santamaria's 1944 report had clearly been circulated more widely following its adoption by the Victorian bishops. Father Lalor had received sufficient copies so that he could place an original into the hands of Ron Richards of the Security Service in faraway Perth, during wartime restrictions that made communications difficult. Presumably, Santamaria had subsequently forwarded copies to Western Australia, using church communication channels.

As we have seen, Jack Blake was definite that the 1945 report had come to him from inside The Movement in Melbourne. So it can have originated from only one of three sources: someone in the inner sanctum; someone in the print shop (which would have been chosen because it was believed to be reliable and, in particular, resistant to CPA penetration); or someone who had received a printed copy *after* its wider distribution following its adoption on 19 September 1945 at the bishops' conference. Whichever source is guilty, Santamaria's prediction that an unreliable element might compromise the bishops' secret had come to pass: the truth was out. By December 1945, the CPA had published revealing extracts of his report in its seminal and influential pamphlet *Catholic Action At Work*.

In the interests of setting the historical record straight, Brisbane's Archbishop Duhig is hereby finally exculpated of

Santamaria's calumny, of which he remained ignorant and therefore unable to defend himself. This was not Santamaria's only recourse to the Stalinist trick of revising history to suit his own narrow political and personal purposes.

BLAKE WAS CONCERNED that the document may have been a provocation—a sophisticated forgery to discredit the CPA when it publicised the report. The party was constantly alert to such tricks, which were regularly used by various intelligence agencies over the years. Luckily, an expert was on hand who could verify it. Blake promptly handed it to his close comrade, prominent Melbourne barrister Ted Hill. A colourless, humourless, and methodical Stalinist, Hill was a well-connected and brilliant barrister. He used his extensive contacts and forensic skills to triple-check the report's authenticity. His investigation rapidly confirmed the document's veracity, and it was only then that Blake forwarded it to CPA national headquarters in Sydney.[16]

The CPA leadership quickly discerned its significance. Blake recalled that it was 'like a godsend for us. It explained the conspiratorial background of what was going on at that time.'[17] As Santamaria had predicted in his 1944 report, the CPA was already aware that a Catholic organisation was working actively in the union field. Communists had been fighting an increasingly bitter struggle with Catholic political activists since at least the outbreak of the Spanish civil war in 1936. Beginning in 1943, the CPA realised that the battle was reaching a new intensity, as The Movement's methodical organisation spewed out massive amounts of anti-communist propaganda and challenged the CPA's hold on many formerly securely held unions.

The report confirmed the CPA's strongly held suspicion that a 'reactionary' Catholic element under the direct leadership of the church hierarchy was subverting the labour movement, disrupting unions, and infiltrating the ALP. The battle was immediately joined, as the communists knew they had a major propaganda coup in their hands. The appearance of *Catholic Action At Work* at the end of 1945 had an electrifying impact across the entire spectrum of the trade union movement.

This sixpenny [$1.70] pamphlet was the first significant public manifestation of the titanic struggle between these two monolithic, highly disciplined, and ultra-secretive organisations. The fight rapidly developed into one of the greatest Australian political dramas of the 20th century. It dominated a significant part of public life for several decades, and still echoes down the years, even a quarter of a century after the end of the Cold War. For example, as a youthful student political activist, the future Liberal prime minister Tony Abbott had a close relationship with Santamaria. In his first speech as a federal parliamentarian, Abbott cited Santamaria for inspiring his interest in politics, later calling him 'a philosophical star by which you could always steer' and 'the greatest living Australian'.[18]

The CPA exposé provided a unique insight into The Movement's genesis and early development, simply by reproducing large parts of Santamaria's report to the bishops' 1945 conference, accompanied by a sometimes tendentious commentary. One historian who studied the original document described it as 'twenty-nine pages of closely typed foolscap'.[19] This could not have been the version distributed to the bishops, but presumably was the *typed* manuscript sent for printing. The copy provided to me by Catholic historian Professor Edmund Campion had obviously been printed professionally at what was called in those ancient, pre-digital days a 'printery'. Campion's copy originated from the official church records of the Adelaide archdiocese, and must be the version referred to in Santamaria's autobiography that he had distributed to the bishops.[20]

The report explained that The Movement 'is the name by which it is known among its members, according to its own constitution'. It had been chosen, 'For obvious reasons', since members 'cannot work publicly as members of a Catholic Action organisation ... but working anonymously ... they perform the highest work of Catholic Action.'[21]

However, the report noted a most significant development in 1944, which had greatly strengthened The Show's effectiveness in organising against the CPA in trade unions: the formation of the ALP's factory-based 'Discussion Groups', the forerunner of the Industrial Groups that officially came into existence in NSW, Victoria, Queensland, and South Australia in 1945–46, specifically to fight communist influence in unions. In the mid-1950s, the Industrial Groups played a major role in the internal factional upheavals that caused the Labor Split. Their original purpose—to oppose communists in the unions—rapidly evolved into Santamaria's vehicle for his plan to control the ALP.

Even in 1945, well before the significance of the Groups was publicly discernible, Santamaria understood with clarity the advantages such an official organisation conferred upon The Show in the fight against its opponents:

It is impossible for us to exaggerate the importance of this change for our activists. Previously in the battle against Communism in the factory, they were compelled to act individually. Wherever they concentrated in groups it was obvious the groups were Catholic ... Today they have the cover of the Labor Party. They carry on the fight as the executives of these factory 'discussion groups' and none can effectively question their bona fides. On the other hand the Labor Party has found that it cannot rely on any other force within the factory to ensure the success of these groups than these members.

A bond of self-interest therefore enables our work to function more effectively in the factory.[22]

Little wonder that Jack Blake and the national communist leadership in Sydney perceived Santamaria's document as a 'godsend'. It not only revealed the church's conspiracy, but predicted with unerring accuracy the form the battle would take. The report's admission about using the ALP as 'cover' was most unfortunate. It would come back to haunt Santamaria in 1954–55 when the ALP disbanded the Industrial Groups because they were effectively controlled by his secretive organisation. The Movement was using the same tactics as the communists to infiltrate, influence, and even control the major workers' party.

The choice of words was unfortunate, too, leading to widespread confusion about two *separate* organisations, both involved in the anti-communist battle in the unions. Even today, seventy-five years since The Movement was born, the demonology of the Labor Split labels almost everyone on the anti-communist side as 'Groupers', so-named after the official ALP Industrial Groups. In fact, the Groups were entirely *ALP* organisations, consisting of both Catholics and non-Catholics bound together by their desire to expel communist influence from trade unions. Some stayed in the ALP after the Labor Split, while others left with Santamaria's forces to form the

ALP (Anti-Communist), later the Democratic Labor Party (DLP). On the other hand, The Movement was a purely *Catholic* organisation, operating under the official aegis and with the financial support of the Australian bishops.

One owed loyalty to Caesar; the other, to God. Where these two forces met and clashed, and how such conflicts were ultimately resolved, would determine many major issues in Australian political life in the second half of the 20th century. This conflict even decided who would govern Australia for the seventeen years between the Labor Split and the election of Gough Whitlam in December 1972, after Santamaria decided to use the DLP to funnel preferences to the conservative parties, breaking a long tradition of loyalty to the official Labor Party by the majority of Catholics.

But in 1945 the issues were not so clear cut, and the contradictions and dangers not so apparent to the bishops. Instead they supported their chief lay advisor, whose smooth presentation and youthful idealism, delivered in person during the evening session of their extraordinary meeting on 19 September, persuaded them that the magnitude of the communist threat required drastic, urgent measures. These secret measures imported many of the positive characteristics of the communists' union organising (discipline, a national structure, and tight, secretive union fractions), as well as their essential negatives, especially authoritarianism and the cult of personality with which Stalinism had infected the Communist Party of Australia.[23]

Over the following years, the two opposing forces increasingly came to mirror each other as the church's Movement assumed its own unique form of Stalinism. This was enhanced by its extraordinary successes in defeating the communists in key trade unions and in building an elaborate, highly efficient, and effective private intelligence network, which the Australian intelligence community utilised in its own operations directed against the CPA.

3

An intelligence agency

The Movement's extraordinary success in defeating communists in trade union elections and effectively limiting their influence in the labour movement has been well documented in numerous books and scholarly journals.[1] This success was made much easier by the formation of the ALP Industrial Groups in 1945–46, providing political cover for Show members to collaborate with Protestants (and others) in the ALP to oust communist leaders from many major unions.[2] The best-known campaigns were those waged to dislodge the CPA from the Federated Ironworkers' Association and the Federated Clerks' Union, but there were numerous other successes between 1945 and October 1954, when Labor's federal leader, Bert Evatt, denounced The Movement, precipitating the Labor Split.

These campaigns were successful largely because of the high level of commitment and close attention to detail of Show members and their allies in the Industrial Groups. Nothing was left to chance, with the preparation of well-constructed, hard-hitting propaganda and meticulous organisational effort, including the canvassing of often apathetic union members in their workplaces and, especially, at their homes.

These operations would not have been anywhere near as effective, however, without the vision, inspirational rhetoric, driving force, and authoritarian leadership displayed by Santamaria. His clarion call to arms to Catholics heightened both their opposition to and deep-seated fear of communism. As Santamaria had observed to the bishops in 1945, it was only the well-organised cadre of Catholics who had transformed the ALP's factory groups into a reliable and cohesive anti-communist force. This was due largely to his understanding that, with the imprimatur of the bishops behind him, Catholics could be organised into an effective fighting force.

Santamaria was an early success story of non-Anglo immigration. Despite—or perhaps because of—his modest lower-middle-class roots and his 'dago' background (a term used then, and later, with barely disguised racism by many Anglo-Australians), he had excelled at school, entering university in the early 1930s when tertiary education was mostly the preserve of the sons (and a few daughters) of the wealthy. His staunch opposition to communism dated from this period. As a young law student at Melbourne University, however, he had been something of a fan of Mussolini's brand of fascism, proposing in his thesis on Italian history that 'there is no intrinsic virtue in political democracy which places it on a plane above more authoritarian forms of government'.[3]

But it was the Spanish civil war that had transformed Santamaria into an inspiring speaker and effective organiser of rank-and-file Catholics, drawing the attention of Melbourne's

Archbishop Mannix, who recruited him to a senior position within the church's official Catholic Action organisation in early 1938.[4] Twelve months earlier, Santamaria's focus had turned firmly to Spain, where General Francisco Franco's forces had launched a military putsch against the democratically elected Republican government in July 1936. This—by extension from his earlier critique of democracy—did not perturb the young Santamaria; nor did the mediaeval and exploitative policies of the Spanish church and its support for Franco's brutal tactics, or Franco's successful request for military assistance from Hitler and Mussolini.

Strongly influenced by Franco's exaggerated propaganda about the murder of priests and nuns by the Republicans, Santamaria performed with consummate skill and flair in a public debate with Republican supporters in March 1937, inspiring the numerically superior Catholics in the audience with his passion, sharp intellect, and moving oratory, delivered in his unique, singsong melodious tones.[5] Typical of the deep political divide of those years, he made no concessions to the opposition's arguments, establishing a lasting pattern in his approach to politics: there could be no quarter shown to communists and their fellow travellers, who, as the church's enemy, were to be ruthlessly defeated.

The only aspect of the CPA that he admired was its phenomenal organising capacity, which Santamaria skilfully duplicated and even extended by marshalling the rigid loyalty that Catholics owed their church by directing them—in an equally rigid and authoritarian structure—in campaigns to defeat his enemy in the battles for control of Australia's unions.

In the context of the 1930s and 1940s, such fierce anti–communism would seem unexceptional, especially in light of Stalin's bloody repression of religion in the Soviet Union.

What was controversial was Santamaria's approach—adopted as a young man in his early twenties—of seeking to impose his narrow interpretation of Catholic social doctrine in the political sphere. As his biographer has noted, 'From his first entry into public debate outside the university, Santamaria made it clear that the Catholic Church should draw no distinction between those matters that belong to God and those that belong to Caesar. This was to become a contentious view in Australia, both within and outside the Catholic Church.'[6]

It was this controversial approach to religion and politics that significantly contributed to his bitter falling out with 'Doc' Evatt in the 1950s.

THEIR RELATIONSHIP had initially been positive. Indeed, Evatt had enjoyed a tactical working relationship with The Show after assuming Labor's leadership in mid-1951. During the early months of 1954, he drew even closer to Santamaria, but, as events unfolded later that year, he found himself under sustained attack from The Movement, and felt he was losing control of the numbers and might be replaced as leader by a Santamaria supporter.[7]

Soon after the publication of Alan Reid's September 1954 exposé of the secret role that Santamaria was playing in Australian politics as the virtually anonymous leader of The Movement, Evatt went on the attack. The essence of his allegation was that it was an outside force, bent on subverting the ALP by adopting 'methods which strikingly resemble both Communist and Fascist infiltration of larger groups' so as to gain control of the party's political and industrial wings, solely on the basis of what he charged was its 'extreme anti-communism'.[8] Santamaria disputed Evatt's assertion that he aimed to control the ALP,[9] but the evidence supports the basic thrust of Evatt's claim: he was correct in asserting that Santamaria secretly wanted to control the ALP; he was wrong, though, about the motive.

There is considerable evidence indicating that Santamaria had been thinking along these lines for many years prior to Evatt's statement. For example, Santamaria's 'Memorandum on the Movement' (written around 1947) spelled out that its aims included extending 'the fight from the trade unions into every organ of public and civic life—political parties, ex-servicemen's organisations, community centre movements, cultural and educational bodies etc.'[10] Catholic historian Father Bruce Duncan quotes from a September 1950 memorandum, written 'presumably' by Santamaria, which 'predicted that, if the Movement continued, "it can be confidently stated" that "soon the programme of the A.L.P. will be in harmony with Christian Social teaching".' In May 1952, The Movement's national conference was so confident of its power within the ALP that it 'determined "to secure control of the [ALP] Federal Executive and Conference by men with a satisfactory policy by July 1952 at latest". Movement members were to try to influence pre-selection for state and federal candidates, and to promote its economic policy.'[11]

In December 1952, Santamaria wrote an extraordinary 'personal and confidential' letter to his closest supporter among the bishops, Melbourne's Daniel Mannix. Santamaria clearly believed that The Movement had achieved much of its original goal of winding back the CPA's position in major trade unions, nationally in the ACTU and in state and regional labour councils. 'The result ... is roughly that the Communist Party, at the present moment, cannot hope to seize control of Australia by revolutionary means', he declared, 'and ... the

Communist grip on the political Labor movement has been checked ... In one sense, therefore, the ... Movement has fulfilled its immediate task.'[12]

Santamaria had no intention of disbanding The Show, however. Indeed, he had another, even more breathtaking, task in mind: transforming the Labor Party into a Catholic-dominated political machine, based on the church's social teachings. He informed Mannix that the previous three years had opened up possibilities that were 'far wider than those of the defensive battle against communism', outlining how control of trade unions affiliated to the ALP made it 'inevitable that as our people obtained prominence in the unions, they would rise also in the political field'.[13] He predicted that:

The ... Movement should within a period of five or six years be able to completely transform the leadership of the Labor movement, and to introduce into Federal and State spheres large numbers of members who ... should be able to implement a Christian social program in both the State and Federal spheres ... This is the first time that such a work has become possible in Australia and, as far as I can see, in the Anglo-Saxon world since the advent of Protestantism.[14]

This letter was potentially dynamite. If it became widely known inside the church and the ALP, it would have sparked bitter differences among Catholics as to the wisdom of its course, and released bitter sectarian feelings among the Protestant majority. How did Mannix respond? As one former Movement priest observed, 'There is no evidence that Archbishop Mannix sent this letter on to the other bishops in 1952 or later; or that the bishops discussed this plan and gave the Movement this extended new mandate to actively influence the political sphere. It seems that it just gradually expanded into this new field.'[15]

Had the issue been referred to the bishops as a whole, such an audacious, strictly party-political venture would certainly have caused considerable controversy and would probably have been rejected if considered at the bishops' regular national conference. This is demonstrated by the motion carried by nineteen votes to six at the January 1956 conference that 'the Movement as an organisation is not a political party nor should it attempt to dominate any political party'.[16] Furthermore, while it is only possible to speculate on this, if the bishops had been apprised of Santamaria's assessment that the 'Movement has fulfilled its immediate task', a majority may well have considered it appropriate to disband The Show—not endorse its expansion into party politics. If Mannix had formally referred this letter to the bishops' conference, it is likely that the course of Australian politics in the second half of the 20th century could thereby have been dramatically different.

In pursuing his strictly political—as opposed to industrial—goals, Santamaria was extremely loose with the truth, even within the ultra-secret confines of inner-Movement forums. For example, in January 1953, a meeting of senior lay and clerical members met to discuss 'pressing problems which their strategy had given rise to'. The central issue concerned whether the bishops' 1945 mandate for The Show included extending its activities into party politics. Santamaria's version of what the bishops had discussed and resolved was at best a revisionist history, and at worst a conscious lie to convince his colleagues of the legitimacy of his ventures into party politics. He claimed that the bishops had agreed to his proposition that The Movement should fight communist activities beyond the unions—that it was given a mandate to extend its remit outside the industrial arena. In a further sleight of hand, he claimed that the organisation's constitution was never submitted to the bishops' 1945 meeting. Neither assertion was true, as the minutes of that meeting make clear: the bishops specifically approved the *'Industrial* Movement' [emphasis added] and nothing further, and the constitution was definitely before them, as it was twice amended, most significantly, to specify that The Movement was to be controlled by a committee of bishops in as far as policy and finance were concerned.[17]

Santamaria's dissembling on these issues had substantial political repercussions. For example, the former Movement priest quoted above was an eyewitness to the consequences of Mannix's decision to slyly give his personal imprimatur to Santamaria's plan without consulting his colleagues. In mid-1954, Father Harold Lalor—the priest who had revealed The Movement's plans to the Security Service a decade earlier and had then become one of Santamaria's close circle in Melbourne—visited his old home base of Perth. A gathering of priests was convened to hear Lalor's analysis of the current state of the struggle, which this ex-Movement priest attended. He remembered, 'quite distinctly', Lalor's words: 'We now have the numbers to replace Dr Evatt, Stan Keon will be the new leader and the next Prime Minister of Australia.'[18]

This was three months before Evatt made his claims about the Movement's intentions towards the ALP. Keon was a staunch anti-communist and, although not officially a member, was a strong Show supporter, who had been promoted by Santamaria as his favoured candidate to replace Evatt as ALP leader. Understandably, he was one of those subsequently accused by Evatt of disloyalty to Labor and of being under Santamaria's control.[19]

Evatt's claim that The Movement's aim was to control the

ALP has been shown—with the benefit of access to several key internal Movement documents and, especially, Santamaria's letter to Mannix—to be correct.[20] He was wrong, though, that this strategy was based exclusively on the negative motive of anti-communism. Santamaria's secret plan to gain control of the party was in order to implement his positive agenda—to transform it into one based on *Catholic* social doctrines. That he could foreshadow such a far-reaching project stemmed directly from The Show's organisational model—based, as Santamaria had designed it, on the CPA.

Santamaria was well informed about the communists' successful penetration of the ALP over many years. Indeed, in the late 1930s the CPA's clandestine influence in the New South Wales ALP had been so powerful that it effectively controlled the numbers on the floor of the 1939 state conference, and was able to elect the key officials and control the state executive. This was achieved by numerous 'double card carriers' whose loyalty secretly lay with the CPA, while publicly they appeared to be staunch ALP members. Communists had also built a powerful machine in the Victorian ALP, and played influential roles in other states.[21]

By 1952, Santamaria had accumulated a decade of practice in clandestine operations, copied straight from the communists' manual. His experience was significantly enhanced by The Show's active collaboration with Australian intelligence services. Much has been written about Santamaria's outstanding intellect and organising abilities that saw the dramatic turnaround in the CPA's fortunes in the unions. Far less, however, has been recorded of the methods used to achieve this.

FROM ITS INCEPTION, The Movement was an intelligence-gathering operation. As seen earlier, its first port of call for this purpose was Australian intelligence. Father Lalor had made contact with the wartime Security Service in Perth in mid-1944, seeking assistance in the fight against communism. He was not the only Movement priest operating in this murky, but fruitful, arena.

Lalor's counterpart in The Show's Sydney branch was Reverend Dr Patrick (Paddy) Ryan, who operated from the Missionaries of the Sacred Heart in Kensington, which, like Belloc House in Melbourne, was something of a second Movement headquarters. Like Lalor, Ryan was a 'militant Roman Catholic priest', an anti-communist crusader, and skilled propagandist. Like Lalor, he had studied for the priesthood in Rome, where he was ordained in 1929. The two priests shared a love of the melodramatic; Ryan's powerful lectures on the dangers that communism posed to the church invariably roused the already fearful faithful. He was also courageous, taking the enemy head-on in legendary debates with prominent CPA leaders, most notably in a famous stoush in 1948 with lifelong Stalinist Edgar Ross in front of a capacity crowd of 30,000 at Sydney's Rushcutters Bay stadium.[22]

Ryan had previously been in charge of Sydney's Catholic Social Bureau, which was a centre of anti-communist activism. The bureau morphed into The Movement's Sydney branch following the bishops' 1945 decision to officially sponsor and finance it. He was appointed as chaplain to The Show's Sydney branch, a post he held until 1953, when he was unceremoniously dumped by Bishop Patrick Lyons (formerly of Melbourne, where he had been Mannix's secretary), causing deep bitterness among the Sydney membership. Ironically, his replacement was Father Lalor, also seen by Sydney as a

'Melbourne loyalist'. A bitter seed had been planted in the fertile ground of the traditional Sydney–Melbourne rivalry.[23]

In effect, Ryan was the key figure in The Movement's Sydney operation, with a seat at the national conference, where at times he pursued a somewhat provincial, Sydney-centric line. Sydney Archbishop (Cardinal after 1946) Norman Gilroy effectively abdicated his responsibilities for the local organisation to Ryan (and for the national body, too, despite his membership of the bishops' committee overseeing The Show's work, which he did not attend).[24] After his sacking in 1953, Ryan emerged as a bitter internal critic of Santamaria, and played a major role in convincing most Sydney Catholics to follow Gilroy's edict to remain loyal to the ALP at the time of the Labor Split, while Santamaria advocated in favour of the breakaway 'anti-communist' party, later the Democratic Labor Party.[25]

While he ran the Sydney branch, however, Ryan was a champion of Santamaria's model for The Movement, justifying the use of strict secrecy and underhanded tactics on the basis that if the communists used unsavoury methods, so could they. In Ryan's world, the CPA's operational model was a mirror of his own. Santamaria's decision to base The Show—lock, stock, and barrel—upon the CPA was his guiding principle. For example, Ryan approved of the distribution of fake ballot papers in union elections—a tactic used by the CPA on occasions, most notoriously in the ironworkers' union—and the stacking of ALP branches, as well as sending bogus members to get the numbers at hotly contested union and university faculty meetings. Anything the communists were doing to impose their control, Ryan argued, The Show was morally justified in copying.[26]

Ryan shared another thing in common with his eventual

replacement as chaplain to the Sydney Movement: like Lalor in Perth, he was the initial point man for relations with the intelligence services in NSW. ASIO's highly censored files on 'Catholic Action' (synonymous with The Movement in this context) clearly establish that, from the early 1940s, Ryan had maintained regular high-level contacts with numerous intelligence agencies. These included ASIO's predecessors, the Commonwealth Investigation Service (CIS, which continued to operate for a few years after ASIO's creation in 1949), and the Commonwealth Security Service (which was active during World War II), as well as the NSW Police Special Branch, Naval Intelligence, and, of course, ASIO itself. This was an impressive array of open doors for a simple Sacred Heart priest to be free to walk through.[27]

One report by the senior section officer of ASIO's B1 (counter-subversion) section in Sydney provides revealing insights into the high-level contacts Ryan had with intelligence agencies. This officer had been recruited to ASIO from the CIS, where his duties during the second half of the 1940s included regular visits to Movement headquarters. His 'dealings were with Dr. Ryan', he reported, and two others 'whose names I do not now recall'. Brigadier Frederick 'Black Jack' Galleghan who, as deputy director-general of security for NSW, ran the Sydney CIS office, and William Barnwell (who later joined ASIO) 'were in contact with Catholic Action in that period also', as were at least three other CIS officers. On some occasions, he recalled, Ryan visited CIS headquarters for meetings with his contacts, who also regularly communicated with Ryan by telephone.[28]

That a civilian leader of a private outfit had such regular high-level contacts demonstrated that the two organisations worked closely on anti-communist operations. Ryan clearly had intelligence of significance to offer the CIS, which, in turn, provided Ryan with information of assistance to The Movement's anti-communist operations. For example, ASIO collected intelligence from its agents indicating that Ryan's CIS contacts—especially with a number of Catholics—were very fruitful. One agent reported that Ryan frequently quoted directly from documents seized in security raids on communists conducted in the early years of World War II (during the CPA's period of illegality under Robert Menzies' federal government).[29]

The files indicate that ASIO, however, sometimes had a somewhat ambivalent attitude towards The Show. The officers with the closest overview of this relationship were delighted with the often-detailed information about the activities of communists supplied by several officially registered agents (who received regular payments for their work, although these were deducted from their Movement salaries). This included obtaining some intelligence gems that were highly regarded at ASIO headquarters in Melbourne.

On the other hand, ASIO was worried by several aspects of The Movement's *modus operandi*. At least one Movement liaison agent with ASIO was viewed as being unscrupulous, and some of his information was classified as unreliable and biased, sometimes deliberately so. It was also quickly established that other wings of the intelligence community had been unprofessional in their relationship—for example, sharing intelligence on a two-way basis by providing official information instead of simply receiving The Movement's. Having established this precedent, Ryan wanted to continue on the same basis with ASIO. Of even greater concern, however, was that the bad habits of these agencies had been imported into ASIO, which had recruited some of their officers.

As troubling as this background was, the early 1950s was a critical period for ASIO in its elaborate operations to penetrate the CPA. By 1953, the first wave of ASIO's agents recruited for this purpose were showing tell-tale signs of exhaustion from the arduous, nerve-racking tasks they were required to undertake. There was an urgent need to replenish this pool. The Show offered good prospects, which ASIO was keen to exploit. There were, however, fears that The Movement might utilise the relationship to penetrate ASIO.

The three ASIO officers most concerned with this relationship were the director-general, Charles Spry; the controller of the Special Services Section (S section, which recruited, trained, and ran ASIO's registered agents); and the NSW regional director, Ron Richards. Having established the first officially recorded contact between the intelligence community and The Movement in Perth in 1944, Richards had been recruited to ASIO and rapidly promoted by Spry to head the critical NSW operation in Sydney, which was also the CPA's national headquarters as well as the base of its largest and most effective state branch.

In 1951, ASIO had the first inklings of problems with the relationship. In late November, Richards addressed a memo to Spry, marked to the attention of Q section (the predecessor of S Section, which ran ASIO's paid agents). Attached to this memo were two reports concerning an agent recruited from The Movement who had worked for the NSW office during 1950. One was written by Richards' senior section officer in charge of running agents (a former CIS officer), and the other by the senior field officer responsible for day-to-day liaison with agents (an ex-Police Special Branch officer).

Their judgement of The Movement liaison agent was not complimentary: not only had his intelligence proved to be unreliable on occasions, but in one instance he had proposed a joint operation with ASIO to commit burglary to obtain supposedly important information. He had also suggested that if ASIO raided a prominent communist's house, he would arrange to have firearms planted there. 'In view of this statement', commented the ASIO officer, 'I considered him to be unscrupulous.' In his favour, when secretly tested by being asked to gather intelligence on a specified individual, his work had been found 'totally correct'. This was established because Special Branch simultaneously subjected the target to 'special surveillance' that corroborated the Movement agent's own information supplied to his ASIO handler.

In response to Richards' memo, in early December 1951, Spry warned ASIO's Papua New Guinea office of the agent's shortcomings (as he had relocated there and was offering his services to the local office).[30] The man was deemed unsuitable for ASIO's methodical and more professional approach towards the invasive surveillance and dirty tricks it regularly used against communists. But even greater difficulties were just around the corner.

In September 1952, Spry and Richards were diverted from their highest priority—investigating the Soviet spy ring that had operated in Australia in the 1940s with the assistance of several CPA members. Instead they were consumed by a 'special investigation ... into irregularities and improper agent control' at ASIO's Edgecliff office in Sydney, centred on the agents employed by ASIO as official conduits to The Movement.[31]

Spry and Richards were deeply worried by the implications of several reports submitted by senior ASIO staff indicating that official intelligence had been obtained by The Show over the previous several years, due to unprofessional methods adopted by officers of both ASIO and its predecessors. This investigation stretched over several years and caused continuing doubts. The intelligence supplied by The Movement—and its potential to provide agents capable of penetrating the CPA—eventually overrode such concerns.

The nub of the quandary was set out in a closely typed five-page memo to Richards from the officer in charge of New South Wales's S section:

> It will be evident that Catholic Action [The Movement], *which is itself an intelligence agency,* by liaison with Organizations, can effect a penetration, especially in the circumstances as set out in paragraph 2 where there is an unorganized liaison and when the degree of information supplied to it would vary according to the discretion of each of the several Officers in contact with it. [Emphasis added.][32]

The danger identified in 'paragraph 2' concerned the 'unorganised fashion' in which officers of the CIS, Naval Intelligence, and Special Branch conducted their liaison with The Show. For example, this officer knew that The Movement's liaison agent with the CIS had improperly obtained CIS intelligence from other agencies to which it had been sent officially. He established this because on at least one occasion The Movement agent had subsequently reproduced the exact same intelligence for the CIS, more or less word for word, that had been supplied by the CIS to other agencies. Furthermore, he had established that The Show had disseminated CIS information to other intelligence agencies, which, in turn, channelled it back to CIS as if it were fresh intelligence. 'While at C.I.S., in about 1948,' he wrote, 'I made a test by supplying [The Movement agent] with some imaginary information and

I later found that identical information was received back at C.I.S., having been channelled to it by Naval Intelligence who obviously had obtained it from Catholic Action.'[33]

This was a deeply worrying aspect of the relationship; it meant that The Movement's sometimes amateurish, bull-at-the-gate, methods could allow misleading, even completely incorrect, information to be circulated throughout the Australian intelligence community.

On the other side of the balance sheet, on many occasions The Show supplied priceless intelligence. A recent example cited in this report concerned three shorthand notebooks 'which contained a record of high level [CPA] meetings' taken by a leading party stenographer.[34] Such a windfall would have provided an eagle's-eye view of the inner workings, current thinking, and strategies of ASIO's principal target.

This officer also reported that the chaotic methods used by ASIO's predecessors were reproduced in ASIO's early days, with a number of officers acting 'independently and on their own initiative' before 'organised liaison' was arranged by Bob Wake, Richards' predecessor as head of ASIO in NSW. Wake had visited The Movement's headquarters and arranged for a 'liaison officer to provide ASIO with information'.[35] ASIO also arranged to regularly pay the liaison agent £2 a week [$100]—a tidy sum in the early 1950s, when the average wage was £10 a week—which was deducted from his Movement salary.[36] Father Ryan approved the arrangement, establishing a formal relationship that lasted for over two decades.

Ryan, however, was not satisfied with a key element of this link. It was not reciprocal—The Show was handing over truckloads of information, but ASIO provided nothing in return. As instructed (presumably by Ryan or Kevin Davis, the lay official in charge of the Sydney office), the liaison agent requested that this be rectified and that ASIO adopt the precedent set by other agencies and provide The Movement with intelligence—strictly on an 'unofficial' basis. In making this request, the agent stated that his predecessor 'had much better access to Government Departments than he himself has at present', including 'open slather with the Navy files and all the usual Departments like Immigration'.

The officer, knowing that ASIO's policy differed from such agencies, cautiously undertook to pass on this request to his superiors. But he also probed as to why The Show might need such assistance, and 'the nature of the enquiries for which he would require information from this Organization'. The Movement agent's response was revealing:

> He was reluctant to answer this particular enquiry, but, after some hesitation, stated that from time to time enquiries were received from Rome and from the Archbishop and 'other higher ups'. He said that he would tell me in strict confidence that recently Dr. BURTON had approached the Archbishop and requested him to arrange for the cessation of adverse propaganda emanating from Catholic sources. As a result of this, the Archbishop had enquired from [Movement] headquarters as to BURTON's background, and the Archbishop was, in turn, informed that BURTON's associations were such that his wishes should not be acceded to. The source had asked me a few weeks previously as to whether or not BURTON was known as a Communist, but had of course not informed me of the reason for his enquiry.

This was an extraordinary conversation at several levels. John Burton had been the head of the department of external affairs when Bert Evatt was the minister during and after

World War II. The principal reason for ASIO's existence was to investigate the spy ring that had operated in the department during Burton's tenure, funnelling top-secret information to the Soviets. At another level, the direct line of communication between the archbishop (Sydney's Norman Gilroy) and The Movement's intelligence apparatus was indicative of the church's knowledge (and presumably approval) of spying as a means to a political end. The mention of inquiries from Rome implied that at some level, at least, the Vatican knew and approved of The Show's activities, although it is probable that the agent was deliberately exaggerating in order to elicit ASIO's co-operation. And the Vatican would have been more focussed on problems nearer to home, especially as the Italian Communist Party was a powerful force in domestic politics.

Despite the sorry picture that emerged from this long and detailed report, the author was sufficiently impressed with this particular Movement liaison agent to conclude that his intelligence was 'productive and worthwhile'.[37] At headquarters, Spry agreed that 'considerable worthwhile information' had been provided by The Show's liaison agent, but was emphatic that 'no two-way information can be considered', even suggesting that 'it would be acceptable to drop the Source should demands become embarrassing'.[38]

Show headquarters was not impressed with this ruling, throwing a monumental tantrum and even threatening to terminate 'the remuneration so that relations between ASIO and Catholic Action would be less formal', although 'this did not mean they would be severed altogether'. The Movement liaison agent expressed the view that he could understand ASIO's reluctance to 'exchange information with every contact, but he felt his employer would believe he would be an exception'.[39] After all, his employer was the Catholic

Church, which conveyed God's wishes, at least in the minds of Movement adherents.

Relations became decidedly frosty. They would get a lot worse, but *realpolitik* considerations would sustain it through several crises.

4

The Show and ASIO

ASIO's refusal to engage in two-way intelligence-sharing with The Movement did not terminate the relationship, but it did truncate it considerably. Spry's rejection of the proposition caused a great deal of sulking at Show headquarters for many months, and the quality of its information was affected accordingly. But when ASIO had its own proposition that The Movement should assist it in a concrete way, the depth of the sulking became only too apparent.

In October 1953 — twelve months after the official rebuff — Spry and Richards found themselves enmeshed in an even more serious probe into improper conduct by intelligence officers in their dealings with The Show. This time, the terms of reference ominously included 'leakage of security information', implying that The Movement had successfully penetrated ASIO. Richards immediately dispatched to headquarters copies of a new report by the senior section officer in Sydney responsible for handling agents.[1]

This focussed particular attention on the fact that

the Movement liaison agent who had been described as 'unscrupulous' and whose intelligence had sometimes been unreliable had been allowed to use ASIO's Edgecliff office to write his own reports. Furthermore, this agent had actually stored his files at the Edgecliff office. The officer reported that he had discovered an extensive cache of his files while 'tidying up an "S" cabinet and destroying a lot of junk'.[2]

'I believe that it can be strongly suspected from the attached material', the officer wrote, 'that not only did [the agent] visit the Edgecliffe [sic] Office for the purpose of preparing reports on information he supplied to ASIO, but that he actually used the Edgecliffe Office for the purpose of doing Catholic Action organisational work.' He was deeply concerned by this revelation, as 'it left ASIO open to grave repercussions' if this state of affairs became known to ASIO's critics, concluding that, 'Such persons could imply that ASIO and Catholic Action were "hand in glove", and working in common to the point of sharing the same office.'

Eerily, exactly this allegation publicly emerged two years later in the aftermath of the royal commission examining Soviet espionage.

Even more disturbing was the suspicion that the officer running the Movement liaison agent had breached ASIO's most fundamental protocol and had passed official intelligence to him; at the very least, the agent 'could have picked up all sorts of information by overhearing discussions when he was in the Edgecliffe Office'. In support of his concerns, the ASIO officer recorded that at least one report supplied by the Movement agent contained intelligence which was 'identical with that on record in our file. It would therefore appear that [the agent] had been supplied by some member of Security with exact copies of the official security reports.' There were indications that this was not an isolated incident.

For ASIO, this was an unwelcome conclusion, and not only because it suggested that some ex-CIS officer—or even officers—now employed by ASIO had leaked official intelligence to an entirely private civilian organisation. Late 1953—when this investigation of high-level security breaches was underway—coincided with a mini-crisis for ASIO's operations to penetrate the CPA. As the officer in charge of S section in Sydney noted in a memo to the field officer responsible for direct, day-to-day liaison with agents, 'In view of recent failures in [censored] operations, and tiredness of sources of long standing, we badly need to develop replacements and understudies.'³

Apparently, some recent operations inside the CPA had been unsuccessful, and this was attributed to fatigue among ASIO's penetration agents in carrying out the delicate and often dangerous tasks set by their handlers. The officer drew his subordinate's attention to the fact that 'There is no doubt that the people [whom The Movement's liaison agent] control, would include a large number of persons who would readily agree to carry out a penetration' of the CPA. So he directed him to 'casually enquire why members of his organisation have not joined the Party'. ⁴

The field officer wasted no time. Three days later, he reported the response, using the Movement liaison agent's exact words:

Our leaders have ruled that our people cannot infiltrate the Party because it would be spiritually and morally wrong to do so. You know, we have had, and continue to have, plenty of opportunities to get people who are in really excellent positions to join the Party, to do so. Some have been very keen and have pestered us to allow them to join. At one stage we became so inundated with requests of this nature that our leaders had to send out specific instructions that all such requests were to be refused. Some people who cannot join are very well placed to do so. Anyone of these people, acting as an individual, may decide to do so, which would be a matter for himself and would depend, I would think, upon the advice given by his spiritual adviser.[5]

In Reverend Ryan's world, it was apparently morally acceptable to use dirty tricks against the communists (for example, by distributing false ballot papers in union elections, and stacking union and student meetings with fake members), but it was wrong to infiltrate the CPA. As a consequence of this logic, he insisted he was protecting the moral and spiritual well-being of the flock he looked after as chaplain to the Sydney Show. But as the field officer noted in his report, the last sentence seemed to be something of a let-out clause, suggesting 'that if we could learn the identities of these persons and then approach them directly, we may recruit from their ranks a few agents'.

His superior mulled over this intelligence during the Christmas–New Year break, and in early January 1954 put the case to Richards. He drew a stark picture, observing that while ASIO's 'coverage' of the CPA 'at present is satisfactory … the tiredness of long standing agents is quite evident. I think that after a certain number of years of service they will be difficult to hold. We could have an alarming situation on our hands at a later date if we were to suffer casualties without being able to replace them, and we now need alternative recruiting measures.' He recommended that Richards should refer the matter to ASIO headquarters for its input.[6]

Richards acted swiftly, discussing the matter personally with the controller of S section, who agreed to the proposition that the Movement liaison agent should be asked to 'nominate a group of his contacts whom he feels are prepared to make an attempt to penetrate the Communist Party ... We will then make a selection of one or two of these and target them into the Party using [censored] as cut-out for the operation.'[7]

The meeting to put this proposition to The Movement occurred in early February 1954. In the meantime, a sweetener had been added to entice a positive response. Remembering the iciness that followed the refusal to conduct a two-way intelligence-sharing relationship, the field officer was instructed to offer The Movement access to the intelligence gathered by those it nominated to penetrate the CPA. When he next met the liaison agent, he said: 'If we made the approach and thereafter did the contacting, we would be prepared to give you a copy of the information received. Under these circumstances would you be prepared to supply to me the names and addresses of suitable persons? You know, we just need to know who to see and where to find them.'[8]

The Movement liaison agent cautiously replied that he thought 'favourable consideration' might be given to the proposal, except that 'the question of the reciprocal exchange of information between the two organisations will be remembered, and will influence a decision on your proposal'. The agent stressed that The Show wanted to achieve 'mutual trust, understanding, and co-operation, with a resultant reciprocal exchange of information', also emphasising that ill-feeling still prevailed from his side who would remember that, 'in the past, you have refused to supply us with information. It has been one-way traffic as far as we are concerned ... This one-way traffic has not made for the necessary feeling of good faith which I think must prevail before we agree to your proposal.'[9]

The answer from The Movement's leaders followed swiftly: a resounding no, based on the same reasoning as before—it was 'spiritually wrong for [The Show] to put agents inside the Communist Party'.[10]

At ASIO headquarters, the controller of the Special Services Section was perplexed by this response. On Richards' memo conveying the news, the controller scrawled a note to one of his officers ('Mr A'), directing him: 'Find out how Victorian office went about it.'[11] This is the only explicit mention in the ASIO files of the Victorian Movement's assent to the placement of some of its members at ASIO's disposal to penetrate the CPA, although a later report demonstrates that this arrangement was definitely put in place in that state.

There are a number of aspects to this apparently innocuous scrawl. First, it seems the spirituality and morality of The Movement's members south of the Murray were not as delicate as in NSW. Second, it has sometimes been argued that NSW was the centre of The Show's relationship with ASIO, implying that Santamaria's Victorian stronghold did not approve of supplying ASIO with intelligence and did not co-operate with its operations to penetrate the CPA. Indeed, in 1971, Santamaria stated unequivocally that 'There was no contact at all with A.S.I.O.'[12] As one historian has noted, however, 'rumours' of The Movement's 'informal links' with ASIO were consistently 'denied', but were 'unlikely to be entirely unfounded'.[13] This judgement was made in 1970, two decades before ASIO's files on The Show started to be released under the Archives Act.

The fundamental question arising from this handwritten note is: *What happened to the files relating to ASIO's successful operations utilising Victorian Movement members as penetration agents inside the CPA?* All inquiries to unearth them have been fruitless, and it must be assumed that either they were lost or destroyed before the Archives Act came into force in 1983.

Stories have circulated for over forty years suggesting that files documenting ASIO's direct relationship with Santamaria were maliciously destroyed to pre-empt the Whitlam government learning of ASIO's 'hand in glove' operations with the ALP's deadly political opponent, which had helped keep Labor out of office for seventeen years. The destruction of such records was variously said to have occurred either in 1973—when then attorney-general Lionel Murphy seized official ASIO records contradicting successive Liberal governments' denials about the activities of Croatian terrorists, and it was feared his next move would be to seize the Santamaria dossier—or, alternatively, when Whitlam established the royal commission into Australian intelligence the following year, and it was feared that the dossier would emerge during its deliberations.

When the Sydney branch of The Show turned down ASIO's request to supply penetration agents in 1954, Spry was underwhelmed, recommending the cessation of contact with the liaison agent.[14] The view from Sydney was rather different; Richards appealed Spry's directive on the grounds that the 'Source is productive' and the 'organisation is a vast one':

[It] can assist us not only by supplying intelligence, but its contacts can be usefully employed in various ways from time to time ... Liaison with the organisation requires careful handling to ensure that we are not "milked" and for various other reasons ... An established routine is operating for proper liaison and it is considered that this is the best means of continuing the association.[15]

Spry, as he invariably did with the recommendations of the highly regarded Richards, quickly approved the suggestion that 'friendly relations should be maintained'.[16]

ASIO's files demonstrate that such 'friendly relations' persisted in NSW for many years, and there are hints in highly censored intelligence reports that ASIO may have eventually recruited some Sydney Movement members as penetration agents inside the CPA, perhaps with the assistance of a Catholic priest.[17] It is well known that, for several decades after the Labor Split of the mid-1950s, ASIO maintained close relations with former members of The Show who had remained loyal to the NSW ALP, as well as with The Movement and other right-wing Catholics.[18]

In addition to the handwritten note indicating that The Movement had co-operated in providing agents to penetrate the CPA in Victoria, there is another document dealing with that state in the publicly available ASIO files. It is a memo written by Spry in November 1957, reminding his Victorian regional director of an allegation arising from the royal commission on Soviet espionage, established in 1954 following the defection of Soviet diplomats Vladimir and Evdokia Petrov. Spry was responding to the Victorian's report that Dr Gerald Caine—The Show's Ballarat leader—was being used to talent-spot potential agents for recruitment by ASIO. In particular, Caine had recommended the recruitment of a non-Movement member for ASIO operations. Spry's response was revealing:

You will recall allegations made after the Royal Commission on Espionage that A.S.I.O. was working *hand in glove* with Mr. SANTAMARIA and the Movement and we have gone to great lengths to ensure that no such undertaking existed, although some Catholic Action [Movement] contacts have passed to us information of Security interest as and when they considered necessary ... we do not desire to have an arrangement where a Catholic Actionist is a talent spotter for A.S.I.O. agent running operations. This could be said to be working hand in glove with Catholic Action and it is this situation we wish to avoid ... You are requested to gradually ease out subject from a talent spotting role although it will be obviously necessary to see him from time to time as a courtesy and you could take any information of Security interest he cares to give. [Emphasis added.][19]

This memo clearly establishes that ASIO's Victorian branch had utilised The Show to recruit agents. It would be extraordinary if Santamaria was not aware of these activities, both as the authoritarian and controlling national leader and because of his total domination of The Movement's Victorian operations. On the other hand, these documents indicate that ASIO's head, Spry, adopted contradictory attitudes towards utilising The Show to recruit agents to infiltrate the CPA. When the NSW branch refused to co-operate with ASIO's proposal in 1954, he was antagonistic to the point of ordering the cessation of the relationship; when he discovered in 1957 that the Ballarat branch was co-operating in just such an enterprise, he ordered it to stop. His reasoning in 1957 does not hold water in light of the evidence of his own direct relationship with Santamaria.

So WHAT CAN be concluded about the persistent claims of Santamaria's alleged close personal relationship with ASIO and, especially, with its long-time head, Brigadier Spry?

One historian has written that much of the information in The Movement's 'Capacious dossiers' was handed to ASIO. According to this account, a senior journalist with *The Australian*—the late David Hirst—had 'taped interviews with Santamaria' revealing 'how he used his information network to supply ASIO with information on suspected communists between 1945 and 1973'. (ASIO was formed in 1949.)[20]

I had a warm professional relationship with Hirst in the 1980s, and knew firsthand that he had extremely good contacts inside the right wing of Australian politics, including with the NCC generally and Santamaria personally. However, if he possessed such 'taped interviews', the question arises as to why this sensational information was never published before Hirst's untimely death in 2013. It would certainly have laid to rest both the fact and nature of the relationship. In the absence of the tapes, this claim must be taken with a large grain of salt.

Some aspects of Santamaria's relationship with ASIO, however, are on the public record. Puzzlingly, the three volumes of the official history of ASIO cast virtually no light on the issue. In volume one, historian David Horner records that, sometime in the early 1950s, Richard Casey, the external affairs minister in the Menzies government, introduced Santamaria to Spry. Horner concludes, however, that 'there is no evidence that their relationship was close'.[21] He does not explain what evidence he reviewed in reaching this judgement. Volume two, by historian John Blaxland, not only contains minor historical errors on the subject of The Movement, but has no meaningful references to Santamaria, while volume three has none at all.[22]

On the other hand, an unpublished volume of the report of the royal commission into Australian intelligence—established by the Whitlam government in 1974—reportedly 'expressed concern at the closeness of senior ASIO officers with NCC [Movement] figures'. Royal commissioner Justice Robert Hope 'believed ASIO uncritically accepted NCC dossiers and information'.[23]

The NCC (National Civic Council) came into existence in December 1957 as a direct reaction to the Vatican's decree that The Movement could not be an official church organisation because of its overtly political character. So the Catholic Social Studies Movement, officially born at the 1945 bishops' conference, simply changed its name and became a strictly lay organisation—at first publicly known as the Catholic Social Movement, and then as the National Civic Council, but still called The Movement or The Show by its members.

For four decades, The Movement denied its special relationship with ASIO. The declassified files prove that this was a lie. It would be extraordinary if Santamaria was entirely unaware of this relationship, especially as it persisted for so long. Nor is it plausible that Father Lalor, who was in Santamaria's inner circle as head of the Institute for Social Order in Melbourne, would not have informed him of his own connections with the Security Service in Perth—that is, if Santamaria did not approve, or even direct, Lalor's approach to Ron Richards. Furthermore, Lalor was appointed as the chaplain to the Sydney Movement in 1953 as Santamaria's 'eyes and ears' to spy on Ryan's independent-minded operation. He would have quickly become aware of Ryan's relationship with ASIO, and informed Santamaria; that is, in the improbable event that he had been ignorant of it prior to that date. Again, it is highly implausible that Santamaria was unaware of ASIO's recruitment of Victorian Movement members as agents to penetrate the CPA.

Santamaria's own version of his relationship with ASIO casts a fascinating light on this shady issue. In 1990, he admitted what he had explicitly denied for so long.

During a lengthy interview with journalist John Lyons for a profile published in the Fairfax magazine *Good Weekend*, Santamaria stated that ASIO head Spry visited him in the early 1960s and 'asked whether he would be prepared to hand over the names of union members he believed were communists or "fellow travellers"'. As a consequence, Santamaria admitted to Lyons that he co-operated with ASIO for four years, providing information 'about suspected communists and "fellow travellers" in the trade union movement'.[24]

No explanation was given as to why he had previously denied ever having such a relationship, or why it suddenly ended after four years. But Santamaria did indicate his bitterness towards ASIO for handing 'to the Hope Royal Commission files which included what he had told them about suspected communists in the union movement', breaching 'what he had understood as a commitment of confidentiality'.[25] Apparently, Santamaria believed that ASIO was above the law when it came to his relationship with Spry, and that it had a duty to defy the royal commission's draconian powers to compel the production of documents.

Interestingly, a search of the royal commission's indices held by the national archives in Canberra does not readily disclose the material to which Santamaria referred. This does not mean that it does not exist in a form not easily discernible from studying the indices. Much of the commission's documentation is still highly classified and therefore is unavailable to public researchers, making a final determination of this matter impossible at this time.

In the publicly available sections of his report, Hope did

make some pertinent comments and a specific recommendation about ASIO's relations with 'private intelligence organisations' that were tailored to The Show, although Hope was undoubtedly also referring to others, including the Returned Services' League.[26] Hope stressed that such organisations should not be used 'as collection agencies for ASIO', especially as they were often well known to the public and were 'generally known to have some particular political affiliation or leaning', deriving from their focus on 'allegedly subversive activities by extremists of the political left'. Hope's words, while carefully chosen, readily fit the description of The Movement.[27]

Hope's recommendation on this question was even more revealing: 'That ASIO ensure that it is in no way beholden to, or develops any kind of special relationship with, private intelligence organizations.'[28] Again, his words were carefully chosen, but one can infer from them that ASIO had previously had a 'special relationship' with such organisations. The files publicly released under the Archives Act unequivocally demonstrate that this was the case with The Movement.

Assuming that Santamaria's account to Lyons in 1990 was accurate—and given the subject matter, there is no reason to question it, at least as far as it goes—the obvious question that arises is why those documents he handed to ASIO over a four-year period, beginning in the early 1960s, are not in ASIO's files and publicly available in the national archives?

Santamaria does not even appear in ASIO's indices. He and the files he handed to ASIO in response to Spry's personal request either were never entered into ASIO's scrupulously compiled filing indices, or were subsequently expunged and no longer form part of the official record. Yet Santamaria was adamant that they had been retained and, to his disgust, handed to the Hope royal commission.

So there are two unexplained gaps in ASIO's records on The Show: the Victorian files dealing with Movement agents used to penetrate the CPA; and Santamaria's own dossiers naming suspected communists and 'fellow travellers'.

An insight into this intriguing situation was provided in a direct communication that ASIO sent me in the 1990s. I had requested access to any files held by ASIO on either the National Civic Council or the Institute of Social Order, which Father Lalor had run in the 1950s. In response, I was provided with an extract from an appendix to part IV of an internal, unpublished history of ASIO. In their explanatory note to me, ASIO stated:

> There is no record of the Institute of Social Order in ASIO indices and records identified on the National Civic Council do not reflect any exchange or communication with ASIO. From the information in the paragraph attached [from the unpublished history], such communication is stated to have occurred. In the absence of supporting records, it must be assumed that contact was regarded as informal and not subject to routine reporting procedures or that records of meetings/exchanges were destroyed, as not relevant to security, sometime prior to the enactment of archives legislation.[29]

The paragraph from the unpublished ASIO history reads:

> Over the years contact with the Institute of Social Order has proceeded for a variety of reasons. By the activity of the National Civic Council in seeking to penetrate organizations which were targets of ASIO concern occasions arose where it became necessary to counter activities by NCC representatives tending to prejudice the success of ASIO

agents in the same area. Moreover the political affiliations of the Council rendered it necessary to ensure that ASIO itself was not penetrated by its representatives. An exchange of information with the Institute of Social Order, at the level of the compilations of unclassified material, maintained that contact. Mr Santamaria was, himself, not a contact of ASIO and was not given any documents. The material supplied to the Institute of Social Order was not supplied for any broadcast by Mr Santamaria—nor did it appear that any was reflected in such broadcasts.[30]

Santamaria had directly and publicly contradicted the assertion that he was 'not a contact of ASIO', unashamedly proclaiming that he was a contact of its most senior officer, director-general Charles Spry, and that he personally supplied information to ASIO for four years. Did Spry not reveal that relationship to others in ASIO? Were Santamaria's files not officially recorded? Did Spry intentionally protect Santamaria from his involvement with ASIO? If so, why then did Santamaria express such bitterness that he had been 'blown' as an ASIO contact when his files were handed to the Hope royal commission? Presumably, he did not invent that story, but must have received solid information from someone either inside ASIO or the royal commission.

Furthermore, whatever material Santamaria provided to ASIO can hardly have been considered 'as not relevant to security' and destroyed on that basis, as ASIO implied in its covering explanation to me. As will be discussed in chapter nine, one of Santamaria's intelligence dossiers in another ASIO file demonstrates that he was a professional who could more than compete intellectually with the cream of ASIO's analysts.[31]

The extract from the unpublished history does resolve the question of The Movement's willingness to penetrate the CPA, notwithstanding supposed 'moral' and 'spiritual' quibbles. ASIO clearly understood from its own experiences the dangers that such Movement penetration agents posed to their own penetration operations, which is presumably why Richards desperately wanted to have control over any sent into the CPA.

The extract also reveals what has long been suspected: ASIO did pass information to The Movement. Even if all of it was, as claimed, 'unclassified material', it still sustains the case of ASIO's critics that it was directly involved in assisting a significant player in Australian politics. That the material was passed to The Movement through the Institute of Social Order demonstrates just how thoroughly it had been under Santamaria's control ever since Lalor was appointed as its first director.

On the other hand, there is no doubt that some ASIO officers did provide The Show with information—including highly classified material based on surveillance and telephone intercepts. Whether this was done informally or officially is not certain, although in at least one case it was so notorious that it would be unlikely that it did not come to the attention of ASIO's senior echelons. This instance involved Jack Clowes, ASIO's expert on trade union affairs. Clowes was a Catholic who, in the 1960s and 1970s, was ASIO's liaison with the right wing of the NSW trade union movement. A former senior Movement official who had extensive dealings with Clowes stated that he regularly engaged in two-way intelligence exchanges with the organisation.[32] It seems unlikely that he was the only officer to do so.

The final intriguing question is why The Show proved such an invaluable source of intelligence for ASIO, even prompting the director-general to appeal directly to Santamaria for assistance, notwithstanding his earlier scruples about ASIO not being seen to have a 'hand in glove' relationship with The Show's undisputed leader.

There are tantalising fragments in the ASIO files that shed some light on this, but the relatively small amount of The Movement's own operational files that are publicly available provides a reasonably comprehensive picture, both of its *modus operandi* and extensive capabilities as an intelligence agency.

5

The conspiratorial method

In September 1952, ASIO's Western Australian office stumbled onto one of the many conspiratorial methods used by The Movement to shield its clandestine operations. In the dark art of secrecy, The Show mimicked—and surpassed—the communists' extraordinary security techniques.

Like all affiliates of the international communist movement, the CPA embraced many of the covert practices developed by the Bolsheviks during the last decades of Czarist rule. In the late 19th and early 20th centuries, the Czar's secret police, the Okhrana, routinely repressed the Russian labour movement. Operating illegally, the Bolsheviks were by necessity a clandestine organisation, utilising tightly organised cells to stymie the Okhrana's numerous penetration agents. A byzantine conspiratorial methodology was developed to protect the revolutionaries' secrets from the state's prying eyes. The organisation was effectively compartmentalised, so that if one cell was compromised, its members could not reveal the identities of those operating in other cells, thereby limiting the damage. After seizing power in 1917, the Bolsheviks—renamed the Communist Party of the Soviet Union—imposed a similar methodology on affiliated parties, including Australia's.

In adopting Santamaria's recommendation to model their Movement on the CPA, the bishops also tacitly approved this aspect of communist organisational practice.

ASIO became perhaps the first outsider to discover one of the key techniques used to protect the security of communications between Show headquarters in Melbourne and state and regional offices. This occurred when several envelopes addressed to 'Mr. R. OLIVER, C/- T.A.A., Perth' remained uncollected and were eventually 'handed to the G.P.O. Dead Letter Office'. They were then transferred to ASIO's Perth office, which was astounded to find that they mostly consisted of half-letters that had been cut vertically.[1] Without the other half, it was impossible to comprehend the correspondence. This method of communication was used by The Show nationwide, and there are many examples of re-assembled letters in the surviving archives of the Adelaide branch.[2]

Inquiries with The Movement's recently appointed Perth representative quickly established that the mysterious 'R. Oliver' was 'a cover name' and that 'the letters had been inadvertently misdirected'. The man in charge of The Show's Perth operations at that time was Frank Malone.[3] He was keen to obtain the missing material so he could re-assemble the letters by sticky-taping the two halves together. ASIO promptly complied with his request to act as postman. In return for delivering the envelopes of half-letters, Malone assured ASIO that 'all information of security interest' crossing his desk would be passed on.[4]

This sudden burst of activity in Perth had been sparked by Father Lalor's recent visit, after a six-year absence in the eastern states as one of Santamaria's senior operatives. At short notice, the local priests were summoned to a specially convened meeting in the 'Archbishop's Palace' to hear Lalor declaiming in typically dramatic style on the dangers of the CPA linking up 'with the communist forces spreading from China down into south-east Asia and onto Australia'. Many of those assembled became chaplains to parish groups, boosting the crusade in Western Australia, where The Movement had previously failed to gain widespread traction among Catholics. Conspiratorial methods were soon *de rigueur*, just as they had been in other states for some years.[5]

Conspiracy sprang from several different requirements. The CPA's influential pamphlet *Catholic Action At Work*—based on Santamaria's 1945 report to the bishops—demonstrated the effectiveness of well-directed, sectarian propaganda. If The Movement behaved like a normal political machine, Santamaria believed, it would be constantly exposed to such negative publicity. By the early 1950s, there was an emerging belief among non-Catholic anti-communists that The Show's *modus operandi* was just as distasteful as the CPA's. This sentiment grew over the following years, contradictorily prompting an even tighter focus on secrecy. As one long-time member commented, 'A lot of people who inadvertently, or perhaps without knowing it, work with the [Movement], wouldn't be doing that if they knew that they were acting on behalf of the [Movement]. So it is a secretive organisation.'[6]

An integral part of the conspiratorial methodology was the adoption of codes for internal communications. For example, people were classified according to an alpha-numerical code: an M1 was a completely trusted member, often also referred to as an SM, or Show Member. 'A communist, on the other hand, would go to the other end of the spectrum and be referred to as a Z.'[7] Individuals in between these two extremes were assigned alpha-numeric codes depending on how they were assessed, such as Movement sympathiser, or hostile non-CPA leftist.

The codes extended to the organisational structure. A clear example of this is found in The Show's Adelaide files:

D.O. refers to propaganda, and is the abbreviation for the title of Distribution Officer ...

C.O., meaning Census Officer ...

V.G., meaning vocational group, is the title we use for Trade Unions. Inner V.G. means Union Group in the Movement. Outer V.G. refers to the Union itself.

N.M.S. — New members' school.

S.S. — Social Survey [the ISO journal].

I.G. refers to Industrial Group ...

E.O. means Education Officer.

M.O., membership Officer and membership.

F.O., finance officer, and finance.[8]

Some of these codes evolved over time. For example, 'G.O.' [Government Officer] was originally used in the period when the ALP was in office in Canberra, but after the 1949 change of government it referred to the 'S.M. [Show Member] in charge of A.L.P. affairs'.[9]

As the organisation rapidly expanded into an efficient intelligence agency, sophisticated filing systems were adopted, using meticulous cross-referencing and index cards to record key information. For example, the Sydney branch used a system of six cards: one 'used for a church census', in which an entire parish would be canvassed to record all Catholics, their loyalty to the church's teachings and practice, their political views and activities, place of employment, and trade union membership, etc.; another card recorded 'the number of our people in each place of employment'; a third recorded 'the number of our people in individual unions'; a Movement membership card also recorded who were ALP members, using the code 'words "sporting club"—that refers to the political party'; and another 'census card [was] used to record details of all Communists or fellow travellers we have on our files'.[10]

The use of codenames in official correspondence was compulsory from the beginning. For example, the regional officer of the South Australian branch, Ted Farrell, signed his letters 'Jack', 'J. Edwards', or 'J.E.', but received letters addressed to 'F. Wilson'. When writing to the national secretary in Melbourne (Norm Lauritz, Santamaria's 'first "recruit"' to The Movement),[11] Farrell addressed him as 'L. Norman', while his principal contact in NSW used the codename 'F. Kayes' to receive correspondence, although he really was Roy Boylan. Commenting on a letter in which Farrell addressed Lauritz as 'Dear Norm', a former Adelaide Movement member described it as a 'breach of security'.[12]

The Adelaide operation was relatively insignificant, compared to the large and powerful branches in Melbourne (head office) and Sydney, and even Brisbane. In this, it mirrored its opponent, which, although wielding a disproportionate influence in South Australia's unions, had a small membership and little impact outside industrial affairs. When The Movement got into its first strides in 1943–44, the South Australian CPA controlled the ironworkers', clerks', seamen's, gas workers', and shop assistants' unions, and had a significant presence on the wharves, in the railways and engineering unions, and in the Holden car plant.[13] Within a decade, The Show had captured the ironworkers' and shop assistants' unions — severe, but not lethal, blows to the CPA.

Despite its relatively tiny membership, Ted Farrell built a well-oiled, efficient, and highly successful espionage apparatus and a solid industrial organisation that caused the communists significant problems in all the unions in which they were active. Farrell was well educated, having obtained a Bachelor of Arts in History and English at Adelaide University after attending the Christian Brothers and Rostrevor Colleges. He then taught primary school students in the public school system, and was president of the Assisian Guild of Catholic Teachers. In early 1946, Adelaide's Bishop Matthew Beovich recruited him to full-time work for The Show, which he had been organising part-time for the previous two years. His broad remit was described as being to 'bring influence to bear on the trade union movement, on the ALP, and, by propaganda, on the ... working community'. Specifically, he was to 'de-louse 4 or 5 trade unions'. Two years later, Beovich appointed him to head the Newman Institute of Christian Studies, which acted as cover for the clandestine political operation. Both bodies were housed in cramped quarters in the Todd Building in central Adelaide, adjacent to St Francis Xavier cathedral. For his services to the church — and his work for The Movement and the Newman Institute — Farrell received the papal Cross of Honour.[14]

A significant portion of the records of the South Australian branch survive, thanks to Professor John Warhurst; they are the only operational Movement archives publicly available. As a young academic at Flinders University in Adelaide in the early 1970s, Warhurst received these files from a youthful priest who had obtained them from some of his older colleagues.[15] They were keen to see them preserved, in defiance of superior instructions issued by Adelaide's Archbishop James Gleeson, who apparently (and correctly) feared they would expose his role in Movement activities. Subsequently, Warhurst deposited them in what was then the Australian National University's Archives of Business and Labour in Canberra (now the Noel Butlin Archives Centre).[16] Even taking account of the fact that they are incomplete, they are a massive record, spanning the period from 1944 to 1961, and containing voluminous correspondence between Farrell in Adelaide and Lauritz in Melbourne and, especially, between Farrell and Boylan in Sydney, who developed a very close relationship.

They also contain a huge, cross-indexed collection of newspaper clippings filed in alphabetical order by subject, covering everything from the Aborigines Advancement League (which begins the collection) and ending with the Zionist Youth League (cross-indexed to the CPA youth wing, the Eureka Youth League), with all manner of subjects covered in between. There are also significant collections of printed material, leaflets, and pamphlets; research reports compiled by Farrell's office; extensive notes on individual trade unions; photographs; and files dealing with prominent South Australian personalities (such as left-wing ALP federal parliamentarian Clyde Cameron, who was decidedly hostile to The Show's operations).

The centrepiece of this archive, however, is the voluminous material collected by The Movement's agents and informants on known or suspected communists, fellow travellers, and sympathisers. Much of this is in the form of handwritten notes, often on scraps of paper held together by rusting pins and paperclips (at the time they were accessed for this book in the early 1990s). This intelligence was compiled in The Show's office on the basis of surveillance reports made by members after observing the movements of suspects, tailing their vehicles, and staking out their meeting places, homes, and workplaces. In this sense, it reflects a classic intelligence operation. One former Movement member recalled that a map of greater Adelaide hung on the office wall, 'in which pins had been stuck to identify where known communists lived'.[17]

The records demonstrate that Farrell was an inspirational speaker who could lead groups of men (and a very few women), with a deep understanding of church teachings and the intersection between religion and practical politics. Above all, he was an excellent political organiser. An insight into Farrell's intelligence-gathering methods is contained in his document dealing with the cultivation of contacts. It is an astute guide, specifically designed for Movement members to demonstrate how to establish and develop contacts to determine the factual state of affairs—such as in particular places of work, and in community and sporting organisations—and then to undertake 'Enquiries' on specific issues of interest to The Show. The purposes of this elaborate system of contacts were to surreptitiously lead such people and use the intelligence gathered to formulate strategies for action.

Farrell's methodology owed much to the Young Christian Workers' Movement (YCW), which stressed the role of independent activity by both individuals and small groups of Catholics—for example, to improve working and social conditions. From The Show's inception, Santamaria had advocated that YCW members be centrally involved in his operations in factories and unions, but he met increasingly fierce resistance from the YCW, which opposed his authoritarian version of the communists' 'democratic centralism'. They were also uncomfortable with The Movement's involvement in politics, in particular its attempts to control the ALP after the communist threat had receded by the early 1950s. But they were especially and vehemently opposed to the rigid discipline imposed on Show members, believing it undermined the independent action of individual Catholics, which was at the core of the YCW's method of operations.[18]

Farrell's adaptation of the YCW model would, however, have met with approval from ASIO's professional agent-handlers, as his document demonstrates:

> The contacts should be sought either at the member's place of employment or in a sporting or social club or some other association where he sees him regularly ... Eventually a member should aim to have several contacts, according to his position in
> 1. his own place of employment;
> 2. other places of employment;
> 3. his occupational association;
> 4. his Parish.
>
> A good man can handle five contacts, but for the moment we will put ours on a quota of 2, but starting with one.[19]

Farrell then gave a detailed, step-by-step account of how members were to be given a practical education on developing their contacts in a series of in-house 'meetings'. He described the purpose of what was, effectively, a training course:

> We must have influence on people, but this can only be done through a series of steps — they must be brought to the stage where they will accept your leadership. You must carefully select the people you wish to influence, gradually develop a friendship with them, and then through your friendship ... influence them to your way of thinking. There is an order through which this can be done, namely Contact, Friendship,

Influence ... until you reach a stage ... where you can bring him nearer to Christ.[20]

The final class in the training course was a practical test for members to elaborate on:

1. What subjects have you heard discussed in your factories or offices, at meals or leisure. Name three subjects most discussed.
2. Recall any conversation in which a wrong attitude was adopted.
3. What position does loose talk, irreligious talk, grousing, occupy in conversation?[21]

After members had demonstrated their capacity for this practical work, they were ready for Farrell's ultimate purpose—'the use of contacts in an Enquiry. In order to answer the questions in an Enquiry effectively, three steps are necessary':

1. Each member must report on the facts at his place of employment (or social club, etc.) as he sees them.
2. He must also obtain a contact in his own place of employment and find out what he sees as the facts there.
3. He should also have another contact (or contacts) employed elsewhere than his own place of employment, and find out from him what are the facts there.

The enquiry questions could then be phrased:

1. What are the facts at your place of employment, as seen by you?

2. What are the facts at your place of employment as seen by your contact there, and as elicited from him by you?

3. What are the facts at their places of employment as reported to you by your other contacts?

In a big factory where there are several workshops, a member's first contact should be in his own shop, and he could even have further contacts ... at the same place of employment, but in different parts of it.

How to take up the matter of your Enquiries. The OBSERVE (or SEE) Section is designed to produce facts, not impressions, on which Judgment is to be made for ACTION to follow.[22]

The intelligence obtained by these means—and by the many Movement members detailed to specific surveillance targets—was extraordinary for a civilian spy apparatus. Taken as a whole, The Show's Adelaide archives resemble ASIO's own files, if in a more primitive, amateurish form. Like ASIO, The Movement clearly made use of official sources to confirm intelligence received from its agents and to gather further information—for example, by using a car-registration plate to obtain the name and personal details of a vehicle's owner. While it is not revealed how such official information was procured, presumably either Show members or sympathisers in government employ were engaged in providing such assistance—or friendly ASIO or Police Special Branch officers may have done so.

As in the case of The Movement's Melbourne, Sydney, and Perth offices, there is clear evidence in these files of a close connection between Farrell and ASIO's Adelaide office.

Farrell's operation was up and running in early 1944, well before the bishops as a body gave their official imprimatur in September of the following year. In early April 1944, Lauritz wrote to Farrell from Melbourne on several union matters, one concerning the political orientation of a suspected communist. Farrell replied that he had 'made enquiries' concerning the target [a Mr McCallum], 'from a reliable source, and the information is that he is a very strong suspect ... he invariably supports moves made by our "friends" in T.L.C. [Trades and Labour Council] etc. I will make further enquiries ... in the meantime regard him as being extremely doubtful.'[23]

By August 1944, Farrell had adopted his codename and was signing correspondence as 'Jack', and there already was extensive correspondence and a considerable movement of personnel between Melbourne, Sydney, and Adelaide as operations in the unions ramped up. Important inner-union documents were already being dispatched from one branch to another.[24] By the end of the year, significant amounts of propaganda were flowing to and from Adelaide, as well as reams of intelligence on communist activities in various unions.[25] One early campaign is recorded in some detail: The Show's effort to stymie the CPA's drive to amalgamate the ironworkers' and munition workers' unions, in which Adelaide provided reliable intelligence to Melbourne.[26]

By mid-1948, Sydney and Adelaide were regularly exchanging information obtained by their respective intelligence-gathering apparatuses. One gem conveyed from Boylan to Farrell was headed 'confidential & unfortunately gospel truth'. Sydney reported that 'Ferguson, State President A.L.P. stated that he would support Communism against Catholic Action. He stated this at a private dinner with three others during an adjournment at the Annual Conference ...

This must be used in a whispering campaign as widely as possible.'[27] This demonstrated The Show's already formidable ability to place its agents in delicate situations to overhear significant political conversations. It also illustrated the type of dirty tactics to be used against its 'enemies'.

By the early 1950s, Farrell was liaising with ASIO, both sharing his own intelligence and requesting information. For example, one of his agents, Bert Kildea, had reported that 'Mr Jack Inspector of Light Houses is a Comm, and also many Keepers.' The comment on this report was 'Good dope for Security'. Another piece of the Light House jigsaw concerned 'Schroeder Mt Lawly Light House. Supposed to be good ALP man, but is frequently visited by Comms.' Then there was the case of Franz Dezman, a recent immigrant from Central Europe, a 'Dachau refugee [who] claims he escaped from Yugoslavia with Map ... is inordinately interested our affairs. Worth check with Security.'[28]

Kildea was a prolific agent, reporting in 1953 that 'A particularly active Greek movement in S.A. coupled with other States is working independently of the Australian C.P., but very well supplied with funds, and supplies the Party with funds when they are short. The Leader (name unknown at the moment) is a very low type, and the general run of the Greeks in it are very bad type.'[29]

Dennis Morrisey, another of Farrell's agents, reported in mid-1955: 'Meeting of local gathering of Reds on Tuesday nights at Margate Street Brighton.' The file recorded that Morrisey 'Will find out person's home from his brother-in-law who lives opposite.' As good as his word, he soon conveyed the required information: 'R.A.J. Dale 25 Margate St Brighton. He owns house where ... meetings [held] every Tuesday night about 9PM. Dale's wife ... married out of church. She is a doctor's receptionist. Dr unknown. DM will inquire.'[30]

As time passed, Farrell's spying activities expanded, both geographically and politically. One of his obsessions was Clyde Cameron, whose opposition to The Movement and work for the Fabian Society rendered him very suspect. On at least one occasion, one of Farrell's agents rifled through Cameron's papers. 'Noted from C.R Camerons (sic) Diary in a quick look is meeting for Fabian Society on Tuesdays, roughly every fortnight—could be twice monthly'.[31]

As his organisation developed in the early 1950s, Farrell's surveillance operations spread well beyond Adelaide. Port Augusta had an active CPA branch, and the Show agent tasked with gathering intelligence there was meticulous:

> Pearl Beatrice BROWN—Teacher Pt Augusta Primary—has been known to loan her car (Vanguard—grey—262–833) to [prominent CPA member] Elliott Frank Johnson (sic) on occasions of his visits to Pt Augusta … Karl Gustav Eckberg … At nights leaves his house with wife & takes devious courses apparently to attend meetings, apparently taking different course each night … James Webb Holdsworth—MacKay St. Cabinet Maker … 55 years 5'9" … fair compl[exion] grey hair. Stooper long arms … Charles … Jarrett—67 Flinders Terrace … 5'4". Strong bld. med comp. grey hair. Associates with members of Com Party. His house held out to be a meeting place for members of Com Party … [Henry Maurice] Stockdale … 7/5/1917. 5'11". Strong bld. Pale comp. brown hair. Hazel eyes. Scar leftside chest. Assisted members of Com Party during last Elections when Elliott Johnson (sic) stood.[32]

This agent's information was largely accurate. Jim Moss was the long-time president of the South Australian CPA branch with a detailed knowledge of its membership. Forty years later, Moss spent ten days closely reading Farrell's archives. Asked about this account of the CPA's Port Augusta branch, he confirmed that it was 'fairly accurate'. He drily observed that the story of Pearl Brown lending her car to Elliott Johnston 'might be right', and that Stockdale, Holdsworth, and Jarrett were CPA members. Moss insisted, however, that Farrell's extensive lists of suspects were not wholly accurate: 'Their net was thrown very broad, their lists are very broad, containing all sorts of people that have got no connection with the party and would be horrified to see their names associated with it.'[33]

For example, Moss did not recognise Hector Goodman, reported by one of Farrell's agents as:

Assistant Station Master Adelaide Railway Station This man is suspected of having Red tendencies at least. According to Dan Laverton he is a subscriber to the [CPA newspaper] Tribune ... about 12 days ago a poisonous screed attacking Dan, the New Group, the Church, BAS [Santamaria], etc was typed and placed on the Notice Board. Dan ... suspected it was typed on the [Assistant Station Master's] typewriter with his connivance.

While conceding that he did not personally know every CPA member, Goodman was one of many examples Moss gave of either incorrect or doubtful identifications.[34]

There was no doubt about Elliott Johnston, however, who was a special target for Farrell. A prominent, effective, and highly regarded barrister, he was in the CPA's inner sanctum from the 1940s to the 1980s. In 1983, he resigned from the party when he was appointed to the South Australian Supreme Court; later, he headed the Royal Commission into

Aboriginal Deaths in Custody. He and his wife, Elizabeth, were under close surveillance by Farrell's agents: 'Mrs Elliot (sic) Johnson (sic), apparently returning from meeting—waiting at [corner] Taylors Rd & H. B. Rd Theb[arton], 10.5pm July 26–54. Information from L. Quinn.'[35] Other agents compiled information that Farrell fashioned into a personality profile:

PROFILE ON ELIZABETH JOHNSTON.
Formerly Elizabeth Teesdale Smith. Was disowned by family when she married Elliot (sic) Johnston in about 1942 ...
    CHARACTERISTICS. Brilliant speaker. Never rattled. Analytical mind. Very good appearance. Could be beautiful if took more care over appearance. Even though dresses very dowdily still manages to make other women look nothing beside her. Good personality. Good leader.[36]

Surveillance of targets extended to suspects' homes. For example, on 14 October 1955, one of Farrell's agents was stationed outside Ern Iversen's house in Highgate. Elsewhere in the files, Iversen is characterised as 'believed Red—Secty AEU [engineering union] Political C/tee ... Behaves and speaks like a Red ... Slim Medium height, sallow complexion—oily manner—dirty fighter.'[37]

The agent took down the car-registration numbers observed nearby, which were 'Given to [name crossed out] 7/11/55'. This contact then provided the full details of the owners' names, addresses, make of vehicle, registration date, occupation of owner, date issued a driving licence, and physical description, for example, 'Age 40. 5ft. 6in. Blue Eyes, Brown Hair.' This information was probably supplied by a friendly Catholic at the motor registry office, although the possibility exists that ASIO or Police Special Branch was its source. There is no doubt that the information was from an official source, as in one case it was reported that 'Other details not available, as index card missing.' The intelligence from this source was then passed to The Show's Parkside section.[38]

The files also indicate that one Movement branch would frequently request another to take action on intelligence gathered on a suspect. One instance concerned Hans Bandler, whose wife, Faith, was a prominent activist in Indigenous affairs. In late 1952, Boylan in Sydney wrote to Farrell:

> According to reliable information we have received, a certain HANS BANDLER has applied for an engineer's position with the South Australian School of Mines and Industries. This gentleman was formerly employed as an engineer with the New South Wales Public Works dept. He is a suspected Communist Party member and security should have quite a file on him. In view of the close connection between the South Australian School of Mines and Industries and Uranium and Atomic Research, Bandler's appointment would constitute the gravest security risk. I am sending you this information in the hope that you might be able to take steps to prevent it.[39]

It is not recorded in the files what action was taken by Farrell in this case, but Bandler never moved to South Australia.[40] In light of the attention Farrell paid to detail and to implementing The Show's conspiratorial methodology, it seems probable that he may have played a role in stymying Bandler's job application.

Much of Farrell's work consisted in monitoring the everyday, often humdrum, industrial and political affairs of factories, offices, and parishes, and meticulously recording the reports of his agents and their contacts. But his dedication to such intelligence-gathering paid handsome dividends in September 1952, when he pulled off a rare and invaluable coup against local CPA president Jim Moss, who had committed a grave breach of the the party's tight security protocols.

6

The jewel in Ted's crown

In early September 1952, Jim Moss, one of the most senior and experienced officials in the Communisty Party's Adelaide branch, hopped onto his motorbike to ride home from work. Having finished his usual Saturday shift, Moss loaded his closely guarded party documents into the haversack on the back of his motorbike and set off. When he arrived, however, he discovered to his horror that his papers were missing.

News of the loss of top-secret CPA documents rapidly reached ASIO's regional director for South Australia, who alerted his superiors in the Melbourne headquarters to this almost unprecedented development.[1] At the end of the month, he conveyed this assessment:

Some weeks ago ... the South Australian State President of the C.P. of A. ... lost a parcel of books and documents relating to C.P. of A. activity with Trade Unions in this State. MOSS has for some time been the C.P. of A. member responsible for the direction of such activity, and the documents in question are of great interest.

2. The information contained in the parcel has since become widely known in industrial circles and it was impossible for MOSS to conceal the loss from the Party.[2]

Ted Farrell's surveillance operations were responsible for procuring Moss's papers. He quickly distributed them, including 'amongst right wing union circles in Adelaide ... also ... the Chamber of Manufactures is aware of the information'.[3] In The Movement's mythology this was one of its biggest coups against the communists. John Maynes, the national vice-president in charge of union affairs, related how Moss had been closely watched by Farrell's agents, who observed that he routinely carried his files around with him on the back of his motorbike. As Maynes told the story, that day in September 1952 Moss had been followed, and the car tailing him had stopped next to the bike at a red light. In a lightning-quick strike, the papers were snatched from the haversack.[4]

The truth is more prosaic. Almost forty years later, Moss still considered the loss of his papers as a 'rather painful experience'. Slight and rather stocky, with a phlegmatic approach to life and politics, Moss was described by one of ASIO's 'usually reliable' sources as a methodical, careful communist, who 'utters no hurried remarks or snap decisions'.[5] Originally from Western Australia, he enlisted in the air force in 1939, and was posted to Adelaide but discharged as medically unfit at the end of 1940. Soon after, he got a job at Popes, which was manufacturing armaments for the war effort, where he met several communists. He joined the CPA in 1942, and rapidly developed into a tough and keenly observant operator.

He did not believe for one minute that his precious cargo

had been 'lifted' by The Movement:

> I used to ride a motorbike around, and on the back I had an army haversack that I'd bolted onto the frame that I could put things in and ride around fairly comfortably. Well, the stitching gave way on this haversack over a period of some time, and it was holding only by a little bit when I put this bundle in. Riding the bike home, the documents fell out. I didn't realise they'd gone until … I got home and found there were no papers in the back. So I turned round immediately and rode off again with the off-chance that I might see them on the road somewhere. When I got to Woodville I got involved in an accident.[6]

It was a serious but not life-threatening crash. A car made a U-turn in front of Moss without looking, colliding with his bike. Moss was thrown off and knocked unconscious, thwarting his search.

While it is certain that the documents were lost, not stolen, there was a kernel of truth to Maynes's story. It is clear that Farrell's agents had kept a close eye on Moss's movements and had probably observed him carrying his files around with him. It is also certain that he was being tailed that day, as recounted by Maynes. This was how Farrell's man obtained the documents: by observing them falling out of the haversack and simply picking them up off the road.

At that time, David Shinnick was a relatively new member of The Show. His family had had a long involvement in the labour movement, stretching back to the industrial upheavals of the 1890s. In the 1940s, Shinnick had spent several years in a seminary, where he became steeped in the church's social teachings. But in 1952 he quit the seminary, approached

Farrell, and asked to join The Movement, taking on the key role of census officer; identifying and interviewing all known Catholics, parish by parish, was a crucial aid for recruitment and intelligence-gathering. As Farrell said, 'From the census we are able to form groups.'[7] Shinnick also put his sophisticated understanding of church teachings to propaganda use, editing the monthly magazine, *Alert*. His recollection was that the Moss papers had somehow come into Farrell's hands, which he remembered as 'a great coup'. He assumed the originals were sent for analysis to Movement head office in Melbourne.[8]

On the other hand, Moss surmised that it would have been miraculous if The Movement had been lucky enough just to pick up his files, so his theory was that someone must have handed them into the police, who forwarded them to ASIO, who, in turn, provided The Show with their set.

Neither Moss nor Shinnick was correct. Contrary to Moss's surmise, the originals went in the opposite direction: from The Movement to ASIO's Adelaide office, which 'deposited' them 'in a place of safe keeping'. There they remained until March 1953, when 'the original documents' were dispatched to ASIO headquarters on the orders of director-general Charles Spry. Contrary to Shinnick's assumption, The Show's head office in Melbourne only received copies of the documents.[9] There is a full set of *photostats* of Moss's papers in Farrell's archive. In light of the size of this set of documents, it seems unlikely that Farrell would have had the wherewithal to make copies for himself, for Melbourne, and for wider local distribution. It seems likely that, in return for receiving the originals, ASIO made at least two copies for The Movement, one each for Adelaide and Melbourne.

The documents were a treasure-trove for The Show, which utilised them in anti-communist propaganda, 'publicising

Communist activities and methods'.[10] More especially, though, ASIO found them valuable from an intelligence angle. They consisted of typed and handwritten lists of names, mostly of CPA members, but also including supporters, contacts, and others with no connection at all to the party; several of Moss's top-secret notebooks in which he recorded, among many other things, the details of those party members responsible for directing CPA activities in particular unions; notes detailing his own personal tasks on a range of CPA matters; notes he had taken at state executive and other party meetings; copies of inner-party correspondence, both of the South Australian branch and also from CPA national headquarters in Sydney, for example, detailing various aspects of party organisation, propaganda, finances, recruitment of new members, and directions on building branches; inner-party organisational documents outlining, for example, the role and functions of branch executives; and material dealing with the wider work of communists, for example, in the peace movement and among women.[11]

The jewel was a document issued by the CPA's central committee secretariat, signed by general secretary Lance Sharkey. It dealt with a number of sensitive political matters relating to tactics and strategy, especially plans to defeat the ALP right wing and build a united workers' party. The Movement gave this document prominence in its propaganda, highlighting its heading: 'This document is not to be reproduced'. As Moss noted, they thought they had obtained 'a great secret document'.[12]

There was a problem, however, for The Movement's propaganda drive. As ASIO's South Australian regional director observed in January 1953:

> While the distribution of copies of the documents ... in industrial and Trade Union circles presented the recipients with a considerable amount of information regarding Communist tactics, it did not cause the general outcry or receive the widespread publicity which the originators obviously desired and anticipated. The persons who received such documents generally believed them to be authentic but, lacking actual proof in that direction, treated them with a great deal of caution and took no action on them.[13]

According to Moss, two factors chiefly accounted for this. The first was that left-wing Labor politician Clyde Cameron publicly cast doubt on the authenticity of the documents when approached by journalists for his comments. At that time, Cameron was leading an anti-Movement campaign inside the ALP, which Moss begrudgingly conceded meant that he was 'playing a good role', if only to 'look after himself'. The second factor was Moss's own response. He steadfastly refused to confirm or deny the loss of any documents, and, as he said with some relief even four decades later, the 'controversy fizzled out'.[14]

There was yet another factor working against the effective public use of the material. The lists of names contained a number of people who were not CPA members, some of whom were actually hostile to communism. A gas company employee, publicly fingered because his name was on one list, was interviewed by ASIO, and disclaimed 'any connections with the Communist Party in this State, and cannot understand why his name should appear on a list of industrial contacts compiled by MOSS'.[15] ASIO quickly discovered that he was not alone in being wrongly accused:

Investigations ... have resulted in the complete identification
of the majority of the persons named in the documents
and several such persons have, at their own request, been
interviewed. The net result of the enquiries into other
than known C.P. of A. members, shows that while in some
instances there may have been a reason for the inclusion of
the name, in others there is apparently no connection with or
sympathy for Communism.[16]

Much to its fury, ASIO also discovered that someone
was spreading rumours around union circles that 'Security'
had advised 'that the original documents were not genuine
and were deliberately "lost" in order to mislead the Security
Service'. ASIO's South Australian regional director assured
headquarters that 'No such advice has been given and this
office has not expressed any opinion as to the authenticity
of the documents.' Even worse, the rumour was eventually
published as fact in a local newspaper, but there was little that
ASIO could do to counter such rumour-mongering, probably
started by the CPA itself.[17] Still, comfort could be found in
the impact the incident had on the CPA's political work. 'The
loss of the documents by MOSS', one ASIO officer noted,
'is having an obvious effect on the Party's activities generally
throughout this State and a definite lull in their programme is
very evident.'[18]

This would have been of little comfort to The Movement.
Farrell and Maynes clearly hoped that the circulation of
the Moss papers would deal a crushing blow to the South
Australian CPA branch. Their disappointment at the relatively
limited news coverage and scepticism of the documents by
other anti-communists was compensated for by numerous
intelligence gems. Foremost among these was the level of

detail about CPA activities in unions—especially confirmation that Harry Krantz, the South Australian branch secretary of the clerks' union, was an undercover CPA member. Krantz was on the top of Maynes's list to be removed from his position, and this intelligence was central to his plans.

One of Moss's notebooks contained a list of communist union officials, detailing their responsibilities for CPA work in their own and related unions. In line with communist security consciousness, Moss only wrote the initials—not the name itself—including 'HK', whose responsibilities were listed as the clerks', shop assistants', and public servants' unions. Another of Moss's handwritten notes was a list of stories to be written for the CPA newspaper, *Tribune*, with the initials of the proposed authors beside them. In this case, Moss had written 'Harry K' next to one story, which provided a more convincing smoking gun for Maynes. Moss confirmed that 'HK' and 'Harry K' referred to Harry Krantz, although proving this—even in the court of public opinion—proved difficult in the early 1950s.[19]

Krantz was a particularly effective opponent, resisting all Maynes's efforts to remove him from office. Indeed, despite the proof that Farrell and Maynes believed they possessed that contradicted Krantz's public denials of his CPA membership, he was never defeated in clerks' union branch elections, retiring in 1984 after serving as secretary for over forty years. He was a secret CPA member during much of that period, and was the only communist to survive The Show's effective campaign in the clerks' union.[20]

Farrell did, however, give in-depth attention to the numerous names in Moss's papers. Considerable effort was expended to establish the details of these people, for example: 'Attached list of some included Moss papers. Addresses, occupations etc checked by [obscured name].'[21] There are long lists demonstrating the care that Farrell took to track down the precise workplaces and union memberships of dozens of those named in Moss's lists.[22] He kept track of names for years afterwards: 'PEARL P in the Moss papers was a Pearl Parfit an invalid who died recently. Obituary appears in [CPA paper] Tribune 6/6/56.'[23]

In its excitement, The Show under-estimated Moss, who displayed a steely resolve under immense pressure, simply playing a dead bat to the many bouncers he faced during the crisis. This allowed him—and the CPA—to tough out what at first looked like a disaster. His combative nature was also useful in fending off the anger of sections of the CPA membership, who were horrified that their names had been publicised as a consequence of his lapse in the carrying out of the party's strict security protocols. As ASIO's director-general noted, 'Moss' lapse has been strongly criticised' in these circles.[24]

Despite what would have been considered a major breach of its internal security measures, the CPA national leadership supported Moss through the crisis, recognising his talents and leadership skills. To temporarily take him out of circulation, he and his wife were called to Sydney for an extended 'holiday'. On his return, as ASIO noted, 'He resumed the position and duties which he had held prior to the loss of the documents; has apparently lost none of his normal self-assurance; and, as far as can be ascertained, was not subjected to disciplinary action.'[25]

THE MOVEMENT KNEW a great deal about Moss, but he knew practically nothing about it. Prior to reading a large selection of Farrell's papers in 1991, he had not even heard his name, nor those of Farrell's staff. This was the ultimate compliment to the success of the 'conspiratorial method'. As Moss said, their 'activities were very hush-hush'. The South Australian CPA branch 'did not wake up to them … in the way we should have' for several years, he conceded. Even the big union battles during the final war years of 1944–45 were viewed as struggles against individuals, not an organisation. It was not until the late 1940s—when The Show's ultimately successful campaign to take over the shop assistants' union ramped up—that the CPA's South Australian branch finally perceived that they confronted a well-run, if opaque, machine.[26]

Having reviewed key elements of Farrell's extensive archives, Moss was complimentary. He had no doubt that The Movement was 'quite a solid organisation' consisting of good operators. Farrell, especially, was 'a pretty shrewd fella':

> It was very much mixed up with the church's teachings, too. He was strong on the idea of combining the apostolate with his work. I would say he'd be a pretty good churchman, but he was also a pretty understanding tactician about what was to be done in the unions—from their point of view. He's quite an interesting character. Wherever he got his training, he was a pretty shrewd character.[27]

Moss was especially struck by Farrell's sophisticated fusion of religion and politics. He quickly discerned that having the church permeate their work was 'very powerful stuff'. He also highlighted the role of the parish census as a 'very important and astute method of keeping in touch with Catholics'.[28]

Farrell ran a school for Show members in June 1947. The idea of such 'schools' was probably adopted from the CPA, which regularly conducted extensive members' courses in Marxist theory and practice. Santamaria made education of members a high priority from the very inception of The Movement, establishing 'a planned educational organisation', including 'a regular course with examinations and diplomas for those qualifying'. These schools consisted of 'systematic lectures on topics such as the general Australian background, social history from the Christian viewpoint, Christian social principles, their application to Australian conditions, actual conditions in Australian factories, union laws and procedure etc'.[29]

As Moss correctly noted, The Movement was alarmed by the CPA's 'materialism', which is 'why they were so focussed on the religious aspects'.[30] The antidote to 'materialism' was evident at Farrell's school, demonstrated by his own inspirational contribution, in which he sharply criticised members for not giving due weight to formal 'Gospel Discussion':

> That is why we do the Gospel Discussion, to help to sustain you, not only in your own section meetings, at the place of work, but so that you can stand up against the filth ... Further, if we are to go from the place of meeting to the districts in which we live, to our places of employment, to the unions, we need [a] link to bridge the gap and that bridge is an intense love of our neighbour. Now you cannot do things unless you have some sustaining force behind you, unless you feel convinced that what you do will not bring you back any extra cash, will not bring you back rewards, but it is the purpose for which you were created. Now I put it to you that the sections are not functioning as well as they ought. How many of them are bridging the distance between them and the rest of the district? ... the function of the section is to work within the district, to Christianise the district. The

first job of Christianising the district is to Christianise the Catholics in it.[31]

There was, however, a political point. In criticising members for leaving too much of the workload on too few shoulders, he likened the key activists to the Apostles. 'I think that we can thank a few apostles in the sections for enlightening these sections and keeping them going,' he proclaimed, 'a few men who are at it night and day, a few men who believe that the [Movement] pledge means something to them. These men are the men you can imitate, they are the ones who are going to save this country for you.'[32] Farrell's reference to the pledge was to the oath taken by Show members, repeated ritually at the commencement of every meeting:

> I pledge myself faithfully to fulfil all the obligations of Movement membership; in particular to attend meetings regularly and to be active in the Union or Association to which I belong.
>
> I pledge myself not to disclose to any person whatever, not being a member of the Movement, any information concerning its existence or activities, either during my membership or subsequently should I cease to be a member.
>
> I make this solemn pledge voluntarily, realising that any breach of it will render me guilty of a serious breach of faith.[33]

'Faith' clearly implied loyalty unto death to The Show as an organisation, but it also had an even more powerful connotation—implying, as it was surely meant to, that a devout Catholic who betrayed this solemn pledge would also betray his or her religious faith, joining those who had rejected Christ's true path.

Farrell's message was reinforced by Father Patrick (Paddy) Kelly, a diocesan priest who edited the local church newspaper, the *Southern Cross*.[34] Having listed Marx, Lenin, and Stalin as communist leaders, Kelly declared, 'Christ is greater than Marx':

> In addition I might say that another leader that they have is the devil. I say that in all seriousness. One would naturally expect to find the devil behind any movement that was denying God and dooming souls ... We have as our Leader a Living Christ ... You have to be united with our Blessed Lord not merely in Holy Communion but throughout the day. You will be a saint if you do it continuously. But perhaps not many of you will achieve that, but all of you can from time to time, turn to Christ in your factory, office, wherever you may be. Turn to him in a renewed pledge of loyalty, with a renewed appeal of love of Christ, even at your Union Meetings say a little prayer to Our Blessed Lord.[35]

Farrell's special guest speaker conveyed the key political messages. Underlining the secrecy with which The Show operated, he did not use his real name. He was referred to as 'Mr Norman', whereas, in reality, he was Norm Lauritz, Santamaria's handpicked national secretary.[36] Like Farrell, Lauritz was an inspirational speaker, and his address demonstrated his charisma and commitment, aiming to reinforce members' belief that they were part of a secret national organisation whose mission was to snatch victory from the jaws of defeat:

> We are a democracy, we believe in government of the people by the people for the people. We hope that by our work we will

make Australia safe for Australians and safe for Catholicism ... as an official of this organisation I have never been one to boast, but I do say this and say it quite deliberately, that had it not been for the setup of this organisation, for the work it has done ... this country would be under the control of the Communists. I say that very definitely and deliberately, because it is the only organisation which is fighting the Communists. Just as you are listening to me tonight in Adelaide just so tonight and in [sic] every night of the week throughout Australia, from the top of Queensland right around the coast, there are meetings similar to this, going on ... We came in when the fight was almost lost, just before the door was slammed, and it is to the credit of this organisation that the Communist Party is no stronger today than it was 12 months or 2 years ago. In fact it is not quite as strong.[37]

Perhaps Lauritz's most important message was that members were not alone. They were part of a noble, larger Movement of committed Catholics secretly working nationwide: 'Every time you get a knock-back, in your Union meeting or A.L.P. meeting, remember that that little set-back is going on all over Australia, you are not in the fight on your own.'[38]

The centrality of religion to The Show's politics was one thing. But practical assistance from the temporal world was gratefully accepted. For example, in March 1953, the Sydney office advised Farrell that 16,000 copies 'of propaganda ... made available to us by an outside body, free of charge' had been dispatched to Adelaide.[39]

This was the start of a lucrative co-operative arrangement with the US embassy to clandestinely supply massive quantities of high-quality anti-communist literature to The Movement—a subsidy worth huge amounts of money at that time. A few months later, Adelaide ordered 10,000 copies of each of four new US propaganda booklets, samples of which Sydney had sent over.[40] It turned out that Sydney had developed a cosy relationship 'with the officer in charge of the embassy' and the US Information Service. By June 1954, Adelaide had upped its orders to '25,000 and upwards' of US embassy-supplied propaganda, with titles including *The Magnificent Accomplishments of the Soviets*, *Behind the Curtain*, and *Who is the Imperialist?*[41]

The supply of such US propaganda to The Movement became a political scandal in April 1955, when the Labor member for the NSW federal seat of Parkes, Leslie Haylen, made allegations during the Victorian state election campaign that resulted in the defeat of John Cain senior's ALP government. One involved his allegation that the Industrial Groups (which were effectively controlled by The Show) had received £7,000 [$340,000] from the US labour attaché Herbert Weiner, who worked out of the US embassy.[42] Such labour attachés operated worldwide under diplomatic cover, and were invariably operatives of the Central Intelligence Agency (CIA). They were often appointed after being vetted by the American Federation of Labor and Congress of Industrial Organisations (AFL–CIO), the equivalent national peak body to the ACTU.[43] As discussed in detail in chapter ten, during the Cold War the AFL–CIO's international department operated as a wing of US government policy, often participating directly in the CIA's clandestine operations against governments and unions considered to be hostile to US interests.

Another claim made by Haylen concerned what he said was a 'link between the United States Information Service in Australia and "The Movement" in subsidising the issue of American foreign policy propaganda'.[44] Santamaria adamantly denied such US assistance had ever been received by The Movement, declaring in 1971 that, 'No money or any similar aid was ever received from U.S. agencies.'[45] The claim concerning Weiner's cash donation remains unproven, but Santamaria was lying about 'similar aid'. In this, too, The Show had adapted the CPA's methodology, which, in its case, involved distributing heavily subsidised propaganda from the Soviet Union, China, and other communist nations. This was also an effective way to launder money to the party, which sold such material to members and supporters, contributing to its coffers, which by the early 1950s were in dire straits, as membership was in an ever-downwards spiral.[46]

The subterranean struggle between the two organisations led to many coups and counter-coups similar to the story of Jim Moss's lost papers. For example, a few years later, in 1958, the CPA would turn the tables on The Movement, pulling off its greatest coup: repelling John Maynes's concerted campaign to wrest one of the biggest jewels from the communists' by-then battered union crown. US-supplied propaganda played a significant part in the CPA's surveillance operations directed against The Show and in the CPA's own propaganda offensive to link it with 'Yankee imperialism'.

7

Spy versus spy: part one

In late March 1958, a well-attended meeting of communist members of the Waterside Workers' Federation (WWF) convened on the Sydney waterfront. The main report was delivered by veteran CPA union leader Ted Roach, who had spearheaded the campaign against shipments of pig iron to Japan in the late 1930s. The campaign resonated down the years; attorney-general and industry minister Bob Menzies had permitted the shipments and was caustically nicknamed 'Pig Iron' Bob, a label the left used to considerable effect all the way to his retirement in 1966 and beyond.

Nineteen fifty-eight was a crucial year in the WWF's internal politics, marking another round in the titanic battle between the CPA and The Movement for control of the union's federal office. By then, The Show was publicly known as the National Civic Council (NCC), but in common parlance was referred to as 'The Groupers'. Under the ruthless direction of

John Maynes, the NCC's full-time vice-president in charge of industrial matters (while also holding the honorary position of Federated Clerks' Union national president), another concerted campaign was secretly underway to unseat the communists. The CPA—despite temporary setbacks in some major branches, notably Melbourne, where the Groupers were strong—had repelled all challenges to their hold on the federal office.

Despite poor health, long-time communist leader 'Big Jim' Healy remained the popular choice of wharfies as union general secretary, with Roach as assistant secretary. Maynes thought he had the perfect plan to defeat them in the looming election and to pluck the CPA's industrial jewel from its already tarnished crown. This involved splitting ALP supporters away from the CPA's 'unity ticket', which had prevailed over the Groupers at previous elections. Maynes believed he had a well-honed tool to bring his plan to fruition: a senior defector from the CPA, a hardened WWF election campaigner who had the confidence of key ALP wharfies, previously members of the left's unity ticket. He was no ordinary defector; this operative had been critical to past communist victories. Maynes firmly believed he had broken decisively from the CPA. However, by late March this plan was in tatters: the defector had proven to be a double agent, delivering Maynes's secrets straight to Healy.

Ted Roach was in vintage form at the CPA meeting that March, speaking for a full hour, outlining one of the most spectacular, and successful, penetration and disruption operations communists had ever launched against the NCC. Even though the ballot was still three months away, Roach was already confident of victory, crediting Vic Campbell with successfully carrying out the operation, directed by 'Big Jim' and the CPA's super secretive 'Control Committee' (known officially as the Central Disputes Committee, the CDC). The CDC was the body responsible for internal party security, vainly attempting to repel ASIO's penetration agents, safeguarding against provocations of all kinds, prying into the private lives of members, and enforcing rigid 'ideological purity'. Supervised by the CDC, Roach crowed, Campbell's work had exposed 'the Groupers as stooges of the Menzies Government, the ship owners, and big business interests'.[1]

At the conclusion of Roach's report, Campbell took the floor, and—as reported to ASIO by one of its numerous agents among the CPA's waterfront members—with obvious satisfaction reminded the assembled comrades that many of them 'had been very critical of him for his association with the Groupers but that they would now understand why he had not been able to take them into his confidence sooner'. Having justified himself, Campbell warned of the negative consequences if news of the CPA's role in directing his penetration leaked out.[2]

Roach and Campbell's speeches launched a tidal wave that overwhelmed the Groupers; the CPA campaign was impregnable. Instead of Maynes's expected victory, Healy's team scored its biggest-ever win—76 per cent of the vote in the July ballot, reducing their opponents to a rump.

IN MANY RESPECTS, Campbell was an extremely unlikely character to have earned Roach's rich praise. Over the years, he had been the target of numerous CDC investigations; a comprehensive dossier had been assembled, among other things documenting his close relationships with gangsters and his alcohol-fuelled bashings that had left many—including several CPA comrades—badly injured, some disfigured.

The name Campbell was Vic's alias. His father was a Cobb & Co driver whose surname was Gore, and his mother had worked as a cook in a Catholic convent. In 1925, after his father was killed, he was placed at the age of eight in an orphanage at Kincumber on the central coast, north of Sydney, but he ran away, was caught and sent to Gosford Boys' Home, but again absconded. His life in the criminal milieu began in 1933 in the tough inner-city working-class suburbs of Woolloomooloo and Surry Hills, where Campbell mixed with wild street boys—apprentice gangsters—and soon came to police notice. Around 1937–38, he was charged with shooting with intent, and was sentenced to twelve months' gaol for possessing a gun, which, he claimed, had been planted on him by the coppers. In 1940, he was again gaoled, this time for six months under the consorting laws, which made it a criminal offence to associate with known criminals.[3]

Campbell was called up into the army in 1943, but maintained he went absent without leave four times, was court-martialled and sentenced to twelve months in a military prison, and was then dishonourably discharged in 1944. Soon after, he went to work on the wharves, and in 1947 joined the CPA at the invitation of veteran communist and Sydney WWF branch secretary Tom Nelson. Nelson admired his courage and brawling skills, and was especially grateful after Campbell came to the aid of party members who had been 'attacked by reaction' (CPA shorthand for right-wing thugs). He rapidly rose through the CPA and union ranks, first as secretary of one of several CPA wharf branches, then in 1950 as a vice-president on the union's Sydney branch executive, and by the early 1950s as secretary of the CPA's powerful Sydney section committee, a communist inner-city stronghold covering the waterfront, seamen, and large factory and working-class suburban branches. Although lacking in formal education, by this time Campbell had already attended two extended CPA ideological and organisational training schools, later—somewhat implausibly—assuming responsibility for education among the section's members.[4]

One prominent CPA wharfie painted a vivid pen-picture of him:

> Vic Campbell was one of the rough-and-tumble, colourful characters on the waterfront. Those years threw up a lot of roughies like Campbell, and he was a bit rougher and tougher than even the normal rough and toughie—and an uncouth sort of a bloke.[5]

He recounted an occasion when he and several other CPA members spent time at Campbell's home:

> We were all drunk, blind as bats. We'd been at the pub till fairly late, and we were still drinking and fooling around, and he produced a bloody gun, and we asked him why he carried it, and he said, 'Protection, brother. You've got to have protection.'[6]

Waterfront politics had always been a tough game. It was often said that whoever wanted to control the WWF had to do a deal with the gangster elements that had infiltrated the workforce decades earlier, especially in Sydney and Melbourne. At one time or another, each of the factions vying for control—the ALP, the CPA, and the Groupers—had to accommodate organised crime, which had the numbers to swing elections to the ticket that promised to look the other way so the criminal elements could get on with their illicit activities. Vic Campbell was a perfect point man for the CPA to liaise with the gangsters. Maynes was equally impressed with his talents. It was little wonder, however, that he was under almost constant investigation by the CDC.

But Campbell's talents stretched beyond his gangster connections. His abilities in industrial campaigns, and especially his successful organising skills in union elections, were duly noted by senior CPA members. For example, in October 1951, the Federated Ironworkers' Association (FIA) elections were in full swing. The CPA was in retreat in the FIA, which it had controlled for the previous fifteen years. The 1949 election had been 'won' through the massive forgery of ballot papers, organised by long-time communist FIA official and Stalinist apparatchik Jack McPhillips. The anti-communist candidate for national secretary, Laurie Short, challenged that result, and his long-running court case was about to end in unequivocal victory after his lawyers proved that forgery had determined the election in the CPA's favour.

McPhillips was deeply worried that the CPA would lose the looming 1951 election, and turned to trusted comrades to keep Short's team at bay. In October, he called a meeting of communist FIA activists in Melbourne. ASIO had an agent present, who reported that McPhillips 'informed them that it had been decided by the C.P. of A. that it was necessary to strengthen the "militant" vote in Port Kembla for the F.I.A. elections, and Vic. CAMPBELL, a Party organiser, from the W.W.F. in Sydney had been sent as an F.I.A. organiser to Port Kembla'.[7] Campbell made no difference; the CPA was defeated, not only in Port Kembla but in its Sydney stronghold, and the recently installed national secretary, Laurie Short, found himself with a majority of delegates to national conference. It was the end of communist power in the ironworkers' union.[8]

This did not take the shine off Campbell's reputation. The following year, ASIO reported that he was a member of the CPA's powerful WWF National Bureau. Effectively, this was the national executive for communist strategy on the waterfront, directing the successful 1952 WWF national campaign, for which Campbell was the 'full-time organiser'.[9] Illustrating his good standing, on 9 September 1952, Campbell attended a high-level CPA 'Political Meeting', chaired by CPA national president Dick Dixon. Campbell had provided Dixon with security protection during the tumultuous months culminating in the narrow defeat of Menzies' 1951 referendum to ban the CPA, and they frequently drank together at waterfront pubs, often in 'Big Jim's' company.[10]

Jack Hughes, the recently defeated communist federal secretary of the clerks' union, who, as a senior member of the CDC, had investigated many allegations concerning Campbell, also attended this meeting. Despite his intimate knowledge of Campbell's unsavoury history, Hughes understood that he possessed street-level political acumen and credibility with the tough waterfront workforce. The agenda was especially sensitive, involving 'work in A.L.P. around 11 citations from A.L.P. Executive on W.W.F. officials'. The ALP had recently charged and later expelled members who had broken its rules by standing on unity tickets with communists in the 1952 union elections. When the full CPA WWF national fraction convened in November, Campbell declared, 'The results of the W.W.F. elections on a National basis were a triumph of United Front tactics.' Those expelled from the ALP were, apparently, necessary collateral damage to shore up the CPA's powerbase.[11]

Not all of Campbell's talents, however, were strictly political. In August 1954, the CPA was working frantically to minimise damaging evidence tabled at the royal commission on espionage, following the defection of Soviet intelligence operatives Vladimir and Evdokia Petrov. One of the CPA lawyers working on the case was prominent Brisbane barrister Max Julius. On 24 August, Julius was in Sydney working on 'Document J', a sensational report written in the Soviet embassy by CPA journalist Rupert Lockwood that was causing considerable embarrassment at the royal commission. The CPA's strategy was to cast doubt on the document's authenticity, insinuating it was a forgery. Campbell's underworld connections had been drawn to Julius's attention, as one of ASIO's well-placed agents reported:

> [JULIUS] wanted to see Vic CAMPBELL and made an appointment to see him at the Waterside Workers' Federation waterfront office, 66 Sussex Street ...
>
> JULIUS wants the services of an expert forger to forge LOCKWOOD's signature and the initials which appear on the side of Document "J" ...
>
> JULIUS wants the man produced ... at 1 p.m. at 66 Sussex Street, on Wednesday, 25 August, 1954.[12]

Throughout these years, as ASIO compiled its large dossier on Campbell, the CDC accumulated an even more massive, parallel file. They gathered evidence of his numerous bashings and violence with various weapons, and also investigated allegations of his collaboration with 'security coppers', with one informant 'pretty certain that he is now a security man'. They collected eyewitness statements of his often-vicious verbal attacks on sections of the WWF leadership (especially on his old friend Tom Nelson), and of the police having 'found a gun in Campbell's place'.

One thread running through the CDC's conclusions was that 'we know from experience that ... Campbell does not always handle the truth in the very straightest manner'. His repeated violent assaults were of particular concern—for example, in one case, 'it appears he acted in a most irrational and provocative manner, indeed a most brutal way, likely to get the Party into serious trouble. ... DID V.C. ENGINEER INCIDENTS?'

A recurring investigation concerned the persistent claim that he had been a provost in the army (a much-hated military policeman). The CDC had accumulated convincing evidence confirming this, but Campbell routinely deflected the charge—for example, by claiming 'that always when he was doing special jobs for the Party, this rumour about him being a provost came up and this always upsets him'.[13] The CDC concluded that Campbell was lying and, as the 1958 WWF elections loomed, this was among the factors that eventually ensured his 'loyalty' to the CPA ticket.

Several CDC investigations, however, were especially intriguing in light of events during those elections: his alleged clandestine co-operation with the Groupers. For example, in July 1955, by-elections were held for casual vacancies for several WWF Sydney branch office-holders. 'There was considerable scramble for the jobs,' according to CPA waterfront organiser, Don Morcom. Bill Brooks, a vice-president elected in 1954 on the CPA's unity ticket, resigned and went into opposition to stand for a full-time position.

Brooks and Campbell were close, having been on the union's Sydney branch executive together since 1950. He thought 'Campbell had plenty of go-ahead and ability and he was a real go-getter ... He drank at the pub next door to the union rooms ... and hung around with tough men, stand over men'. But, as he said, 'I got on well with him.'[14] At the time of the by-elections, Campbell was in Western Australia, but, as Morcom reported to the CDC:

[I]n the middle of the problem, Campbell suddenly reappeared from the West, and it was obvious only to have a hand in the matter. (It is suggested that he had meetings with the opposition.) We had produced a special How to Vote ticket—yellow card board with green printing, to make it distinctive. One of the samples usually put on the outside of the bundles went off, and the opposition produced an identical How to Vote card. Campbell is strongly suspected. Also too Campbell approached me and said he was picking up Brooks' written propaganda to be used on election day. He put the proposition that he knock it off; I agreed. He suggested it be burnt at 93 [Sussex Street—CPA waterfront headquarters]. I made an appointment to see him, but told him if I didn't turn up, he knew what to do with it and I suggested it be dumped in the Harbour. I did not turn up; he claimed he dumped it in the Harbour, but it was noticeable that they had more stuff than they could give out on election day.[15]

Despite this suspected treachery, Campbell retained his CPA membership. An ugly incident at Easter 1956 threatened his position when, after yet another heavy drinking session, he severely bashed a prominent—and much smaller—CPA member. This time there was serious talk of expelling him from the CPA. A CDC inquiry was launched by Jack Hughes, who, in the end, again let him escape the ultimate punishment, noting that it was his 'last chance'; that he would be barred from holding any party or union executive positions for twelve months; and that he had to 'actively prove himself'.[16]

Despite the damning evidence, Campbell successfully appealed 'against the harshness of the penalty'. In mid-June 1956, the Sydney district executive endorsed 'the decision ... that Comrade Campbell was guilty of uncommunist conduct that could have had most serious consequences for the Party'. Strangely, in light of the vehement censure thus far expressed by everyone involved in the investigation, the executive waived the actual punishment, expressing confidence that Campbell would, miraculously, transform into 'a diligent Branch member', and suspended the decision barring him from holding official positions.[17] He had, however, already been removed from the unity ticket for the 1956 WWF Sydney branch election, which must have stung, as he had been a vice-president since 1950.

But he had survived this further self-inflicted crisis. A week later, a CPA central trade union committee meeting was held to discuss waterfront tactics. This was an official sub-committee of the party's highest body, the powerful central committee. It brought together the most senior communist unionists (dealing with issues across the entire trade union movement). Present were the CPA's industrial supremo, former ironworkers' union official Jack McPhillips, along with many senior unionists, including Ted Rowe (engineering union), Tom Wright (sheet metal union), Pat Clancy (building union), Matt Munro (Sydney WWF), Ted Roach (national WWF), and Vic Campbell who, apparently, was still treated as a loyal, if misguided, comrade.[18]

Throughout 1957, however, Campbell's performance continuously perplexed the CPA's leadership. His skills as an election campaign manager continued to be held in high regard, but more and more his loyalty to the party came under close scrutiny. His hostile attitude towards Tom Nelson, in particular, caused widespread consternation. In the winter of that year, his relations with the party were at their lowest ebb in his decade of membership.

By December 1957, things had crystallised. Don Morcom, the CPA waterfront organiser, had assembled a concrete case, reporting that he had come 'to the conclusion that Campbell is an agent'. Morcom believed that Campbell was working for Security. He reviewed many of the previously recounted incidents. Tellingly, he reported to the CDC that Campbell had refused to even speak to him since August 1957, although he had tried to talk to him several times: 'We are still considering what should be done about it—whether he should be brought in for a discussion, or whether he is trying to manoeuvre some provocation.'[19]

This was especially worrying, as preparations for the July 1958 union elections were well underway, and all the signs were pointing to a hotly contested campaign. Even more concerning were growing suspicions that Campbell was surreptitiously working *against* the CPA and had, in fact, defected to the opposition.

8

Spy versus spy: part two

It was no coincidence that Vic Campbell had stopped talking to CPA waterfront organiser Don Morcom after August 1957: he had, indeed, clandestinely defected to the Groupers, making contact with Jim Macken, a senior Sydney-based NCC member and official of the clerks' union. Macken had spent time in Movement headquarters in Melbourne before going on the full-time payroll in his hometown of Sydney at the end of 1948 where, in the early 1950s, he was one of Father Ryan's liaison agents with ASIO.[1]

In September 1957, Macken worked closely with Maynes on union affairs. When Campbell turned up, he did not like the look of him, and 'was very circumspect' because he did not trust him. But he concluded that Campbell had not been 'sent in by the CPA'. He judged that Campbell 'was under immense psychological pressure and had contacts with criminal elements', so he sent him 'off to Maynes and Alford' as quickly as possible—'they could have him'.[2] Gus Alford was the most prominent, effective, and popular Show activist on the waterfront, who was running the 1958 WWF campaign, closely supervised by the NCC's industrial supremo, John Maynes.

Around this time, Campbell also approached Bill Brooks. The two had remained friends, and Campbell knew that Brooks retained considerable personal popularity, which would be crucial in defeating Tom Nelson, who by this time was Campbell's personal *bête noire*. According to Brooks, at least part of Campbell's alienation from the CPA was deeply personal. 'Campbell fell out with Nelson over Carol Knox,' he stated, 'whose husband Charlie was a wharfie, but she went off to live with Campbell, and Nelson was hostile about it.' According to Brooks, 'Nelson and Campbell finished with one another … Campbell was very hostile to Nelson, and he came to me and said he was going to break with them and go into opposition.'[3]

On the other hand, a long-time communist wharfie experienced Nelson's hostility to Campbell in a different context. These two men had an altercation over the allocation of tickets to the union's annual sports carnival. According to this wharfie's vivid recollections, Campbell 'grabbed me by the throat. So I kneed him in the groin and there was a terrible row … Nelson came in as Campbell pulled the gun … a big gun, which I saw him pull three times, an old-fashioned gun … Nelson really told Vic off that day … He said: "I've had enough of you, Vic, you just cut it out."'[4]

In January 1958, Macken dispatched Campbell to Maynes and Alford in Melbourne, where he formally offered his defection. Before leaving Sydney he created a powerful bargaining chip, meeting with the group of wharfies who would form the core of Sydney's team to oppose the CPA in the local branch election. (National and branch ballots were conducted simultaneously.)[5] Sydney was critical, as the CPA's vote was strong there, while Alford's team had built a solid base in Melbourne. Campbell promised to deliver the most influential ALP supporters from the CPA's unity ticket to the Groupers, who would then be able to run their own 'unity ticket'. Campbell's second bargaining chip was his vast—and successful—experience in organising union election campaigns, which Maynes and Alford were only too eager to embrace.

In mid-February, the first public skirmishes began, with the Groupers bombarding the Sydney waterfront with posters attacking Nelson:

"TRAFALGAR"
NELSON'S
ONLY
VICTORY
PUT THE
RED EXECUTIVE
OUT
NEXT JULY[6]

But, just as Maynes's and Alford's campaign was gathering momentum, the CPA sprang its trap. By early February, Healy, Nelson, and Morcom had enough evidence to conclude that Campbell had defected. They were worried; if he could not be pulled back into line, the election result might be too close for comfort. So, according to a well-placed communist wharfie, a simple but brutal plan was hatched: they would stand over the arch standover merchant. The man chosen to confront Campbell was another CPA wharfie, Jack Hartley. He was one of the rare breed who could go toe-to-toe with Campbell in a brawl and survive the battering, as one of his comrades remembered: 'Jack had been to sea on American ships during the war, so he spoke with an American accent. They called him the "Woolloomooloo Yank", but he was able to handle himself in a street brawl. He was a big bloke, quite fearless.' Returning to Sydney after the war, Hartley became 'a close associate of Nelson'.[7]

In mid-February, just as the Groupers' posters were plastered up, Hartley was ordered to shirt-front Campbell when he was drinking at the workers' club. Hartley was primed for the confrontation:

> The word was out that Campbell was mixed up in some funny business, and he complained to Jack about it, and he said: 'What's this all about me being a copper?' And 'Big Jack' said: 'Well, you are, ain't you?' By this time they'd accumulated evidence, and Jack had knowledge of it. So Jack laid it on the line and Campbell went to water, because his other associations outside the waterfront meant that he was in extreme jeopardy ... because he was a gangster, and gangsters don't muck around, they'll fill you full of lead. If the union had dropped the fact that he was working with the coppers, it would've been public knowledge, so everyone would've known, including his associates ... So they did a deal — Nelson and the others involved ... and the result was that Campbell made this statement, and to cover Campbell they said they'd asked him to go in and spy on the Groupers ... Campbell blew his guts and told them a lot about what the Groupers had been doing.[8]

In fact, from this point onwards, Campbell revealed

everything to Hartley about the Groupers' plans.[9] Hartley's initial report to the CPA indicated the extent to which he had 'spilled his guts'. For example, Hartley listened in while Campbell spoke to key Show organisers on the phone, reporting in particular on his call to Jim Macken, who informed him that Maynes 'would be arriving in Sydney on Wednesday next, February 19th' for a meeting at the Metropole hotel 'to organise opponents to the Federal Officers. C[ampbell] is alleged to have the job to produce people to contest these positions— 1 from Fremantle and two from Sydney ... C. got a list of names from Makin [sic] of Group supporters who have indicated that they will support the groupers. This of course was placed in the hands of the G[eneral]. S[ecretary].'[10]

From this time onwards, Jim Healy knew the names of the Groupers' key supporters, receiving detailed reports about their plans soon after they were decided. Under tight CPA control, Campbell continued to act out the role of *bona fide* Grouper, picking up Brooks on 19 February and driving him to the Metropole, where Maynes reported 'that he had had a discussion on the previous night with the ... Group in Melbourne and they had asked him to find out the present position in Sydney and what progress had been made in working out the nominations for National positions in the Waterside Workers' Federation elections', and whether someone had been lined up to go to the national conference in Melbourne in early March to finalise the campaign. Maynes reported that he was on his way to Brisbane and Rockhampton on clerks' union business, and would arrange for delegates from those ports to attend the Melbourne meeting, and that Adelaide, Hobart, and Launceston would send representatives. Campbell outlined the arrangements he had made for a Fremantle delegate, and reported that four would attend from Sydney.[11]

Maynes was clearly impressed, believing that for the first time a truly national campaign—uniting the anti-communist forces—could credibly challenge Jim Healy's team. He announced that the Melbourne meeting would decide the candidates for national officials, reporting that the Melbourne Groupers proposed that Sydney should field candidates against Healy and also for federal president. Brooks got down to business, pointedly asking where the money would come from. Maynes assured them there was 'unlimited finance coming in'. He reported that £1,000 [$30,000] was available for the campaign, but 'stressed that money would have to be raised also by the various branches, that this was essential in case questions were asked as to where the money for the campaign was coming from'. Melbourne proposed that Alford do a national tour after nominations closed, to 'ginger-up' the campaign; according to Maynes, 'he had research and legal people preparing statements' on the team's policies, which 'would be available a few months before the elections'.[12]

Unwittingly, Brooks greatly assisted the CPA by insisting that Sydney should be independent of Melbourne, which 'was well known as the Industrial Group, but the Industrial Group had practically no support in Sydney. If the Sydney organisation were to be openly known as the Industrial Group it would be doomed.' He appreciated the financial and other support of the Groupers, but was adamant Sydney should not be publicly associated with them, although the clandestine link should continue. He proposed establishing a 'central force in Sydney' and, while he would attend the Melbourne meeting, was emphatic that it 'should be kept quiet'.[13] In one single contribution he had given the communists all the ammunition they needed to publicly destroy his credibility.

Maynes's role was pivotal, demonstrated by the fact that, in early March, Campbell took delivery of a clerks' union car for use during the campaign.[14] Maynes thoroughly trusted him, leaving it up to him to select two additional Sydney delegates to attend the Melbourne meeting (along with Campbell and Brooks). The CPA ordered Campbell to take two low-key party members, John Burraston and Jim O'Brien. Thirty-six years later, Burraston was still perplexed by his involvement, recounting how communist WWF official Bobbie Bolger had approached him:

> He said: 'Would you do something for the party?' I said: 'Yeah.' I thought it was just handing out leaflets or something. He said: 'Do you think you could go down to Melbourne tonight or tomorrow morning?' I said: 'Oh yeah.' I probably met them at the airport, and that was where I met Vic Campbell … They just explained to us that the Groupers were being supported by Shell Oil Company for somebody to oppose the communists. And they said: 'We want it to be you.' Well, I couldn't speak. I don't know why they ever picked me—it was stupid. So we went down to Melbourne, and there were all these people there, and I had to get up and say that I hated communists, and that was it … We had a good time while we were there, drinking and lairing up.[15]

On 7 March, the Sydney delegation flew to Melbourne, staying at the Parade hotel in Fitzroy with all travel, accommodation, and living expenses paid by the Groupers.[16] When the meeting convened, Campbell was elected chairman, and a national committee was appointed with Alford as secretary and Campbell as president. A bemused Burraston was endorsed to stand for general secretary against 'Big Jim', and O'Brien for president.[17] Two CPA members had been endorsed by the Groupers to stand for the most senior national positions. Burraston recounted the surreal experience:

> I was picked to oppose Jim Healy ... You see, I had no politics ... for me to oppose Jim Healy was just too silly for words ... The Groupers didn't seem to be suspicious ... We were accepted as genuine anti-communists trying to get rid of the WWF leadership.

The best-known actual Grouper, Alford, was picked to contest the position of national organiser.[18]

Alford delivered the finance report, 'but first appealed to delegates to not allow any of his report to go outside the meeting, indicating that if the "comms" got hold of it, it would destroy the groups'. It was dynamite. About £42 [$1,250] per week was collected on the Melbourne waterfront, he reported, but this was Group money, whereas 'the organisations to be now set up in the other ports are to be completely divorced from the Industrial Groups'. Alford's wages and work expenses were said to be £600 [$18,000] per year, and the Melbourne committee established for the campaign had £800 [$24,000] in hand. Alford then dealt with the most damaging aspects of the money's real source, which would prove deadly when later publicised by the CPA.

The advertisement regularly placed in the Groupers' waterfront newspaper *Vigilante* 'by Shell Oil Company brought in £28 [$835] per issue, and Shell Oil also donated to their funds. He stated that in view of the criticisms of the advertisement that it may be adviseable [sic] to withdraw it, but the company had assured him that the donation would continue.' He then revealed another bombshell, reporting that they also received donations from members of the Liberal Party, assuring 'delegates that there was plenty of finance coming', and appealing 'to delegates to approach business people and shipping companies in their ports who were sympathetic to them'.[19]

There could be no doubt that the bosses were bankrolling the campaign. This was underlined by the relationship the Groupers had with Jim Shortell, a former senior right-wing union official who had been supported by The Movement (as a non-Catholic) before being appointed by the Menzies government to the Australian Stevedoring Industry Authority (ASIA). Maynes arranged with Shortell for the Sydney campaign to be provided with an ASIA office, handily located in Customs House at Circular Quay.[20] His role in Maynes's plans would be used to devastating effect among the membership, who saw ASIA as a tool of the government and the bosses.[21]

The Melbourne meeting was the endgame for Maynes's dream of wresting control of the WWF from the CPA. The icing on the cake was information Campbell provided to Hartley about anti-communist propaganda supplied to Macken by the US labour attaché (technically a diplomat, but usually a career CIA officer), 'proving' the involvement of US imperialism in plotting against the union.[22] The propaganda value of the US connection was demonstrated in an official union leaflet distributed on 13 March calling a general members' meeting for the following Sunday in the union hall. The leaflet was the first public indication of the devastating attack about to be launched, utilising Campbell's intelligence as conveyed to Hartley. After recounting earlier incidents of the Groupers' 'anti-union' activities, the leaflet levelled a series of damaging allegations:

They now have organised a secretly controlled nerve centre; a conspiratorial body with U.S.A. backing to pull the strings and unite, on top level, shipowners, the A.S.I.A. and notorious reactionary forces outside the W.W.F. such as Maynes and Co. of the Clerks Union ...

And of course they are responsible for the organisation of groupings, enemy agents, disgruntled and ambitious people and sponsorship of lying, rumourmongering [sic] to confuse the membership as to who is responsible for the many attacks upon their precious work conditions ... and trade union rights.

To consider all these matters, fellow members, a meeting has been called in the Union Rooms ... this Sunday 16th March where Jim Healy ... will make exposures of the organised attack.[23]

The same day that this leaflet hit the waterfront, the CPA bulletin, *Wharfie*, launched its own attack, claiming that the ship-owners and ASIA 'finance and give material support to their "Vigilantes" in the ranks of the workers who seek to split the workers and turn them against their leaders. For this reason, *Wharfie* welcomes the special meeting which has been called to expose the splitters and disruptors within the Federation.'[24]

Maynes, Alford, and Macken still did not suspect Campbell's hand in this decidedly disastrous turn of events.[25] The next phase of the trap was sprung on 15 March. Macken went to Campbell's home, where a heated argument occurred during a lengthy telephone conversation with Alford and Maynes in Melbourne. The CPA had orchestrated a letter to Maynes and Alford from the Sydney candidates, 'demanding that Alford ... not run on the ticket'. Alford and Maynes insisted he should, but they capitulated three days later, fearing that their 'unity ticket' would otherwise disintegrate.[26]

The Groupers had been comprehensively out-manoeuvred and were in disarray, but the penny had not yet fully dropped. Campbell concluded that his double game was at an end. On 26 March, Alford arrived from Melbourne, confused, uncomprehending, and still blindly trusting Campbell. At a meeting with Alford and Macken, Campbell was actually given control over the Groupers' nominations. The CPA's WWF National Bureau was hastily convened, deciding to lodge the nominations but to then have Burraston and O'Brien 'go to the Federal Office and make a statement for the reasons for them not standing'.[27] The Groupers would then have to scramble to assemble a full ticket, ensuring it would be Melbourne dominated. (Alford was forced to nominate against Healy, meaning that three candidates were Melbourne based.) Even more damaging, their ticket would be openly Grouper dominated, because the candidates who were supposed to provide their 'unity ticket' had withdrawn.[28]

On 29 March, Campbell informed Alford that the Sydney candidates were pulling out, and, 'after pleading with him', Alford 'thanked him for letting him know and stated that he would come up to Sydney to nominate against the General Secretary'. In response to Alford's question about the withdrawals, Campbell stated they 'did not want to be mixed up with the people from outside, such as Shortell, Makin [sic] and Maynes ... Alford pleaded with him not to mention anything about Shortell.'[29]

Macken was very upset at the withdrawals, and 'continually phoned C[ampbell] over the week-end but he would not answer the phone'.[30] On 31 March, Campbell finally rang Macken, who told him that Alford's nomination had been officially lodged.[31] The two men met for one last drink in the Dumbarton Castle hotel. 'Campbell was very apologetic about the whole thing and claimed that he'd been stood over by the party, and been threatened with exposure as having been a provo during the war.'[32]

Bill Brooks heard a similar story, and was sure the CPA must have had something on Campbell:

> I believe he definitely was with us. A man couldn't act that well. He was too sincere—in everything—that he had to be with us. I did hear later … that they got over the top of him because they had too much on him … concerning his intrigues … I genuinely believed he had defected from the CPA and was a big help because he was a good organiser and the type of bloke we wanted … he would have pulled a lot of left-wing votes away from the CPA.[33]

In the end, the reverse was the case: the CPA–ALP unity ticket pulled a lot of votes away from the Groupers. In the months between the exposure of the Groupers' plans in mid-March and the ballot in early July, the communists drilled it into the rank and file that Alford and company were in the pockets of US imperialism, the Menzies government, and the bosses, in the pay of big business, and aimed to undermine their hard-fought-for working conditions.[34] The last word was left to 'Big Jim' Healy when he presented his report to the union's Seventh All Ports Biennial Conference on 22 September 1958:

> Before proceeding with my report let me first express my appreciation of the very encouraging vote of confidence expressed in both the leadership and our national policy at the recent Federation ballot.
>
>   I have now been General Secretary of the Federation since

November 1937 ... The 17,228 votes accorded to me out of
a total of 22,544 votes recorded, which equals 76 per cent or
¾ of the members' voting is an all-time record. It provides a
complete answer to the daily press and other enemies of the
Federation who were prophesying that the membership was
tired of the present leadership and opposed to the national
policy. Their wishful thinking even caused them to express
the belief that I was old, tired and ill and that I might not live
long enough to hear the result of the election. The facts speak
for themselves. The overwhelming support given to myself
and the other federal officers shows quite clearly that the
policy we have followed and the results obtained therefrom
have been satisfactory to the overwhelming majority of the
membership.[35]

In light of Healy's popularity among the membership, due
in large part to his legendary common touch with ordinary
wharfies, it seems probable that he would have won without
the huge leg-up provided (under duress) by Vic Campbell.
The result may have been far closer and, had a Grouper unity
ticket stood, as envisaged by John Maynes, other members of
Healy's ticket may well have been defeated; there was a distinct
possibility that Campbell would have ousted the rather aloof
Tom Nelson as Sydney branch secretary.

Healy's victory at the subsequent election in 1960 would
be his last; in July 1961, he died from a stroke at the tragically
young age of 63. The CPA's decision to stand Nelson in the
by-election to replace him was a disaster; he was not that
well known, or well liked, outside his Sydney base, and was
defeated by ALP unionist Charlie Fitzgibbon. As the popular
and charismatic WWF national industrial officer Norm Docker
remarked, if he [Docker] had been the CPA's candidate,

Fitzgibbon had stated he would not even have run, and the communists would have retained control of the union's federal office. In the end, neither they nor their sworn enemy, The Movement, won the ultimate battle. Fitzgibbon stayed in office until 1983, when Docker finally succeeded him, but by then the CPA was a shadow of its once-powerful self.[36]

The man at the centre of this story of intrigue, blackmail, and double dealing was also a shadow of the once influential communist he had been for almost a decade from the late 1940s. In the wake of the election, it seems the CPA allowed Campbell to quietly let his membership lapse, only to mysteriously re-admit him a year or so later. Although he was briefly involved in some industrial matters for the union, he spent most of the next few years engaged in menial tasks, such as collecting unsold goods from fundraising events, on behalf of the party in which he had once exercised considerable political authority.[37]

He ended his days a broken man, ravaged by alcohol, and kept at arm's length by both his old CPA comrades and The Show, to which he had genuinely defected. By the second half of the 1960s, Vic Campbell was a resident in the somewhat Dickensian-era Morissett psychiatric hospital (originally called the 'Asylum for the Insane') on the shores of Lake Macquarie, south of Newcastle. From there he wrote to one of the Groupers' supporters, promising to reveal everything about his role as a double agent in the 1958 union election. His offer was never taken up; after all, he was in a mental institution, and who would believe the ramblings of a mad man?[38]

9

The ghost of Stalinism

By the early 1970s, the CPA was a shadow of a once-formidable political and industrial organisation. Split into three separate parties, with an ageing and shrinking membership, and its power in the trade unions greatly diminished, the influence of its ideology in Australia was at its lowest ebb since the early 1930s. The party had suffered two catastrophic splits: the first in the early 1960s, and the second a decade later, both centred on the legacy of Stalinism.

In the early 1960s, a small but influential section left to form a pro-Beijing party, embracing Mao's line that Stalin had basically pursued the correct communist line, and stridently denouncing Khrushchev's condemnation of Stalin's crimes. In the mid-1960s, an even greater upheaval occurred when a new generation of CPA leaders criticised Moscow's embrace of neo-Stalinism after Brezhnev purged Khrushchev in 1964. Simmering tensions boiled over when the CPA leadership supported Alexander Dubček's Prague Spring and condemned the 1968 Soviet-led invasion that crushed Czechoslovakia's experiment in 'socialism with a human face'. Eventually, one-third of the membership—including many key union leaders—formed a pro-Moscow party in 1971. The hatreds generated by these splits left deep scars.

Santamaria followed these developments, rightly discerning the immense possibilities they opened up for The Movement's union operations. By then, his organisation was widely known as the National Civic Council (NCC), and this is the name by which it will be frequently called from this point forward, although members still affectionately called it The Movement or The Show.

In December 1970, ASIO obtained Santamaria's sophisticated analysis of 'the divisions in the C.P.A.'[1] In what reads like an ASIO 'Position Paper' written by one of its top analysts, Santamaria observed that the latest CPA split offered 'vast opportunities in the unions and elsewhere, but only if there are sufficiently trained "cadres" to exploit it':

> If the anti-Communist forces had the resources and handled themselves carefully, there could be nothing but very great gains in this particular field. At the moment, it seems that practically everything in the field of anti-Communist organisation ought to be subordinated to widespread recruitment and training of every possible person who can gain full time positions in unions.[2]

Santamaria correctly observed that Stalinism was at the core of the divisions. He also understood that bitter personal rivalries invariably surfaced during such factional battles. 'Fights are not always about the issues which are invoked in the course of the fight,' he wrote. 'Fights are often about purely personal issues which are embellished into struggles of principle.'

In the following decade, the consequences of modelling The Movement upon the CPA would consume his own seemingly monolithic organisation, ending in an equally bitter split focussed on a form of 'Stalinism' in the NCC. This began in the mid-1970s with deep feuds involving John Maynes, whose authoritarianism caused divisive upheavals in NCC-controlled unions. Maynes had loyally served as Santamaria's second-in-command as vice president (industrial), but in the early 1980s they had a severe falling-out when Santamaria effectively turned his back on unionism. Maynes was a long-term NCC staffer. For over twenty years, he falsely claimed he was the full-time federal president of the Federated Clerks' Union, for which he actually only received an honorarium.[3]

JOHN GRENVILLE was a key figure in the first phase of the NCC's divisions. Like many who had been drawn to The Movement from the early 1940s onwards, Grenville came from a middle-class Melbourne family. He was educated by the De La Salle brothers at Malvern, then as a boarder at the Marist Brothers-run Assumption College in Kilmore, central Victoria. The Labor Split occurred while he was at Assumption, and inevitably he was drawn into the furious arguments that arose. This greatly influenced Grenville's views when he enrolled at Melbourne University in 1957 and became active in student politics. He was a founding member of the university DLP Society, and joined the Australian Labor Party (Anti-Communist)—later the Democratic Labor Party (DLP). The NCC recruited him at the end of 1957.[4]

He was soon a regular at NCC headquarters, where

he first met Santamaria. Steeped in the church's anti-communist and social-justice teachings, Grenville was drawn to the organisation's fight 'against the totalitarian left in the trade union movement'.[5] After a period of political inactivity following his marriage in 1963, his value to the NCC emerged when he became a key player in this fight, demonstrating his credentials as an industrial advocate for the municipal officers' and teachers' unions, drawing him to Maynes's attention.

In early 1964, Maynes had helped Mick Jordan succeed Vic Stout as secretary of the Victorian Trades Hall Council (the Trades Hall), the peak body of Victoria's unions. In return for delivering the NCC's votes, Maynes requested that one of his trusted people be appointed to the Trades Hall staff. When the position of research officer became vacant in 1966, Maynes asked Grenville to apply, and Jordan appointed him.[6]

Working closely with Jordan gave Grenville the opportunity to learn sophisticated industrial skills, also providing a bridge so that NCC policies could be implemented and the communists' (of various factions) resisted. Strategy and tactics were decided at NCC caucus meetings prior to the weekly Thursday council meeting, which all affiliated unions could attend. The agenda paper would not be issued until Thursday night, but the Trades Hall executive debated and approved it on Wednesdays, giving Grenville advance knowledge. If the agenda was deemed to be of sufficient importance, the caucus would be convened to determine how NCC-controlled unions 'were going to vote, who the speakers would be, and the general gist of the type of argument that would be put forward'.[7]

It was impossible for Grenville to hide his real allegiances, even though he publicly denied his NCC membership. As he said:

One is immediately known by the other side because of the policies you pursue, stands you take, and any one particular ideological argument is always noted by the other side. I would say that I can always tell a member of the Communist Party who claims that he isn't, in terms of the way he's performing. So that they would have known exactly the way I was performing. Now, put that into the broad spectrum of the middle group that you might talk about in the Trades Hall situation, they were well and truly advised by the extreme left that I was an undercover member of the NCC.[8]

Many communist delegates to Trades Hall were hostile to Grenville, personally as well as politically. Others were polite, even helpful. One in particular summed Grenville up perfectly. George Seelaf, a staunch CPA member, was the Victorian secretary of the meat workers' union, and, as Grenville recalled:

He came into my office one day and introduced himself. He said to me, 'I've been telling Jordan for a long time that we need someone in here with your type of qualifications. Mind you, I didn't exactly have you in mind and if I get half a chance I'm going to cut your fucking throat from ear-to-ear. But while you're here you might as well learn something,' which he proceeded to impart. I could often go and talk to George about an industrial issue, and he was very competent and his working knowledge of the Victorian system was invaluable, and he made no secret of the fact that he was more than happy to impart it to me. In fact, there was never evidence that George was cutting my f-ing throat from ear-to-ear![9]

When Jordan died suddenly and unexpectedly in 1969, Grenville won the subsequent election for assistant secretary of the Trades Hall. 'And that of course was a predetermined situation in that the NCC operatives ... with votes at the Council had caucused and determined that I should be the candidate.'[10]

By this time, Grenville was a member of the inner sanctum, sharing a close political relationship with Santamaria and attending his weekly lunch at NCC headquarters at Riversdale Road, Hawthorn. These brought together the most senior political and industrial operatives, including Santamaria and Maynes, and DLP leaders such as Senator Frank McManus, Jim Brosnan, and Frank Dowling. While not a formal executive, these lunches functioned as the forum in which the week's key events were discussed and analysed, often focussed around the issues that would appear in Santamaria's influential News Weekly column and TV commentary, Point of View. When industrial issues came up, Grenville was a key voice, reporting on events at the Trades Hall, and assessing the prospects of winning the NCC's position or defeating the left's proposals. Following these lunches, responsibility for garnering the numbers fell to Grenville.[11]

But in September 1971, the pressure of 'wearing an overt hat and a covert hat' told, and Grenville resigned. Jordan's death had also completely changed his situation: he had no rapport with his successor. He said the whole experience was 'rather intense and it does have an effect on you, your physical and mental condition, your family life and so on and it got to the stage where I felt personally that in view of the fact that I was meeting myself coming back it was time to take a breather'. The reaction of his NCC colleagues was intense, and 'a great deal of pressure was put on me to stay', including 'accusations of high treason' from some, as well as from 'sympathetic but disappointed people wishing that I would have stayed'.[12]

Grenville's first preference was to resign and take a position in an individual union. Sam Benson had recently become the national secretary of the Merchant Service Guild, and offered him the position of industrial officer. However, nothing came of this. Benson later told Grenville that he had informed Santamaria of the proposed appointment, who pressured him to withdraw the offer because of Grenville's important role at the Trades Hall.

Much later, Grenville was amazed to learn that Santamaria had earlier been prepared to unceremoniously dump him. US state department records revealed that in December 1969 Santamaria had met with US labour attaché (and almost certainly a CIA officer) Emil Lindahl:

> ... at a lunch at the Victorian Employers Federation where Santamaria was speaking. Santamaria was, according to Lindahl, 'his usual erudite self'. In a private discussion, Santamaria talked about whether to sacrifice one of his followers John Grenville as the price of achieving unity of the anti-communist forces in Victoria.[13]

Back in 1971, Grenville knew nothing of Santamaria's ruminations concerning his 'sacrifice', or of his role in canning the job with Benson. He had been a member of the clerks' union up to this time; but, with no immediate job prospects, he decided to take his young family overseas, so he resigned from the union.[14]

In October 1972, he returned home, and soon found himself once more at the centre of the NCC's industrial operations. As he recalled, having been back in the country for less than twenty-four hours, 'I went to nine o'clock mass at Saint Dominic's Church at East Camberwell and I quietly drove around the block to have a look at Melbourne town, which I hadn't seen for quite a while. In the course of that I saw Michael O'Sullivan mowing his lawn outside his house.' O'Sullivan was well known to Grenville as 'a full-time operative of the NCC', of which he later became Victorian president, working closely with Maynes on industrial issues.[15]

At this time, the NCC was rejoicing that long-time clerks' union federal secretary Joe Riordan was finally moving on after fourteen years, entering federal parliament at the December election that brought Gough Whitlam to power. Riordan was a special hate-figure for Maynes because, as a committed ALP member, he had obstructed Maynes's plans to completely dominate the union and use it as an ideological springboard in the union movement. O'Sullivan's warmth towards Grenville was based on the fact that he 'would be a good replacement'.[16] This proposal coincided with Grenville's need for full-time work. But in order to achieve this, Maynes had to perform several dodgy manoeuvres.

The first was to ensure that Grenville was a financial member of the clerks' union, which he duly re-joined on 23 November 1972. The official union receipt indicated that he was employed as a clerk by John I. Taylor and Associates Pty Ltd, Consulting Land Surveyors and Town Planners.[17] John Taylor's brother, Peter, was the NCC's national finance officer, through whom Maynes made this arrangement. As Grenville said, 'I never received any salary … from this source.' But he did need to earn a living while waiting for the clerks' union job to become available, so, 'in order to keep me on ice, I was given a desk job in industrial affairs in NCC headquarters'. This job made him eligible to re-join the union, but, as he wryly observed, 'It wouldn't have looked too good when one is re-joining the clerks' union for the purpose of becoming federal secretary to have on one's application card that the employer is the NCC. So this particular subterfuge of the dummy employer was invented—not by me—for the purpose of concealing the operation.'[18]

Maynes's second manoeuvre involved postponing the effect of a new rule that would have required Grenville to have been a financial member continuously for twelve months to be eligible to stand for elected office. Once that had been achieved, he was elected by the clerks' union federal council on 19 February 1973. This was a significant triumph for the NCC. As Grenville commented, now that the federal secretary 'was in the hands of a safe, secure, and loyal operator, the position ideologically in the union could change ... the union could become a springboard federally for pushing NCC propaganda and policy and be the keystone apparatus in its activities in the trade union movement.'[19]

But he soon discovered that things were far from satisfactory. In theory, the NCC's activities in the union were directed by a caucus consisting of members of both organisations. In practice, this caucus did not function. 'People are told what to do from the top,' Grenville recalled in 1977. 'Some degree of window-dressing, of course, is indulged in, but this is simply to enable people to get their riding instructions rather than for them to have any great say in the affairs of the union.' As Grenville rapidly concluded, 'I was in the situation where I was second in command to the NCC head office industrial structure.' Maynes, as federal president of the union, insisted 'that he had to be on one hand treated as the chief executive officer of the union and on the other hand was the NCC's national industrial officer, and I—in the notional sense as federal secretary—would be the conduit for orders down the line and feeding information back up the line. So it was pretty much a Stalinistic type of structure.'[20]

The irony was not lost on Grenville:

> The situation as far as I'm concerned was that I was involved in a fight against totalitarianism. Now, that can emanate from the left or the right, but at that time, of course, being on the right, I thought it was strictly the preserve of the left. But the longer I stayed there the more I recognised that we were making exactly the same errors and denying the individual his rights in the democratic sense in exactly the same way as the totalitarian left had deprived members of the clerks' union of their rights over a period of time prior to the accession of the NCC into the leadership.[21]

The Movement had been founded in the 1940s because senior Catholic bishops believed that the CPA was using its control of unions to advance communism's political and ideological cause as a stepping-stone to revolution. But Grenville discovered that the NCC was now manipulating unions it controlled for its own narrow political and ideological purposes.

The tension frequently felt by many communist union officials between purely industrial issues and the political and ideological demands of the party were mirrored in Grenville's experience:

> It was a nuisance, in the obvious sense that I was much more concerned to get on with the industrial job. But the other side of the work was always constantly nagging you. You would be right in the middle of a real industrial situation and working on it, you know, twelve, fourteen hours a day,

trying to achieve something. And you'd get some of these stupid NCC-type requests coming across your table that have absolutely nothing to do with what you had been paid to do by the members of the union. And you had to, in effect, don another hat and attend to one of these political-type operations that wasn't necessarily in the interests of your particular organisation in the industrial sense.[22]

One of the major distractions faced by Grenville involved Maynes's operations in other unions. One critical intervention in which he became embroiled concerned a faction fight inside the Shop Distributive and Allied Employees' Association (the shop assistants' union). This was one of the unions won by The Movement from the left in the late 1940s and early 1950s, and was 'regarded as one of the two major springboards for their ideological offensive'. As Grenville candidly explained, 'I was part of the hatchet job that was done on Barry Egan, the shop assistants' national secretary.'[23]

A long-time ALP member who was also a loyal—but undercover—NCC member, Barry Egan had been a senior manager in the retail industry before becoming NSW secretary of the shop assistants' union and then, in 1970, federal secretary. His rise had been made possible by the NCC's control of the union's federal executive.[24] By the mid-1970s, Egan's decision to take a course decidedly independent of Maynes's authoritarian control caused a brutal backlash, involving—as Grenville witnessed first-hand—'the extraordinary expenditure of thousands and thousands of dollars in litigation in that union to destroy Barry Egan'.[25]

At Maynes's direction, the NCC loyalists illegally removed Egan as federal secretary, a manoeuvre that was overturned by the courts, but which only prolonged the inevitable conclusion

of the struggle: Egan's eventual demise in October 1978.[26]
Egan's determined opposition to Maynes's domineering
behaviour coincided with a similar brawl in the clerks' union.
As Grenville stated, it was 'absolutely essential' that Maynes
'remain in control of the clerks' and shop assistants' unions'.[27]
To achieve this, Maynes destroyed three loyal NCC members
who refused to toe his line down to the last minute detail, two
of whom held critical positions as federal secretaries of their
unions, and the third as secretary of a powerful union branch.

These three senior unionists were united in their opposition
to Maynes's capricious exercise of the dictatorial powers he
possessed as the NCC's industrial supremo and, especially,
his profligate misuse of members' funds to pursue ideological
campaigns far removed from their industrial interests.
One major focus of their mounting anger was Maynes's
extraordinary globe-trotting jaunts, in which he linked up with
discredited international 'unionists' whose real loyalties lay
with the US government, and who actively participated in the
increasingly unsavoury operations of the CIA.

10

The Show, the CIA, and international unionism

The titanic internal struggles in the clerks' and shop assistants' unions were rooted in John Maynes's undemocratic power, exercised over the unions' affairs from his office at NCC headquarters. He was able to enforce this power through his authoritarian control of the considerable force of cadres who—as a condition of their NCC membership—were 'pledged' to blindly follow the orders of the national vice-president directing industrial affairs. But at its core were the competing priorities of the industrial interests of the unions' members with the ideological priorities pursued by NCC headquarters. For unionists who believed their first job was to serve the members' interests, Maynes's pursuit of extraneous ideological issues inevitably resulted in bitter conflict.

In both unions, the conflict was brought to a head by the international activities of Maynes and his closest supporters.

These involved both the clerks' and shop assistants' unions in expensive and politically disastrous affiliations with international trade union organisations that effectively operated as arms of the United States government, often at the direction and with the financial assistance of the CIA. As news of the CIA's involvement in such operations seeped out, it caused considerable alarm to the federal secretaries of these unions—John Grenville and Barry Egan. The revelations coincided with a barrage of negative publicity about the CIA's numerous illegal 'dirty tricks' operations—involving, among other things, the covert overthrow of democratically elected governments, the use of mind-bending drugs such as LSD in experiments on innocent people, and assassination plots against America's political enemies. In the mid-1970s, such scandals reached a crescendo, resulting in a series of US congressional and other official inquiries that cast the CIA in a decidedly negative light.[1]

The two international organisations that prompted bitter internal fighting in NCC-controlled unions were the International Federation of Commercial and Technical Employees (known by its French acronym as FIET), which had affiliates representing white-collar workers in the Western world, Asia, Africa, and Latin America; and the International Federation of Petroleum and Chemical Workers (IFPCW). Both were part of elaborate schemes designed and funded by various US government agencies to establish a network of international unions capable of acting in America's political and economic interests. Operating under the auspices of the anti-communist International Confederation of Free Trade Unions, such organisations were seen by many Western unionists as vital cogs in the Cold War fight against the communist-dominated World Federation of Trade Unions and its international unions.

But several, including FIET and IFPCW, were largely pawns in the hands of American unionists who effectively worked at the direction of US government agencies.

From the late 1960s, their clandestine operations began to leak out.[2] Congressional hearings later exposed IFPCW and FIET's roles in CIA-directed intelligence operations. This not only caused considerable embarrassment to the US government; it also fuelled a widespread debate inside the Australian trade union movement, especially among those affiliated to FIET and IFPCW. It rapidly emerged that IFPCW had been a CIA-funded and -directed organisation since its inception in the early 1950s, and that its leader, Lloyd Haskins, had utilised the organisation to carry out clandestine CIA operations that favoured American companies and US government policies.[3] It was also established that FIET, through its leading American affiliate, had also been involved in several clandestine intelligence operations, most particularly in using CIA funds to prolong a politically motivated strike in British Guyana that helped to topple a leftist administration in 1964—a goal that suited US policy aims in the region.[4]

Under Maynes's direction, the clerks' union had affiliated with FIET in 1958, followed soon after by the shop assistants' union. Maynes always insisted on exercising total control of the clerks' union's international operations, especially as they related to IFPCW and FIET. This obsession grew after 1973, just as the scandal surrounding their involvement in covert intelligence operations grew to breaking point. 'It must be understood that most of the relationships were channelled by him, through him, and to him,' John Grenville said, having experienced this first-hand.[5] In effect, Maynes was the point man for both his own union and the shop assistants', sitting on the FIET international executive with the shop assistants' Jim Maher, another of the unionists under Maynes's control in his role as the NCC's industrial czar.

Maynes was especially close to another FIET international executive member, Gerald O'Keefe, the head of the department of international affairs of the Washington-based Retail Clerks International Association. O'Keefe actively participated in operations directed by the CIA and other US government agencies. Together the two men co-ordinated FIET operations, especially in Asia, where Maynes was Asia–FIET's vice-president. One matter that occupied their time was Barry Egan's emerging independence from Maynes. In September 1973, Maynes wrote to O'Keefe, suggesting they meet ahead of an impending FIET executive meeting in London to discuss the shop assistants' NSW branch which, under Egan's influence, had raised objections to the union's affiliation with FIET.[6]

Egan had attended an Asia–FIET meeting in Singapore earlier in 1973, delivering a paper on multinationals. He came away underwhelmed, refusing to attend another 'because of my observations at that meeting and the response of members to my report'. Indeed, he actively campaigned for the shop assistants' union to disaffiliate from FIET, loudly objecting to 'the involvement of Australian union officials ... when foreign countries are involved with commercial and political interests conceivably not in the best interests of the Australian people'. By 1977 he was scandalised by the huge amounts of money being spent by the shop assistants' union on its affiliation with FIET, estimating that over five years it had incurred hundreds of thousands of dollars in affiliation fees, airfares, and related travel costs.[7]

His campaign to end what he viewed as the wasteful expenditure of members' money hit a brick wall called Jim

Maher, the shop assistants' federal president and Victorian branch secretary. As Grenville witnessed first-hand, Maher got his 'riding instructions on how to handle Egan' directly from Maynes. In June 1974, Grenville and Maher travelled together to attend an Asia–FIET seminar in Kuala Lumpur, where 'the whole operation between Maher and Maynes was designed to ensure that the biggest can possible would be tipped all over Egan in terms of his reputation in the eyes of … other international trade union people'. One shop assistants' official 'even told the doorman of the hotel what a louse Egan was. So that's how far that particular operation went … and it was designed to destroy Egan in the international field, especially in relation to FIET where Maynes wanted to have total control insofar as Australian representation was concerned.'[8]

In mid-1977, the Australian union movement was rocked by intense media coverage revealing the extent of US government—especially CIA—infiltration of international unionism, including within Australia. For a number of years prior to this scandal reaching a crescendo in 1977, Egan had been especially concerned by the evidence demonstrating 'that FIET was receiving funding from the US government'. In response, the shop assistants' NSW branch had 'put up a proposition to the national executive that we should not participate in FIET's international conferences and cease paying affiliation dues'. But when the national executive convened, 'Maher as presiding officer overruled me, stating that this wasn't worth discussing and he then proceeded to the election of three delegates and three observers' to a 'series of international conferences in Seoul, Tokyo, and Honolulu', including a FIET executive meeting. Egan was furious, particularly as key officials were absent during a period of intense industrial campaigning by union members.[9]

THE SHOP ASSISTANTS' was not the only NCC-dominated union involved in Maynes's international operations and expensive junkets. They also had ramifications inside the clerks' union. Maynes and other clerks' union officials bolstered the contingent of up to twelve Australian unionists to attend this particular set of international meetings. Along the way, they linked up with representatives of the US government, who also wore hats as officials of American unions and FIET executive members. As Grenville recalled, 'The international aspect was becoming something of a scandal.' Deeper resentments about being treated as Maynes's cipher were central to Grenville's growing disenchantment, but 'Maynes's version of the need for the NCC, per medium of the shop assistants' and clerks' unions, to be operative in this international arena led to very sharp divisions ... In fact, [it] led to the schism in the National Civic Council.'[10]

Grenville was strongly in favour of policies and actions 'to combat multinationals', and believed 'that people who have had a little bit of exposure to other parts of the labour movement around the world are all the better for it'.[11] But when it came to Maynes's international activities:

> We are talking about a continuous stream of trips abroad which don't appear to relate in any great substance to the needs of the clerks' union at the particular point in time ... which was one that really had still to be fought in the grass-roots situation back here in Australia. So it is very dubious that any real benefits were accruing to members. This was the debate: what are we getting out of this junketing?[12]

Grenville's answer was that the union's members were getting nothing out of Maynes's international activities, but that his role in FIET 'gave the clerks' union a base in South-East Asia, which meant it gave the NCC a base in South-East Asia, and it was a conduit right through to the executive-board level of a relationship between people like Maynes and the NCC dealing with a number of very interesting people who appear to have links right throughout the world with that government agency known as the CIA'.[13]

The debate was brought to a head in 1974 by the visit to Australia of Charles 'Chips' Levinson, the secretary of the International Chemical Workers' Federation (ICF). After assuming this position in 1964, the distinctly anti-communist Levinson had re-built the moribund ICF into a dynamic organisation that quickly overpowered its competitor—the CIA's creation, the International Federation of Petroleum and Chemical Workers (IFPCW). Grenville had a long meeting with Levinson in Sydney, together with John Forrester, the secretary of one of the clerks' union's larger and more important sections—the Central and Southern Queensland branch. A skilled operator who had learned his politics in the hard school of the NSW ALP as an undercover NCC member, Forrester was brought up in The Movement. His father had been a founding member in the early 1940s, and the son, in turn, joined in 1951.[14] Forrester supported Grenville during his confrontations with Maynes, who declared all-out war because of their refusal to obediently follow his instructions.

Levinson's presentation was devastating. 'We were acquainted with the full story, which totally discredited the IFPCW,' Grenville recalled, and 'as the federal secretary of the union, it was something of an acute embarrassment to learn about our association with this discredited organisation. Along with Forrester, I ... recommended we cease our association with the IFPCW as quickly as possible and affiliate with the

International Chemical Workers Federation'—the course taken by the shop assistants' union under Egan's influence.[15]

The reaction was volcanic. 'Brother Maynes hit the roof and said that we had no right discussing this type of thing because international discussions were his preserve.' Later in 1974, when Grenville visited the International Labour Organisation in Geneva (where the International Chemical Workers' Federation headquarters were also located), Maynes instructed him 'to make no contact whatsoever with Chips Levinson'. The battlelines were by now drawn between Maynes and his clerks' union loyalists, and Grenville and Forrester. As Grenville rhetorically asked, 'Why is it that there was a strong insistence that the clerks' union remain affiliated with the discredited and rump organisation called the IFPCW and why have resolutions been carried ... to not go into the ICF?'[16]

This heated debate was not confined to the clerks' union's affiliation with the CIA-controlled IFPCW. It extended to the entire range of Maynes's international operations. Grenville and Forrester had touched a raw nerve. In May 1974, Maynes circulated an extraordinary document to the union's federal executive. Headed 'Where I Went and Why', it was a five-foolscap-page defence of his then-recent five-week international junket. As Grenville ironically noted:

> It reads like a regular Cook's Tour. It includes a visit to Geneva, Singapore, Rome, Indonesia, London, Washington, Denver, San Francisco, Tokyo, Hong Kong and you name and I'll play it.[17]

The most revealing section dealt with Maynes's meetings in Washington. These included a *Who's Who* of American unionists who worked under the direction of the CIA to promote US political and economic interests. Most had been directly involved in clandestine CIA operations to undermine and destabilise unions and governments that posed a perceived threat to such interests. At the apex of American unionism were the senior representatives of the AFL–CIO, the equivalent national peak body to Australia's ACTU.[18]

The AFL–CIO's international department was the controlling headquarters directing the clandestine operations of active CIA agents inside US unionism. As Grenville drily commented about Maynes's Washington connections, 'So we find ourselves meeting people like Harry Goldberg, Jay Lovestone, and Ernest Lee of the AFL-CIO. I understand they wear some other hats from time-to-time.'[19] Indeed, their activities were so notorious that the organisation came to be known among its growing band of critics as the 'AFL-CIA'.

Goldberg, Lovestone, and Lee, however, wore their CIA hats as badges of honour. As head of the AFL–CIO's international department, former communist leader Jay Lovestone directed the CIA's union operations worldwide over several decades. Goldberg was the AFL–CIO's Asian expert with a special focus on Indonesia—where he had run the CIA's labour operations since the early 1950s[20]—and Australia (which he visited several times). Lee had a similar background, playing a key role, for example, for the CIA in destabilising British Guyana in the early and mid-1960s. Furthermore, Maynes held discussions with prominent CIA unionist Gerald O'Keefe of the Retail Clerks International Association, senior State Department officials—including the head of the Australian desk—and US Labor Department personnel.[21]

The important role of Indonesia in The Show's international operations emerged clearly from Maynes's report. In Jakarta, he met with Agus Sudono, who had been installed as head of the country's tame-cat union movement in the aftermath of the brutal military operation that brought Suharto to power in Indonesia, resulting in the murder of at least 500,000 communists and leftists in 1965–66, and the destruction of independent trade union organisations. As vice-president of the IFPCW, Sudono had been a key CIA operative for many years, working closely with Goldberg. Goldberg had played a clandestine role that helped pave the way for the military coup, and then arrived back in Indonesia a few months later to ensure that Sudono took charge of the remnants of the union movement. Throughout 1966 he wrote a string of revealing reports, including informing his colleagues back in Washington of Sudono's leading role in the mass killings as head of the Workers' Action Front.[22]

Goldberg's initial visit to Australia occurred in March 1960, at the invitation of Laurie Short, the head of the ironworkers' union.[23] In Honolulu on his way home, he wrote a lengthy report for his colleagues in Washington. Somehow the Labor barrister Lionel Murphy—later elected to the Senate—obtained a copy and passed it to a CPA member.[24] It emerged in full in the initial edition of what was described as *Underground Tribune*, under the heading, 'Price: What You Can Afford'. Goldberg was scathing about Australia, Australians, and their prime minister:

Let me say bluntly ... in some of the most fundamental values, and in the chief issues activating our world, this country is backward, in a backwash it hasn't gotten out of yet, isolated, insulated, provincial, etc ...

The average Australian is ... rather narrow visioned, and extremely short on theory, sensitivity and sensibility ...

We saw a [Prime Minister] Menzies' performance in

Parliament. This is a puffed-up politician, not a statesman, supercilious, arrogant, smooth and slick, who tries nothing so much as to imitate Churchill in his oratory and mannerisms.[25]

Goldberg's attitude towards the ALP and ALP unionists was even less complimentary. 'They, more than anybody,' he wrote, 'illustrate the softness and complacency in character, as well as the ignorance in theory, which help to explain why the communists are so influential in Australia.' They were described as displaying a 'gutlessness' because 'they want to maintain their positions and if they need the support of the commies to do so, they'll play ball with them. It's as simple as all that.'[26]

The Show was practically the only ray of sunshine Goldberg observed on his visit. He met Archbishop Mannix in Santamaria's company, and also had a long one-on-one discussion with the NCC head. Of Santamaria, he wrote:

> Well, he certainly is quite a guy. He's brilliant, forceful, speaks very well, logically, etc. It was quite a heart-to-heart talk we had ...
>
> As to Santamaria himself personally, his moral integrity and sincerity, I can't offer myself as an authority after one session. All I can say, for what it is worth, is that he impressed me as sincere and that he's thought of highly by all the Victorian Labor boys, with whom I met, and who are the minority opposition in the Trades Council, and most of whom ... are members of the DLP.[27]

Goldberg attended a rowdy meeting of the Victorian Trades Hall Council, during which he was given an especially hard time by communist and other left-wing delegates. Maynes stood up and defended Goldberg, who wrote glowingly of him in his report: 'A good one, obviously the floor leader of the anti-commie minority.'[28] This was the start of a close personal and political relationship that stretched over many years. Goldberg concluded his report:

> I think we ought to pay more attention to Australia than we
> have in the past. There are some things we can do. I have a
> number of proposals I'll want to make when we get together.[29]

Apparently, one of the proposals involved cementing NCC-controlled unions into the 'AFL-CIA's' international labour operations, which is precisely what Maynes obsessively did for three decades, expending vast sums of union members' money on international junkets to advance the NCC's ideological agenda.

By the time Maynes visited Washington in 1974, there was a mountain of publicly available information about the AFL–CIO's clandestine role, demonstrating that its agenda was to further the interests of US government policies. This often also involved advancing the interests of US corporations in their worldwide operations, including gross exploitation of workers, especially in developing countries. This, of course, was the very behaviour that international unionism had been established to oppose in defence of workers' rights. Likewise, significant evidence had emerged of the CIA's use of US unions as the cover for clandestine operations around the globe. Maynes was willing to destroy three of the NCC's most senior operatives rather than abandon his close working relationship with such US intelligence 'assets'. However, by persisting with these links to such thoroughly discredited organisations, he was also sowing the seeds of his own destruction.

11

The NCC schism

For twenty-five years leading up to 1975, John Maynes had undisputed control of the NCC's industrial operations. In The Show's authoritarian structure, his word was final in matters relating to trade unions. He expected John Grenville, Barry Egan, and John Forrester to buckle under his orders and cease interfering in what he considered to be his sole prerogative to run the international affairs of NCC-controlled unions, even if that meant turning a blind eye to the CIA's anti-union operations.

Maynes's verbiage in his extraordinary report 'Where I Went and Why' was supposed to be the final word. But it did not quell dissent within the clerks' union, as Grenville recalled:

> The tensions started to mount. The day-to-day management of the union was becoming increasingly more difficult given the machinations of Maynes and the fact that he wished at all times to be treated as the chief executive officer of the union with the federal secretary, in effect, playing office boy.

Now you can take that for a while, but if you are doing your job you become totally immersed in the industrial needs of the union, which means that friction must arise under those circumstances.

And it did.

There was a very real concern about this international thing. Our resources were quite limited and we couldn't afford to be squandering them on all sorts of peripheral things that appeared to have no great worth or relevance in the current set of circumstances.[1]

Even worse, Grenville discovered that Maynes had corrupted the clerks' union's industrial integrity by accepting cash donations for the NCC from employers, who clearly believed that in so doing they were buying industrial peace.

For example, during an industrial dispute over equal pay for women airline clerks, Grenville had returned from Sydney to Melbourne late one evening to be confronted by a very angry member of Ansett airlines' senior management at the company's head office. Grenville had phoned ahead to Terry Sullivan, the union's assistant federal secretary, asking him to attend the meeting. This was to ensure he had a witness for what he anticipated would be a heated argument. At first, Grenville was very satisfied with what quickly became an acrimonious scene. As he drily observed, 'It meant that our tactics were working.' But it was what happened next that really startled him, as one of the managers snarled, 'If you keep carrying on like this — not another fucking penny for the NCC.' In other words, the clerks' union was seen by senior management as a 'tame-cat' union, and the vigorous campaign to achieve equal pay for women workers violated the established rules.[2] As Grenville commented:

It goes right to the very heart of where the NCC raises a tremendous amount of its finance—namely from the bosses. People thought they were buying industrial protection in terms of that particular type of finance, and they found to their horror that there were people in the clerks' union who were fair dinkum. Now that of course led partially to the friction in the union, so the political end result had its genesis in an industrial situation.[3]

This was not the only occasion when Grenville's work on behalf of members was undermined by Maynes's corruption. In early 1975, Grenville and Forrester were spearheading a campaign to organise clerks in the health-insurance industry, commonly known as health funds. This campaign—just one of Grenville's hectic round of industrial activities—also engaged many state branch offices, because the health-funds industry had numerous state or local components. Having been authorised by the union's federal executive, Grenville served a national log of claims on every health association or group; there was nothing unusual about this. The employers banded together to resist the claim; there was nothing unusual about that. The employers, though independent of each other, collectively hired a senior barrister to advise on the best way to oppose the claims. His opinion—which included a concrete plan on how to combat the union—was forwarded to each fund.

One small Western Australian fund responded to the opinion with considerable annoyance. Incorrectly assuming it contained more union demands, the correspondence was re-addressed to the local clerks' union branch, with a note unequivocally stating that it wanted nothing more to do with this activity. The problem for the employers was that this 'return to sender' mail landed on the desk of the union's branch secretary, who immediately forwarded it to the federal office in Melbourne. As Grenville later recalled, he 'could not believe [his] good fortune. The entire strategy of the employers was laid bare.'[4]

One aspect of the barrister's opinion was dynamite, advising the employers that, as a consequence of the union's log of claims, 'A strong and militant union will be establishing its influence in the industry for the first time.' The barrister went on to advise his clients that, 'It is possible that internal union politics may alter union policy later in the year. It is thought that any change could only be for the better in reducing the present militancy.'[5]

Clearly, someone inside the clerks' union had advised the employers that moves were afoot to rein in the troublemakers. As things emerged, there was a very close relationship between the 'someone inside the clerks' union' and the way the legal opinion arrived in the union's federal office. Grenville stated that he received a phone call from the Western Australian branch secretary, informing him that the correspondence had been received in Perth and that he was sending it on. Grenville was naturally delighted, quickly sharing this bombshell with the federal president (Maynes), who coincidentally happened to be in the union's federal office that day. (His real office was located next to Santamaria's at NCC headquarters in Hawthorn.) A clearly angry Maynes responded that he had ordered the Perth office to send the document to him directly, bypassing Grenville. It was apparently strictly an NCC matter, and Maynes was 'pulling rank' as The Show's union supremo. In other words, another 'bagman' operation was in the making; there had been a separate discussion that had excluded Grenville, who was not supposed to know about the barrister's opinion.[6]

Grenville firmly believed that this incident showed that 'approaches had been made to the bagmen of the NCC that they wanted to see a little less of this strong industrial approach now being perpetrated on them. So it was quite obvious from this document that undertakings had been given that the people who are responsible for the strong industrial policy were going to be curtailed, were going to be leg-roped.'[7] Once again, Maynes expected the dissidents to fall into line.

As a result of such incidents, and the enduring scandal of Maynes's international junketing, the early months of 1975 were dominated by a continuing brawl between Maynes and Grenville. Things were poisonous, and it was clear that something had to give. On 13 May, a caucus of NCC members who also held full-time positions in the clerks' union was convened in Melbourne ahead of a federal executive meeting scheduled for the next day. It turned into a running brawl. Grenville raised his dissatisfaction with the manner in which Maynes ran caucus as his own private fiefdom, dispensing orders that he expected everyone else would obey and unquestioningly implement.

Forrester, who had already developed 'an independent position away from the dictatorial control of Maynes', threw his support behind Grenville, only to be disingenuously informed that the meeting was not an official NCC caucus, 'but was merely a meeting of Movement members'. The brawl continued for several hours, during which Grenville raised the odious stink surrounding Maynes's international junkets. Referring to his latest trip, Grenville stated, 'On this occasion you were away for four weeks, yet I can only account for six days.'[8]

This sent Maynes into orbit, and he issued a public ultimatum to Grenville: conform to his dictates on all matters by 4.45 the following Friday afternoon, or 'You have had it.'[9]

After a fruitless three hours, the caucus reconvened over dinner in a restaurant in inner-city Carlton. Halfway through the meal, Maynes erupted again, issuing ultimatums freely to those who had dissented from his dictates.[10] He particularly turned once more on Grenville, who recounted the threat in a letter to Santamaria two days later:

At dinner, Maynes commenced to talk about some of his recent overseas activities and then returning to what I had said at the caucus meeting turned to me and said, 'If you ever raise that aspect of my activities again, I will cut your fucking throat'.[11]

The dinner finally broke up in an unseemly public outburst, as recorded by Forrester a few days later in his own letter to Santamaria:

The next thing I heard abusive language with frequent obscenity coming from inside [the restaurant] and I thought that Grenville had blown his top. Ultimately they both came out of the restaurant but to my amazement it was John Maynes continuing this in the street in Carlton in a manner I have never ever heard him employ before. Grenville got into his car and John [Maynes] even went as far as to push his head inside the door and continue the abuse.[12]

Grenville and Forrester had agreed in advance that the caucus meeting was the appropriate forum to bring matters to a head with Maynes. They had also agreed that it was time to bring Santamaria directly into the conflict, so they had both spoken to him earlier in the day—Forrester in person and Grenville on the phone. Santamaria agreed that the whole mess needed to be considered and, hopefully, resolved by caucus. Realising that the confrontation would be extremely difficult and would go late into the evening, Santamaria gave Grenville his private number, telling him to phone, irrespective of the time, to report on how things had gone.[13] Late that night, Grenville rang Santamaria at his home to brief him on the tumultuous events:

> I put it to him that in the circumstances that were developing in the union, with the industrial pressures on the one hand and the political pressures on the other, it was all becoming too much for me and that I proposed to resign. I pointed out that the situation was one where, on the one hand if I did something, Maynes said I had no right to do it without consulting him and, on the other hand if I didn't do something I was being abused for not doing it.[14]

According to Grenville, Santamaria listened with obvious concern and then, without prompting, compared it with the situation within the NCC's national office, telling Grenville that, 'If I thought I had problems in the rather narrow confines of the clerks' union they wouldn't hold a candle to similar problems that he was experiencing vis-a-vis Maynes's activities in respect of the NCC as a whole. He asked me if I would draft a report concerning these things.' At the same time, Forrester 'sought an audience with Santamaria and expressed similar views to my own. Again he received the assurance of Santamaria, as I did, that we were both right and indeed we were encouraged to bring the matter to a head.'[15]

Assured by Santamaria that he would support them in his supreme capacity as NCC national president, Grenville and Forrester dutifully wrote lengthy reports on the state of affairs in the clerks' union; in Grenville's case, a twenty-two-page handwritten document signed off 'Warmest regards John G'; in Forrester's, a six-foolscap-page, closely typed personal letter, supplemented by a lengthy report on what he saw as the deteriorating situation of the NCC's wider political and industrial activities. Both were clear that the situation was now impossible and that the authority exercised by Maynes as the NCC's industrial czar had to be terminated. Grenville proposed that a democratic national structure replace Maynes's domination of industrial policy.[16]

He also appealed to Santamaria's notion of fair play in relation to Maynes's ultimatum that he should conform or get out: 'The Show is perfectly entitled to come to the conclusion that I must "conform or get out"—not John Maynes,' Grenville wrote to Santamaria. 'If that is the conclusion then I will very sadly tender my resignation.' In other words, there should be a proper process to determine the matter, not Maynes acting as accuser, prosecutor, jury, judge, and executioner. But on the crucial question, Grenville was adamant: either Maynes disappeared out of clerks' union affairs, or he would.[17]

Grenville and Forrester were also clear on the role that Santamaria had to play. 'We predicted that there was no way you could bring this man Maynes to heel in terms of the discipline and participation as a member of a caucus unless ... Santamaria ... was prepared to direct Maynes to toe the line and accept the discipline of that particular organisation in the same way as I did and as Forrester did,' Grenville remembered. 'He accepted that it would be difficult but nevertheless encouraged us—indeed, directed us—to continue on with this plan.'[18]

To their disgust, every time they attempted to bring Santamaria back into the situation 'by way of disciplining

Maynes to the extent that he would in effect chair a court of appeal', Santamaria squibbed it, refusing to attend. The week after the caucus meeting, Santamaria asked Grenville to meet with him in his office at NCC headquarters to discuss the contents of his letter. Just prior to this meeting, Santamaria rang and suggested changing the venue to Belloc House, citing Maynes's proximity to his personal office. But the meeting never happened. Instead, Santamaria again phoned Grenville to say that he had suddenly become 'terribly busy' and that their get-together would have to be re-arranged, promising to be in contact with a new date.[19]

Grenville never heard from him again.

Subsequently, a senior NCC member informed Grenville that Santamaria claimed that he had never received the communication that he had himself requested Grenville to supply—the twenty-two-page handwritten letter with a copy of Forrester's report attached. Grenville stated that he hand-delivered these documents to Santamaria at his home in Burke Road, Kew, and that it was the occasion on which he was introduced to his wife, Helen.[20]

Grenville and Forrester then made another attempt to involve Santamaria in mediating the crisis. Santamaria visited Brisbane in late May on other NCC business. Forrester requested that he should attend a meeting of NCC members who operated inside his branch of the clerks' union. Grenville flew up for this meeting, only to discover that Santamaria had snuck out of town without saying a word to Forrester, but that Maynes had somehow gotten wind of the arrangement and was hanging around, spoiling for another confrontation. Santamaria clearly wanted to dodge that prospect. Presumably, he had decided that Maynes was too powerful for the time being and that a full retreat was in order, notwithstanding the firm pledges of support he had given to Grenville and Forrester.

Instead of joining the battle, Santamaria delegated his role to his handpicked, lame-duck intermediary—the head of the NCC's Queensland operation, Brian Mullins. Having been instructed by Santamaria to chair a meeting of Maynes, Grenville, and Forrester, and to 'instruct' Maynes to refrain from interfering in Forrester's branch, Mullins instead readily admitted that he could not 'issue an instruction to Maynes. You know that he won't take any notice of it.'[21] Grenville concluded that:

> Any further sense of responsibility towards the NCC could no longer be contemplated because it was quite obvious that there was no such thing as a coherent organisation called the NCC. Here we had a clear-cut admission—continuous from 13 May onwards—that there was no disciplinary action that could be taken by the NCC through its major operatives in respect of the activities of Maynes; that he was completely a Stalinist operator who was not subject to anyone's control, who did not have to render an account of his stewardship, who was not to be treated as an equal member of a [union] caucus situation.[22]

The first consequence of Santamaria's failure to honour his commitments to Grenville and Forrester was Grenville's resignation as a member of the NCC. Forrester, however, persisted, again arranging for Santamaria to attend a meeting in Brisbane of clerks' union activists—with the same result: Santamaria again squibbed it. As Forrester wrote in a letter to Santamaria in mid-August, 'Your failure to "front" again during your recent visit to Queensland on the basis that you did not have the time is in its own way a most impressive performance.

Unfortunately it has impressed people against you.' In a cutting comparison with Maynes, Forrester informed Santamaria 'that many ... people respect his courage particularly when placed against your non-appearance'.[23]

Grenville—now seeking new employment—was caught in the middle of the increasingly heated antagonism between Maynes and Forrester. He also found himself a political and social outcast, sent to Coventry by a directive issued from the Maynes camp that all communication between Grenville and NCC members had to cease. This meant that the industrial and clerical staff—who, under the union's rules, technically reported to him as federal secretary—now took their orders directly from Maynes. Apparently, this direction extended to Grenville's wife, Mary, who, on one occasion (at a church social function), also found herself sent to Coventry. The wife of a senior NCC operative—with whom Mary was conversing—was directed by her husband to cease any further dialogue. The parting words were, 'We aren't supposed to be talking to you.'[24]

With his working and social life in turmoil, Grenville submitted his resignation as the clerks' union federal secretary, effective at the end of August 1975. He resigned simply because of the impossible circumstances in which he found himself, thanks largely to what he saw as Santamaria's gutlessness. Soon after his resignation, his union membership dues were returned to him—meaning not only peremptory expulsion but also, effectively, exclusion from the industry—and his shares in the union's credit union were cancelled simultaneously.[25]

Maynes had ensured that Grenville was left with nothing: no job; no ticket to work in the clerical industry; no long-time comrades in industrial struggles; and no credit union to offer a loan to tide him through the tough times he now faced. As he ruefully observed later, 'I was being played as a pawn in what was really going on in the NCC.' In the context of the by-then two clearly defined factions—one led by Santamaria, the other by Maynes—'I was being used by one to beat the other … I was used by Santamaria as part of the mounting challenge to the Maynes position within the NCC.'[26]

SANTAMARIA'S FAILURE to come in behind Grenville left Forrester isolated in Queensland. Theoretically, he had a powerful union branch structure to support him, but Maynes quickly marshalled the even more powerful NCC machine against him. Again, Santamaria stood by and watched.

Grenville's departure was the signal for Maynes to mount 'a vicious sectarian campaign to destroy Forrester and his colleagues because [they were] exhibiting an independence of mind, an independence of control, and an independence of policy which could not be tolerated'. Wielding the extraordinary authority he had vested in him by the national executive—and Santamaria personally—as the NCC's industrial czar, Maynes directed the entire machine, both inside the union and the NCC, into a campaign to destroy Forrester and his supporters.[27]

The first step was to put the 'Fear of God'—literally—into Forrester's supporters. 'People were told that they had to conform or they would be destroyed.' As the battle raged between Forrester's forces and Maynes's, a letter was sent out to the dissidents by Brian Mullins. Mullins demanded that Forrester's supporters indicate by a certain deadline 'whether each individual member desires to fully recognise the constitution of The Show and its legitimate officers in governing bodies and to continue his or her membership'.

This none-too-subtle blackmail concluded with the revealing punchline: 'I now await your decision ... with the sincere hope that you will do nothing wittingly or unwittingly to give aid and comfort to the enemies of God and country.' Apparently, God was sitting on the right-hand shoulder of the NCC's self-appointed, unelected 'officers', and anyone who dissented from their 'official' pronouncements was *ipso facto* an enemy—unless, of course, they agreed to conform to dictates from on high. 'God and country' was 'their medium to coerce people back into line'.[28]

The lengths to which this campaign extended is revealed in another Mullins letter sent to the principals of all Catholic high schools in the archdiocese of Brisbane (and more widely in Queensland). It was in response to an offer made by Forrester 'to provide speakers to the Catholic Secondary Schools on the subject of Trade Unions'. Mullins reminded the principals that the NCC's lectures in Catholic schools had been approved by the archbishop, which, to many of the faithful, was almost the word of God. He also advised:

> Insofar as Mr. Forrester's offer is concerned ... we would strongly recommend that such offers would be declined. Mr. Forrester is no longer associated with our organisation and the branch of the Union which he administers has changed character over the past year. The union now has links with left wing elements of the trade union movement including a body called the Women's Trade Union Committee. In the circumstances we would advise you to place your requests with us ... we may be relied upon to give informative talks which are either related to or consistent with Christian social teaching.[29]

Under intense attack from Maynes and his local supporters, Forrester did not take a backward step. In August 1976, he wrote an incendiary letter to the clerks' union federal secretary, declaring that his branch would no longer pay its share of Maynes's international junketing:

Re: INTERNATIONAL

It is difficult to know where to start in view of the amazing series of documents which have been flogged about by John Maynes and yourself on this subject in recent weeks. I am sure you will excuse the fact that I have waited for the pens to run out of ink before replying in one total document rather than wasting the time and money of this Union in the way that you and Maynes have done. Of course, I can understand the difficult situation under which you are working in view of John Maynes' present emotionally disturbed state ...

I think it is nearly time we cut through the continuing propaganda of Maynes that only he can manage the international sphere and that myself and others, such as ... Barry Egan, the National Secretary of the Shop Assistants' are destroying twenty years of topgrade work by himself. Probably, the greatest condemnation of Maynes' international travel ... came from the lips of Mr B A Santamaria in my discussions with him on 13 May 1975 ...

Santamaria advised me that Maynes' continual overseas tripping was producing no results for the National Civic Council and was causing embarrassment to him ... Santamaria further stated that he had had to cancel an overseas trip for later in the year on defence matters which he considered of the gravest importance because of the 'scandal' (his word) that Maynes' international tripping was causing amongst other officials of the National Civic Council.[30]

Forrester's defiance was in the shadow of the executioner's axe. Having either expelled or disciplined the dissidents who supported Forrester, and launched what Grenville termed 'a vicious sectarian campaign' against a fellow Catholic, Maynes's next step was to challenge Forrester in the branch election at the end of 1976. The NCC's campaign cost thousands of dollars, resulting in the defeat of Forrester and his supporters. An angry John Grenville asked a simple question: 'Did the little people who give their $10 and their $5 and their $20—all of whom are listed in [the NCC magazine] News Weekly's fighting fund—know that that money would be used, not for the cause which was advertised, but to destroy another Catholic in the trade union movement who simply represented an independent point of view and who would not be dictated to—or see his union destroyed by—an outside influence?'[31]

In the short term, Maynes had won: he had forced Grenville from the federal secretary's position, and defeated Forrester in a key clerks' union branch. In mid-1977, however, Grenville made a brave prediction:

By adopting this totalitarian approach, they have actually sown the seeds of their own destruction which now can be brought home to each and every individual member of the clerks' union and we can have a situation in the future, I am sure, where this type of totalitarian control can be destroyed. You see the most ironical side of the story is that this type of operation ... goes back to the days when the communists controlled the union. I for one thought that I was joining a team that was totally opposed to the type of control that was manifest in the operations of the communists when they controlled the union and I now find that I was party to the perpetration of similar acts. The attempts that are being made to prevent scrutiny of who really controls the clerks' union will fail and in the not too distant future the clerks' will be one of those unions that will ultimately be a democratic operation.[32]

In mid-1977, those words appeared to be extremely optimistic. The Maynes machine was firmly in control of major unions, notably the clerks', but also the shop assistants' union (in which he destroyed Barry Egan in 1978), the Victorian branches of the Federated Ironworkers' Association, and the Amalgamated Society of Carpenters and Joiners. Santamaria had stood by and watched while Maynes pursued a vicious factional fight—the second large-scale split in The Show's thirty-three-year history, following that of twenty years earlier in the midst of the Labor Split of the mid-1950s.[33] In doing so, it appeared that Santamaria had recognised that his power derived from control of such unions, and that he needed Maynes more than he needed Grenville, Forrester, and Egan.

But, beneath the surface, major trouble was brewing. The faction fight had disastrous consequences for the NCC's control of the clerks' union. A few years later, sections of the union fell to the left, whose tickets triumphed in two of the major branches. The first to fall was Forrester's old stronghold, the Central and Southern Queensland branch. The group Maynes had promoted—led by Joan Riordan—lacked Forrester's industrial and political skills, and were swept aside in 1982 by a team led by the competent and efficient Bernadette O'Callaghan, a mere branch organiser. Subsequent well-funded, concerted efforts to unseat her were unsuccessful.

Then, in 1988, Maynes's stronghold of Victoria fell to a team led by the charismatic Lindsay Tanner, later one of the most effective senior ministers in Kevin Rudd's federal Labor government. In his riveting account of the long struggle to wrest the branch away from the NCC, Tanner's commentary echoed Forrester and Grenville's earlier critique. In the decade since Forrester's defeat in Queensland, and Grenville's resignation as federal secretary, nothing had changed on the international front. In a letter Tanner wrote in 1986, he lampooned 'the "adventures of Mickey Maynes" in his globe-trotting crusade against international communism', which still expended huge quantities of members' money on pursuing relations with CIA-controlled international bodies.[34]

Having won a by-election for the position of assistant branch secretary in 1987, Tanner's pen-picture of Maynes was redolent of Grenville and Forrester's observations in the mid-1970s:

> State Executive meetings were quite extraordinary. John Maynes dominated completely, sometimes launching into monologues from the chair which lasted up to three-quarters of an hour. [Branch Secretary] Harry Darroch usually presented most of the agenda items, generally practical industrial and organisational matters. Maynes would then pronounce a response from on high ... These pronouncements were often so out of step with reality that poor Darroch was left with a "solution" impossible to implement. The organisation was paralysed by an almost total separation of power and responsibility ... the key decisions were made by a man who had no involvement in running the branch and whose grip on reality was tenuous to say the least.[35]

Tanner could hardly believe the union's industrial tactics that, again, were consistent with what Grenville had confronted and had struggled so hard to change. 'In representing members,' Tanner wrote, 'the FCU [clerks' union] often ignored or overrode their wishes, presented them with a fait accompli, or did a deal with the boss behind their backs.'[36] Nor had things improved in the airline industry; during the 1988 union election campaign, 'A leaked memo from Ansett Airlines Employee Relations Manager Michael Gay, in which he referred to "the overriding concern we have for the continuation of the current union leadership", was used with telling effect' against the Maynes ticket.[37] Maynes had done nothing to alter the union's tame-cat status since Grenville's confrontation with Ansett management fifteen years earlier. Unsurprisingly, airline clerks voted overwhelmingly to eject Maynes's team, electing Tanner and his ticket. Despite the membership's clear-cut decision, however, Maynes refused to recognise the election result, utilising similar tactics to those wielded by arch Stalinist Jack McPhillips to frustrate Laurie Short after his victory in the ironworkers' union almost forty years earlier:

> The National Office endeavoured to deprive the newly elected Victorian Branch Executive of every major function critical to running a branch of a union. They prevented us from getting access to Branch funds and Branch cars. They tried to take control of Branch staffing matters and assisted and encouraged Branch staff to go on strike and establish a picket line. They acted to deny us control over our own premises and then tried to stop us moving the Branch office ... They used the union journal to bombard us with outrageous propaganda including baseless accusations of ballot fraud and tried to prevent us producing our own journal. They appointed our ex-organisers as National officials and instructed them to continue acting as de facto Victorian branch organisers ... They tried to remove our right to represent the union in the Victorian industrial relations system. And they tried to undermine our only avenue of appeal against these

outrages—recourse to the Federal Court—by prohibiting us from spending any more than a small amount on legal fees and requiring us to pay their legal costs as well as our own ...

These were the same people who in the 1940s and 1950s stood for 'morality' in trade unionism and crusaded against alleged Communist ballot rigging and malpractice. Most of them imagined themselves to be deeply religious. In fact they were almost completely amoral, prepared to stoop to any lengths to retain control of a union which they regarded as their personal property. Their response to our election victory was simple: a union branch without control of its staff, premises, cars, legal representation, funds and journal, and without the capacity to represent the union in the industrial relations system. In other words, a shell. And the people orchestrating the process, National President John Maynes, and National Secretary Terry Sullivan did not have to face membership election and remained in office only because of a corrupt and unrepresentative electoral system, and had both been defeated candidates in the Victorian Branch elections. The pure cynicism and lust for power inherent in their actions was breathtaking.[38]

Despite such loud echoes of Stalinist tactics, Tanner's team persevered and, as Grenville had predicted in 1977, a large measure of democracy was eventually restored to the union. In his book, Tanner paid tribute to Grenville's not inconsequential role in helping achieve this from the sidelines, providing advice, encouragement, and practical support. After Tanner's team won, Grenville was finally reinstated as a union member and, in recognition of his services to the clerks' union, was appointed as branch returning officer to ensure that democracy was restored to the union's elections, including conducting often long-overdue ballots for workplace shop stewards.

The authoritarian control exercised by Maynes in the clerks' union largely sprang from the inculcation of Stalinism into The Movement in the early 1940s. The ghost of the organisational framework that Santamaria had imported from the Communist Party of Australia would haunt him for the rest of his days, as his own organisation splintered and became largely irrelevant, just as his enemy had already done.

By 1988, when he lost the Victorian clerks' union branch, Maynes had already personally experienced just how brutal Stalinism could be when used by a ruthless opponent who exercised the levers of organisational power. In 1982, a further split inside the NCC witnessed the arbitrary expulsion of Maynes and his supporters by Santamaria, just a few years after he had informed Grenville and Forrester of Maynes's destructive role in the NCC's national office. In effect, Santamaria had concluded that communist control of unions was no longer the problem: it was unionism *per se*.

An indication of the bitterness involved in the Santamaria–Maynes feud was provided by *News Weekly*, in which the demise of Maynes's clerks' union machine was greeted with barely disguised glee. Santamaria danced all over Maynes's political grave, pointedly claiming that, 'From 1982 onwards, the National Civic Council had offered logistic support to the Maynes group, in an effort to win the Victorian and Central and Southern Queensland branches … Hundreds of NCC members were willing to participate in this effort. Without exception, these offers of assistance were rejected after being referred to the FCU's [clerks' union's] National Office [i.e., Maynes].'[39] But this was mild in comparison to the harsh words exchanged between the combatants at the height of the factional battle in 1982–83.

12

The cult of personality

The Movement had only been functioning for a few years before it began to mimic one of communism's least admirable characteristics: the elevation of its leader to cult status. It was, like so many other aspects of The Show's development, inevitable that this would be so, as Santamaria had predestined himself for the role when he chose to model it on the Communist Party. But in the cult that he fashioned, encouraged his supporters to embrace, and then accepted—with suitable modesty—he did not merely emulate but surpassed the communists' cult of personality. Like the CPA's general secretary, as undisputed leader of The Show he wrapped himself in an aura of infallibility; unlike his communist opponents, this was even to the exclusion of his closest colleagues.

Stalinist leaders like the CPA's Jack Miles and Lance Sharkey would deliver lengthy keynote reports to the party's national congress as general secretary, sometimes lasting for several hours. But then other senior leaders—such as national president Dick Dixon, who would deal in depth with industrial and union activities—would deliver substantial reports on major aspects of the party's work since the previous congress. The general secretary was acknowledged as the ideological and organisational supremo, but only within the framework of collective responsibility, entrusted to the national leadership as a whole.

Not so in The Show.

In May 1992, a conference observing '50 Years of the Santamaria Movement' was held at the State Library of New South Wales. Gerard Henderson—once a protégé of the 'Great Man'—presented an acerbic critique of his former mentor. He titled his paper 'B.A. Santamaria, Santamariaism and the cult of personality'. Henderson recounted the extraordinary events of The Show's March 1954 national conference, held over five days:

> The meeting commenced with an announcement that the [Movement's] national officers had decided that the entire first two days of the conference should be devoted to the delivery of four papers by B.A. Santamaria ... The papers encompassed the whole gamut of the Movement's work—political, industrial, economic and international.
>
> There was some tension at Santamaria's almost total domination of the conference. The minutes of the meeting record that eventually a Sydney delegate, Fr Paddy Ryan, moved a resolution to the effect that in future no one speaker should give all the key addresses. During the course of the ensuing debate he said that it was 'not true' to claim that 'no other persons' were available to deliver talks and that he could name 'six straight off' who could do the task. Fr Ryan's modest suggestion that

Santamaria was not the only prophet on the Movement's land failed to impress. His motion was defeated 30 to 4.[1]

Just over twenty years later, nothing had changed inside The Show, of which Henderson was then a member. In October 1974, a two-day National Civic Council seminar was convened, as Henderson recalled:

The original agenda, as circulated, listed a total of eight papers to be delivered—two of which were to be given by Santamaria.[2] I had a particular interest in this since I was scheduled to deliver *A Critique of the Movement*. Over previous years I had become regarded as a somewhat irreverent internal critic of the Movement and at last I was to be given my say. Or so it seemed.

On arriving ... I received my name tag, meal voucher, draft conclusions and revised agenda. Lo and behold I discovered that my paper had been dropped by the [Santamaria] powers that be. Bob Santamaria was now listed as delivering all the papers except one ... For the rest it was to be Santamaria, followed by Santamaria, followed by Santamaria. He justified this format by claiming that, unfortunately, there was no one else capable of delivering the papers in question. It was just like two decades previously.[3]

So 'Santamaria spoke all day on the Saturday', and the 'same format was repeated up to the early afternoon on the Sunday'. Henderson eventually overturned the ban on his paper and spoke last, delivering a 'very tough' critique of The Show. 'In the discussion period that followed it was made clear to me, by one and all alike, that any criticism of Santamaria or the Movement was out of place.' As would have occurred in the CPA several decades earlier, it was no surprise that Henderson was expelled from the NCC shortly after.[4] But by then the CPA had rejected Stalinism, and manifestations of the cult of personality were looked upon with disdain, while they were still firmly entrenched in The Show. Santamaria believed that only he could deliver the sermons from the mount, and his loyal acolytes — like those of successive North Korean dictators — implicitly believed that 'The Respected and Beloved Leader' possessed infinite wisdom.

It was not only his own adherents who heaped adulation on Santamaria. As recorded in chapter two, former Liberal prime minister Tony Abbott described him as 'a philosophical star by which you could always steer' and as 'the greatest living Australian'.[5] His predecessor, Malcolm Fraser, was also a vociferous admirer. Along with over 1,000 supporters of Santamaria's, Fraser was at Moonee Valley racecourse on 13 August 1981 to mark the fortieth anniversary of the foundation of The Movement. He delivered the keynote address, a homily of praise to Santamaria and the organisation he had founded, moulded, and led since its inception:

> For one person to have given leadership and guidance of such a calibre to an organisation of this kind for such a long period must surely be without parallel in Australia's history. It is impossible to talk about the NCC without talking about Bob Santamaria ... In *Against the Tide*, your President says that when he was asked to play a part in the movement at the time of its foundation he was puzzled to understand what practical use was seen in him. I might say that I think that is the kind of modesty that has typified Bob Santamaria throughout his life ...
>
> But if Bob Santamaria was puzzled, I think it would be fair to say that if there was any basis for puzzlement at any

time, it was not going to last for very long. Without doubt, the first thing to be said about this organisation is that from the beginning it took a stand against communism. It dedicated massive and sustained efforts to the achievement of free trade unions. It worked for the wellbeing of all families and especially the underprivileged in the Australian community, and it emphasised the need for defence and foreign policies which would encompass Australia's long and short term security ...

Let me say that whatever people may think of your President there can be no doubt that through his ... tenacity and forcefulness, his foresight and his faith, through his moderation, and through his modesty, he has achieved a substantial place in the history of Australia.[6]

Fraser was joined by a multitude of adoring fans, including future Liberal prime minister John Howard and several other members of federal cabinet, as well as leading personalities from the business community, the legal profession, the Catholic and Anglican churches, the media, and, of course, the trade union movement that had given birth to The Show.

The presence of Fraser, Howard, and other senior Liberals caused considerable grumbling among those who thought The Show was an integral part of the labour movement, not the conservative side of politics. One disgruntled member wrote a letter to the faithful. Addressed to 'Longterm Participant', he highlighted that 'there is a long-standing principle governing the operation of The Show that the organisation is "as far removed from party politics as it is above party politics". (The words quoted are Bob's and have been a governing principle all along.)'[7] This was not strictly correct; as seen in chapter three, Santamaria planned to take over the ALP, and, when he failed in this endeavour, formed the breakaway DLP as a party-political operation that was essentially an extension of The Show's operations.

Nevertheless, this internal critic was horrified that the NCC was being tainted by such a close association with the Liberal Party and that Santamaria's new ideological direction was opaque to the membership:

> Many are worried that Bob is ill-advised by those few national officers physically around him day by day ... and by *their big business finance connections*.
>
> I suggest that there is a problem nowadays for the intelligent interested person associated with The Show who seeks to discover the new policy of a new executive; the problem is how to find out about it. NEWS WEEKLY says nothing about it and supporters are not advised. [Emphasis added.][8]

Beyond the discontent with the celebration's close association with the conservative side of politics, there was another fundamental problem. Allegedly, the celebration was scheduled on the fortieth anniversary of the foundation of The Movement. But was it really forty years? In his 1964 book, *The Price of Freedom*, Santamaria wrote that:

> The initial meeting of the organization, later known as 'the Movement,' which was held on 14 August *1942*, brought together about twenty unionists from twelve Melbourne suburbs. [Emphasis added.][9]

By the time his autobiography was released in 1981—conveniently, a few months before the date he had personally selected for the celebration—Santamaria had slyly altered this passage:

> The initial meeting of the organization, later known as 'the Movement,' which was held on 14 August *1941*, had only four people present ... The next meeting brought together about twenty unionists from twelve Melbourne suburbs. [Emphasis added.][10]

This was no minor slip of the pen, or a passing lapse of memory. It was a classic example of historical revisionism, specifically designed for a political purpose. It was yet another example of the lasting effects of Santamaria's importation of the Stalinist model into The Movement.

The historical timeline clearly demonstrates that the version Santamaria gave in *The Price of Freedom* was correct as to the year the endeavour began (although the precise day and month cannot now be accurately established, as all the participants are dead). It is impossible that things got moving a year earlier, in 1941, in the manner he claimed in 1981. That would have left a significant political hiatus between the first meeting of laymen to discuss establishing the organisation and Santamaria's first annual report of early 1944.[11] There is no doubt that Archbishop Mannix approved of the idea in late 1942–early 1943. The other members of the Victorian hierarchy subsequently discussed it in late 1943, but there is nothing in the available records indicating that deliberations—by either laymen or bishops—occurred earlier than this.

There is, in fact, a wealth of evidence demonstrating that work on forming The Movement actually began in late 1942, not one year earlier. For example, in early 1959, Norm

Lauritz (Santamaria's 'first "recruit"' to The Movement and the founding national secretary),[12] gave a detailed, tape-recorded speech to a gathering of NCC members, recounting the organisation's genesis, in which he had personally participated:

> In about the end of 1942 and the beginning of 1943, a small group of Catholic laymen met as a research group into Communist activities in Australia ... We compiled this report and we submitted the report to the Archbishop [Mannix]...
>
> The Archbishop naturally then said to us ... 'Well, what do you propose to do about it?' And in the rest of the report we submitted a suggestion that we should begin an organization based on the whole set-up of the Communist Party ...
>
> The Archbishop then gave us permission to set up an organization in Melbourne in 1943.[13]

Lauritz also stated that Mannix subsequently approached the bishops of Ballarat, Sandhurst, and Sale, who, in late 1943, agreed to establish The Movement in their dioceses, effectively transforming it into a Victoria-wide organisation. According to Lauritz, it was these bishops who recommended to the September 1945 extraordinary bishops' conference that it be endorsed as an official, national organisation.[14]

Lauritz's recollections — recorded more than twenty years before Santamaria chose 1981 to celebrate the 'fortieth anniversary'— are confirmed by the official minutes of the May 1943 meeting of the Episcopal Committee on Catholic Action (comprising a small group of bishops), which considered a report prepared by Santamaria. The minutes contain a specific reference to 'the *special work* [Santamaria] has been undertaking in the last six months'. [Emphasis added.] As one well-informed Catholic historian has noted, '"Special work" was one of the euphemisms used for the Movement.'[15]

Virtually the same terminology appears in Santamaria's first annual report of early 1944. As discussed in chapter one, in mid-1944 Father Harold Lalor provided Ron Richards of the Security Service's Perth office with a copy of that report, in which Santamaria referred to 'an earlier memorandum' outlining 'the reasons for the *special action* which has been taken since'. [Emphasis added.] Although I have not been able to locate this earlier document (undoubtedly the report to Mannix, referred to by Lauritz in his 1959 talk), its timeframe is explicit from Santamaria's 1944 report. 'It was obvious from the general trend of Communist policy', Santamaria wrote, 'that 1943 was intended to be the vitally important year.' This indicates that the 'earlier memorandum' was written from the perspective of late 1942–early1943. This is reinforced by the content of Santamaria's report of early 1944, which, after recounting developments during 1943, lays out the 'programme for 1944'. There is no mention of activities conducted in 1942, which would have been expected if the organisation had been formed in 1941, as Santamaria claimed almost forty years later.[16]

In fact, Santamaria's second annual report—considered at the bishops' September 1945 extraordinary conference—explicitly dated the organisation's establishment to mid-1943. On page one, in paragraph one, Santamaria wrote:

In presenting the Second Annual Report on the anti-Communist Campaign, I believe that it would be best to direct attention again to the salient features of the Report that was presented a year ago. In that Report it was pointed out that the organisation dealing with this work was brought into existence in the *middle of 1943* to face a critical situation which threatened the conquest of every major trade union in the country by the Communist Party. [Emphasis added.][17]

There is no trace of a document specifically headed 'First Annual Report'. From the publicly available material, the logical conclusion is that Santamaria's report of early 1944 is the same as the one he labelled the first annual report, especially as it was headed 'Report on anti-Communist Campaign', using precisely the same terminology as for the second annual report. In handing this report to Richards, Lalor explained it was 'a summary of the proceedings of a [special] conference of Roman Catholic Bishops which was held in Melbourne towards the end of 1943'.[18]

The available documents—corroborated by a critical eyewitness account—leave no doubt about the timeline for The Movement's formation:

- Late 1942: initial discussion of the need for such an organisation;
- 1943: the organisation takes its first steps, establishing its Melbourne branch;
- 1944: Santamaria compiles his first annual report, based on the detailed plan presented to the Victorian bishops in late 1943, extending its operations throughout Victoria; and
- 1945: after considering Santamaria's second annual report, the Australian bishops endorse The Movement as a national organisation at their extraordinary conference.[19]

The sequence of events also indicates that it took a few years for The Movement to solidify into the organisation that it eventually became—an unexceptional process, given the political climate and logistical problems in the midst of World War II, and the enormity of the task. As Gerard Henderson pointed out in his 1992 paper, yet another Santamaria account—published in the Institute of Social Order's magazine *Social Survey* in 1960—probably provides an accurate version, asserting that The Movement *evolved* during 1942 and 1943, rather than having been 'formed' on a particular date.[20] If there was to be an official, fixed date, it probably would be 19 September 1945, when the bishops extended their official imprimatur at their extraordinary conference in Sydney.

SANTAMARIA HAD A particular reason to backdate his own conception of the date. The purpose of his resort to historical revisionism was simple: to get the fortieth-anniversary celebrations out of the way before he engaged in yet another Stalinist manoeuvre—a good old-fashioned purge of dissidents.

This occurred in August 1982, exactly at the time the fortieth anniversary should have been celebrated at Moonee Valley racecourse. It involved the purging of Santamaria's long-time deputy, John Maynes, and his key supporters, including their removal from their elected positions and from full-time NCC employment. This purge of veteran cadres was conducted with the type of brutal efficiency that once accompanied the exercise of Stalinist power in the CPA. It demonstrated the Bolshevik principle that he who holds the levers of power can exercise them decisively at any time against those who are the nominated enemy. In this case, it was a simple formula: power was held by the NCC's national president (Santamaria) and national secretary (Peter Westmore), and was exercised against Maynes and his group, who did not have their hands on the administrative levers or control a majority of the carefully handpicked delegates of national conference.

The bitter split between the two sides was quickly brought by those purged before the Victorian Supreme Court, where the NCC's dirty linen was aired in public. John Grenville had been predicting just such a major schism since 13 May 1975, when he had complained to Santamaria about Maynes's dictatorial behaviour in the clerks' union. Unprompted, Santamaria informed Grenville that his own problems with Maynes were even worse. In 1975, Santamaria had not acted upon his assurances to Grenville and John Forrester that he would back them in their confrontation with Maynes. In 1982, he acted decisively.

When things eventually split asunder in October 1982, Grenville had a hunch that the documents filed by the two parties in the Supreme Court would be surreptitiously removed from the registry as soon as the case was concluded, unless an early effort was made to obtain them. Fortunately, he did just that, applying for and obtaining copies of some of the key documents before they mysteriously 'disappeared'—presumably removed clandestinely at the behest of one (or perhaps both) of the parties who wanted to cover up the mess as far as possible. It is a toss-up whether this was Santamaria or Maynes, who pointedly was not among the five plaintiffs, instead hiding in the shadows behind his supporters, who instituted the case.[21]

What emerges from the surviving documents is revelatory.

The immediate causes of the split first surfaced in August 1980 when, according to the Maynes group, Santamaria informed other senior members of his 'view that there were tensions in the organisation which were affecting the way in which it was working'.[22] In notes distributed to his hard-core supporters at this time, Santamaria indicated that the 'entire disturbance in the organisation' arose from the refusal on the part of Maynes and his group 'to accept legitimate authority', by which he meant their alleged 'insubordination' in the face of his self-declared right to run the organisation unhindered, wielding the powers of a supreme leader.[23] Santamaria traced the causes further back in the past, in an official statement claiming that 'The original difficulties went back beyond 1975, and have been the subject of repeated attention by the various national bodies of the organisation', confirming what he had told Grenville in 1975.[24]

While not explicitly stated, the inference can be drawn that, by 1980, Santamaria had finally had enough of Maynes: there simply was not sufficient room in one organisation for two authoritarians with giant, competitive egos, each adamant he was correct on all issues. As discussed in chapter nine, Santamaria had demonstrated considerable insight into the motives of individuals engaged in bitter factional disputes, concluding that they were often caused by 'personal issues' as much as matters of 'principle'. This could now be applied to his own organisation and to himself.

Yet, as in the case of the CPA splits, 'struggles of principle' also lay at the heart of the NCC schism, with Santamaria determined to change course, while Maynes clung to past verities. According to the Maynes version of events, 'In April 1980 … Santamaria called for the removal of the industrial staff from the NCC payroll and for their transfer to union jobs.' This proposal was not accepted by the Maynes group. So, in June 1980, Santamaria demanded that the NCC be formally divided into two separate bodies. This was also rejected.[25] In July, news of Santamaria's manoeuvres was leaked to *The Bulletin*:

The proposal, reportedly, is for the organisation to drop those of its 30 organisers concerned with full-time union work and to have them re-employed on the staff of sympathetic unions. This would mark a shift in emphasis in NCC work—away from direct involvement in unions and towards organisation on issues such as family policy, university activism, women's questions and defence and foreign affairs.[26]

In August 1980, Santamaria, Maynes, and their respective supporters among the NCC's officers came to an accommodation—of sorts—and signed a formal agreement.[27] This divided the organisation into two practically separate political operations, but still united under the NCC banner. One was defined as those people 'performing or attached to the industrial, women's and youth work', and the other to those 'performing the work of News Weekly, the Family Association, the Universities'.[28] The ideological division had been clarified: Santamaria had effectively ceded control of trade union work—the original catalyst for establishing The Movement—to Maynes. As one disillusioned ex-member said, 'To Santamaria it's no longer communism in unions that's the enemy, it's unions as such. His attitude is that we wallowed too long in industrial relations.'[29] Santamaria wished, instead, to concentrate on Catholic moral, social, educational, and propaganda issues.

The separation was not just political. The personal element of the struggle was starkly illustrated by the agreement's provision for a physical separation of the two factions, with the industrial operatives relocating from NCC headquarters in central Melbourne and transferring to Carlton, with similar arrangements established in other cities.

The agreement was specified to run for two years, from

the date it was unanimously ratified by the NCC's national conference (3 September 1980) until 3 September 1982. As is usual in such bitter splits, the organisation's assets—property, money, files—were uppermost in the dispute. The agreement provided that if unity and full reintegration were not achieved during those two years, at its conclusion 'the income of the NCC for the next succeeding 2 years would be divided as to one-third' to Maynes's faction 'and as to two-thirds' to Santamaria's, and subsequently the dissidents 'would be allocated one-third of the NCC's assets'.[30] This, not ideological disputes or personality clashes, was at the core of the court case brought by Maynes's supporters: they wanted their 'fair share of the loot' that, they implied, they had spent years helping to accrue.

It seems that Santamaria's plan all along was to dud them. The 1980 national conference had endorsed personnel changes as part of the deal. One of these was that Maynes's most senior supporter, Gerald Mercer, relinquished the administratively powerful position of national secretary to Santamaria supporter Peter Westmore. Santamaria was re-elected as national president, and Maynes as national industrial officer. The Maynes group was adamant that the NCC's constitution provided that such elected positions were for a term of three years, at which time the subsequent national conference would convene and new elections would take place.

However, having gotten the fortieth-anniversary celebrations out of the way a year earlier than should have been the case, Santamaria sprang his trap just before the expiry of the two-year agreement. As is so often the case in such schisms, each side gave wildly different accounts of what had occurred, finely calibrated to appeal to each faction's core supporters and to achieve maximum influence on waverers.

The Maynes faction claimed that, 'As the two years drew
to a close, officials from the Industrial Headquarters sought
discussions with ... Santamaria about reunification. He said
that "tensions" (between officials) had not abated, and that
reunification was not possible.' They claimed that he also
rejected their plan for a further two-year interregnum, aiming
for a phased but 'complete reunification'. In this version of
events, 'Santamaria's sole proposal was that all staff would
be "re-employed" by the NCC, on condition that they gave a
signed undertaking to accept his sole authority as to the work
they would in future undertake.'[31]

Santamaria's version, in a masterfully crafted letter to
NCC members, claimed that the division of property and
income provided for in the 1980 agreement applied only
during 'its currency ... After the expiry of the limited period of
the Agreement, the right to invoke these provisions expired'.
According to Santamaria, he provided Maynes with six weeks'
notice of his intention to terminate the agreement at a national
conference to be convened at that time. 'The six weeks' notice
was to give him ... ample time to invoke the separation clause
before the Conference, and before the Agreement's expiry date.'
Neither Maynes nor any of his supporters did so, Santamaria
reported. 'Their reason was obvious,' he wrote. 'No supporter
would long continue to subscribe to an organisation split in
two. Invoking the Agreement would thus achieve no practical
result.'[32]

Which begs the question: what was his purpose in signing
the agreement? If he believed that invoking the property and
income clauses 'would achieve no practical result', was it not
disingenuous to sign it in the first place?

With negotiations stalled, Santamaria gave formal notice on
11 August 1982 of a national conference to be convened ten

days later. The principal purposes of the meeting, according to both sides, were 'Recission [sic] of the resolution carried at the 1980 Conference ratifying the Agreement of September 3 1980' and the election of a new national executive and national council—twelve months before they were due.[33] Despite Maynes's several letters opposing the agenda and his vociferous objections at the meeting itself, Santamaria had the numbers by a wide margin—more than three-to-one, or 37 to 11 on the critical vote.[34] A new election therefore resulted in Maynes being removed from his decades-old position as national industrial czar. Santamaria was in complete control of the organisation, which he considered he had always owned.

The next move was simple: issue the dissidents with conditions of continuing employment that Santamaria knew they would never accept. When they inevitably rejected his demands, they were sacked by vote of the national council, ordered out of their offices, and instructed to return official property and files.[35] Maynes's supporters cloaked their court challenge with justified allegations of substantial breaches of the NCC's constitution and denial of natural justice. The nub of their purpose, however, was simple: they wanted orders reinstating them, or else the payment of damages, which, in their dreams, involved obtaining their one-third share of the organisation's assets and one-third of its income for the subsequent two years, as had been agreed in the 1980 document.

Santamaria's letter to the dissidents of 26 August contained one condition that revealed the depth of his Stalinism. As Mercer stated in his affidavit filed in the case:

The condition which required [Mercer] (and other officials) to accept direct responsibility to the President [Santamaria] according to a resolution passed in 1966 which purported to give him powers not subsequently incorporated in the 1970 revisions to the Constitution, was in my view unconstitutional, and unreasonable, and amounted to requiring an open-ended commitment of loyalty to one man. I find his request morally repugnant.[36]

Santamaria claimed that, 'No such undertaking has ever been demanded of anybody. It would be utterly unconstitutional. It would be both unprincipled and irrational. Not one single official would give it if any President were sufficiently irrational to demand it.'[37] In fact, he had done precisely this: his letter insisted that if Mercer wanted a continuing role on the NCC's payroll, he had to accept 'direct responsibility to the National President [Santamaria] ... and to no other person'.[38] In denying this fact in his letter to NCC members, Santamaria was simply lying. He muddied the waters by hiding behind decisions taken by national conference and national council to request every officer to accept direction about how they were to be deployed and what duties they would be assigned. But, as he candidly admitted, as 'chief executive officer finally responsible for carrying out the decisions of National Conference and Council, I must actually implement the decisions of those bodies'.[39]

Father Paddy Ryan would have been muttering 'I told you so' from Heaven, reminding all and sundry of his own purging as chaplain to the Sydney Movement in 1953, and of his complaint aired at the 1954 national conference that Santamaria had dominated, speaking for two whole days when Ryan believed others could have delivered the papers just as well. Then, as in 1982, Santamaria's cult of personality held sway and, more importantly, on each occasion he had the numbers against those impudent enough to dissent from his self-obvious greatness.

On 21 October, the court made an interim judgement, concluding that the Maynes group had established a *prima facie* case that the elections held at the 1982 national conference were unconstitutional and, consequently, that the national council which had dismissed them was not properly constituted. It also found that a *prima facie* case had been established that they had not been afforded natural justice.[40] Maynes and his supporters had won a moral victory. However, the orders they had sought—demanding reinstatement—were refused, because the judge concluded that in the event that the Maynes group won the case when it came to full trial, an award of damages would 'be adequate' compensation. In so concluding, the judge also resorted to his acute understanding of *realpolitik*:

> I am also influenced by the fact that the defendants [Santamaria and his supporters] have what might be described as 'the numbers' so far as the members of the Council of the N.C.C. are concerned, and, it would therefore seem unlikely that in the end result the plaintiffs [Maynes's supporters] will again be employed as paid officials of the N.C.C.[41]

In effect, the Maynes group failed to obtain reinstatement, but had substantially dented Santamaria's moral standing by demonstrating his refusal to abide by the NCC's constitution and to follow a fair process in sacking them. The full trial would finally determine the merits of the case and, perhaps, award them substantial damages. The case, however, did not proceed to trial. Instead it was settled by consent between the two factions, with 'Orders that each action be dismissed without any other Order being made'.[42] No other details were forthcoming at that time, but it is now known that the settlement included providing the Maynes group with 'sufficient funds to set up an organisation'.[43]

So it did not bring peace. On the contrary, both sides now resorted to an increasingly vituperative propaganda campaign. The Maynes faction resigned from the NCC as part of the settlement, but immediately formed the Industrial Action Fund (IAF) to continue its trade union work, while leaving the NCC 'to do its work of commenting on public issues through "News Weekly" and "Point of View" and in the Australian Family Association, and amongst University Undergraduates'.[44]

In appealing for funds from NCC members and supporters, the IAF made many allegations against Santamaria, who, in order to silence them, instituted defamation proceedings against key dissident figures, claiming their publications had labelled him 'dishonourable ... untrustworthy ... a thief ... who refused to honour a promise ... who has betrayed ... the ideals of the National Civic Council ... who has led the ... National Civic Council away from the ideals which were established within its Constitution for his own personal ambition'. It was an attempt to stand over his former colleagues, and it largely worked. The writs against the various Maynes supporters were not actioned; but, as most of them did not have the means to defend a lengthy defamation trial (having worked for many years on the meagre salaries paid by The Movement, similar to those of CPA functionaries), the proceedings had the effect of frightening them into refraining from further public criticisms of Santamaria. This was obviously his intent.[45]

'Bitter' would be an understatement of what had come to pass between Santamaria and Maynes, who had been intimately associated in the anti-communist cause for thirty-five years.

More than three decades after these tumultuous events, two sets of allegations made by the protagonists endure. Despite Santamaria's lengthy, nit-picking, point-by-point rebuttal of Maynes's accusations, he did not specifically deny two damaging quotes attributed to him from June 1980, when the agreement between the two factions was under negotiation:

> I regard it as absolutely dishonest for any group of persons regardless of the side which they have adopted in a situation of fundamental division to attempt to possess themselves of all the assets of the organisation facing those who might not wish to work with them with enforced compliance or resignation.[46]

And:

> I would regard any attempt to appropriate all the assets of the organisation by any single group, on the specious basis of offering employment to those they know will not accept it, as attempted theft.[47]

If accurate, these statements indicate that Santamaria regarded what occurred in 1982 as being 'absolutely dishonest' and 'theft'. Presumably, if he felt confident of his facts, he would have specifically repudiated the Maynes group's attribution of these words to himself.

Santamaria had his revenge. In his letter to NCC members, he outed Maynes, who for decades had publicly denied that he was a full-time official of The Show. This was one powerful reason he had not put his name to the court case seeking the reinstatement of paid officials, of which he was one of the longest serving. In a letter to members, Santamaria exposed Maynes's fraud:

> The payout to those who left … was $73,735.63! The Movement had to go into debt, from which it will take a long time to recover. They received full superannuation payments at the highest discretionary level permitted by the Superannuation Trust Deed. For instance, *Mr Maynes' superannuation payment amounted to $56,000* the highest ever paid to any individual official of the organisation. What more could be done in the interests of equity? [Emphasis added.][48]

To rub salt into Maynes's wounds, Santamaria concluded by comparing his erstwhile comrade's 'mendacious leaflet' unfavourably with the old enemy:

> In all the years, not even the Communist Party or any of its members has said that of me. I did not expect to see it said by once-trusted colleagues.[49]

After almost four decades of shared struggle in the anti-communist cause, it had come to this: Santamaria was branded by his own words as 'absolutely dishonest', and Maynes had sunk to a dishonourable level that not even the communists would stoop to.

The Show was over.

Postscript

At the time The Show suffered its devastating split in the early 1980s, its decades' old symbiotic relationship with the CPA was at an end for all practical purposes. The weaker the communists became—as they tore themselves apart in their own splits, stretching over twenty years from the early 1960s—the less reason there was for the NCC to persevere with its anti-communist struggle. By the time the Santamaria–Maynes schism ultimately occurred in 1982–83, after at least ten years of tension and disharmony, the CPA and its two offshoots were so small and divided, their presence in the trade union movement so diminished, and the future of international communism so shaky, it was becoming clear to many observers that the end was nigh for Australian communism.

Shortly after the NCC's own split, another round of defections occurred from the CPA, with Victorian leader Bernie Taft leading a significant group into the ALP. By the early 1990s, all that remained was a rump party of died-in-the-wool neo-Stalinists with virtually no influence in the wider labour movement. The CPA's once powerful and large cadre of full-time union officials had, in the main, ceded their control of key unions back to the left wing of the ALP.

SO WHAT WAS LEFT for The Show? As the split hardened in the wake of Santamaria's purging of its industrial cadres, one of Australia's most insightful anti-communist intellectuals summed up the crossroads it had reached. Frank Knopfelmacher, an irascible, forceful émigré from Czechoslovakia, invariably found the words to encapsulate the state of affairs in any given political situation. In the aftermath of the Victorian Supreme Court's interim judgement of October 1982, he forensically analysed the NCC in his heavy, somewhat menacing Central European accent:

> My feeling is that one wing—the industrial one—clings to the old verities that the principal battlefield for the committed Catholic trade unionist are the trade unions and the Labor Party, whereas Mr Santamaria, and those who go with him, feel that our society is changing—the industrial working classes ... and the trade unions are no longer the decisive agencies of social change and social organisation—and that it is important to exercise influence in those institutions which influence the thinking of the white-collar strata—that is, in universities, in publishing houses, in the mass media, in the press, and so on.
>
> In other words, the Santamaria view seems to be that the principal function of the NCC is an ideological apostolate in favour of traditional, fundamentalist, intelligent conservatism, whereas the old-time wing of the NCC wants to continue the good old struggle in the unions. If the word conservative is to

be used in any meaningful sense, I would regard the Maynes wing as being the more conservative in the sense that they want to stick to what is habitual in our world, but Santamaria's outlook is more oriented towards the new emergent elites, the white-collar, opinion-making, manipulative elites in the media and in the universities and so forth.

May I add ... that in my opinion the NCC, in places like the media and the universities, has no future because it has not come to terms with modernity. It adopts towards modern society an attitude which Hans Kuhn [sic], in his famous book on Germany, called cultural despair—they reject modernity. Now, if you want to influence modern people, you cannot reject the basic presuppositions of their existence and their basic assumptions on how to live.[1]

Knopfelmacher's analysis and predictions were unerringly accurate.

First, to the Maynes faction. In appealing for financial support from those NCC members whose orientation was to the struggle in the unions, Maynes coined the catch cry 'Keep the fight going.' It was defined succinctly as, 'The work is the fight against left-wing supremacy in unions.' The problem for this formulation was that such a supremacy was non-existent. As early as December 1952, Santamaria—in his letter to Archbishop Mannix—had declared that The Movement had virtually broken the back of communist control of the unions.[2] The left never recovered from the series of defeats it suffered in the period 1945–1954. Put simply, it was the right who exercised supremacy in 1982. So, in claiming—as Maynes did in 1983—that 'Constant organisation, vigilance and the grooming of moderate leaders for senior posts are needed to preserve moderate leadership', he was living in the past.[3] The left and right would never again swap the control of unions in bitter election campaigns in the way they had in past decades. Except for the occasional one-off victory—usually in state branches, such as the Victorian and Queensland clerks' union branches, not federal offices—there would never again be any significant alteration of the balance of forces in the union movement. The strength of the ALP right wing, however, could only be consolidated by what happened next.

For some time, the ALP right in the union movement had foreseen where things were likely to end inside the NCC. They had developed a carefully planned strategy to bring Show-controlled unions back into the mainstream. This involved their re-admittance to the ALP, re-uniting the right-wing forces that had been divided by the Labor Split of the mid-1950s, thus augmenting their numbers so effectively as to permanently wrest control of the Victorian branch of the party from the left wing. By the early 1990s, with a massive campaign of union amalgamations underway, the discernible force of The Show in unions had all but disappeared, as could also be said for the communists. The situation had returned to its normal position before the CPA became a major force in the unions in the decade after 1935: the ALP right ran things.

Knopfelmacher, however, was correct in another sense. At the time of the NCC schism of the early 1980s, membership of trade unions in Australia represented roughly half of the workforce. By 2017, the figure had slumped to 15 per cent, with membership in the private sector down to 11 per cent. As Knopfelmacher analysed the situation in 1982, 'The trade unions are no longer the decisive agencies of social change, and social organisation.' Today—with the industrial and manufacturing sectors of the economy in seemingly terminal decline—they barely survive at all.

The only notable former Show-controlled union with any political clout in the 21st century is the shop assistants', which—bloated by sweetheart agreements with major retailers that provide a version of compulsory unionism—exercises disproportionate influence in ALP policy-making. Its main preoccupation is negative: to resist what Knopfelmacher referred to as 'modernity' and to attempt to revive a conservative, traditionalist form of Catholic social policy.

This union's obsession with such issues—including same-sex marriage, abortion, stem-cell research, and in vitro fertilisation—has often come at the expense of its members, many of whom are low paid and young. In industrial deals with food chain McDonald's, and retail giants Woolworths and Coles, for example, the union has sold out the people who pay their dues (often as a condition of employment), depriving many of penalty rates and in some instances agreeing to hourly payments below those legally required. On the other hand, employers have received stern correspondence from the union opposing their public support for same-sex marriage.[4]

Despite Santamaria's disingenuous claim that 'trade unions would remain [the NCC's] main area of work',[5] the NCC never again played an influential part in union affairs—apart from a quixotic, expensive, but unsuccessful attempt in the early 1980s to unseat Laurie Carmichael, one of the last prominent CPA union officials left standing. Santamaria's indifference to the fate of his once-mighty industrial army was summed up in the overt encouragement he gave to the idea that it should re-unify with the ALP—the once-hated enemy from which he had withdrawn the unions he controlled in the wake of the Labor Split to pursue the fight against the CPA and international communism, and to advocate for Cold War defence and foreign policies.[6]

The priority that Santamaria allocated to trade union work in the 1980s was made clear in his paper 'The Movement into the Eighties', distributed with the invitation to the 'fortieth anniversary' celebration in August 1981:

> Apart from the normal daily responsibility of maintaining the existing base we hold within the trade union movement, our major responsibility in the immediate period ahead will be to defeat the attempt to destroy the uranium industry in this country, an operation ultimately organised by the Communists and their allies ...[7]

As John Grenville ironically commented, 'It must be very, very comforting for all those chaps in the industrial wing to know that for the '80s their role will be to defend the barons of industry via the uranium industry.'[8]

Santamaria's new priorities were enunciated in this paper. He did not long dwell on international communism—his obsessive preoccupation of bygone decades—merely asserting the proposition of 'the clear danger ... of the imposition of Soviet hegemony as a result of the growing political/military superiority of the Soviet Union'.[9] By the early 1980s, exactly the opposite was the case: the communist economic and political system was sclerotic, on the verge of disintegration, and its military technology, especially in nuclear weapons, was light years behind the West. But as far as Santamaria was concerned, the danger was even greater than in previous years.

His real focus, however, was not on the communist enemy, but on the 'enemy within'. He headed his treatise 'the West's "schism in the soul",' which took as its motif the collapse of Western civilisation caused by 'corruption from within'. According to this assessment, the 'fundamental cause' of this development was 'the true Cultural Revolution of the late 'sixties and of the 'seventies; not the shoddy but brutal political power play which Mao inflicted on the Chinese people, but the profound moral transformation which came about within the Western world itself'.[10] His worldview was informed by the history of failed civilisations:

> No truly great civilisation, as that of the Christian West once was, ever collapses as a result of external attack. If external attack appears to be the immediate cause, it has been preceded by long decades, sometimes even centuries, of corruption from within. Of the various types of corruption, none is more profound in its effects than the loss of intellectual clarity as to the ultimate truths and principles by which it is worth living, or for which it is finally worth dying. It is around these truths only that the cohesion of societies, as small as the family, as large as the State, can finally be built ...[11]

What Santamaria was railing against, as Knopfelmacher had correctly noted, was modernity itself. What he favoured was a return to the past—a past in which Catholic social, moral, and religious precepts formed the basis of the kind of society and economy that contained 'the ultimate truths and principles by which it is worth living'. What had replaced this and had now to be overturned was the victory of 'the humanist revolution' caused by 'the assault on the principle of authority' and the corruption of the legal and educational systems. The moral issues he identified were 'abortion, divorce, homosexuality'. But married women in the workforce was the demon that had opened Pandora's Box, handing education to the corrupt secular world and changing society's 'view of normality—and morality', especially as they related to things such as 'lesbianism, abortion, contraception, pre-marital sex', and imparting 'a new, and quite deliberately anti-Christian morality under the pretext that you are teaching biology'.[12]

These types of ideas were at the core of Santamaria's new direction for The Show and, as he explained:

> This why this Movement has made such a heavy investment of personnel, time and resources in the struggle on the university campus and in teachers' unions in defence of sound educational philosophies and against the abuse of the classroom; why it has worked against Modernist and Marxist influences within the Christian churches, whose purpose … is to empty the supernatural content out of religion.
>
> We have not, and will not abandon the trade union and political struggles which brought us into being. But there is more to it than that. The 'eighties are not the 'forties, and our responsibility is to be present, not where we would like the action to be, but where the action really is.[13]

In this, too, Knopfelmacher was correct. Maynes represented a conservative view of where the battles of the modern world were being—and would continue to be—fought, whereas Santamaria favoured fighting on the battleground where his traditional, fundamentalist conservative ideology was under threat of demolition. As Santamaria summarised his position at the end of his paper, 'There is no point in fighting the battle in the unions … unless we simultaneously impose a check on the forces which underly [sic] the disintegration of the family.'[14] The Movement's failure to make any ground in this struggle since he expounded this position has simply been due to its inability—as Knopfelmacher saw clearly—to connect with people who live in and, most importantly, *want* to live in the modern world, not in the semi-mediaeval world idolised by Santamaria. For example, in the thirty-five years since Santamaria's paper was distributed, many Catholic women have behaved like their sisters of other Christian faiths. More sophisticated and tertiary educated, they have entered the workforce in greater numbers, planned smaller families, and largely eschewed the church's most conservative social doctrines.

Never was the title of an autobiography more apposite: Santamaria was battling 'against the tide' of modernity.

As the 1980s progressed, the tide became bigger and much more powerful. The Hawke–Keating governments' economic reforms took society further away from Santamaria's idealised past. He suddenly found himself in sympathy with many of the ideas of old foes who, like him, clung to vanishing verities. For example, he found he could have a friendly dialogue with long-time Victorian communist leader Bernie Taft. As their interlocutor wrote in his report of their meeting, 'What intrigued the two old enemies was the extent to which their economic and social views had converged since the collapse of the Soviet system and the rise of fundamentalist free-market economic orthodoxy throughout the English-speaking world.'[15] Much to Taft's amazement, Santamaria veered towards a Marxist view of class, which would have been condemned in earlier years as anathema to basic church teachings:

> I am very sympathetic to Marx's view that unless we are very careful we will find that the State is run by the dominant class. At the moment I have no doubt at all that the State in Western society is run largely by the multinationals and the great investment banks whose economic power exercises a veto over the authority of the State, and that their policies suit a particular group of people.[16]

At the end of his life, Santamaria reflected on the bitterness of his failures, although he insisted that at over eighty years of age he had no regrets, and still worked 'as hard as I ever did for the ends that I want to see realised'. But, he said, 'My honest belief is that I have achieved little or nothing at all. The things that I have been deeply interested in, and worked very hard for, are more remote today than when I started.'[17]

John Forrester, who joined The Movement in 1951 and worked for Santamaria's cause for twenty-five years—much of that time as a secret member inside the ALP—echoed this verdict. 'In the long term we lost', he declared. 'Overall I don't think we Christianised society. I think the ideals and the aims were not achieved—and many of them perhaps shouldn't have been achieved. But certainly we failed in that area. We didn't produce this Christian millennium in Australia.'[18] Forrester, however, lamented that, under Santamaria's leadership, The Show had abandoned the church's core principles: 'We ended up—and this is why so many of us are disillusioned—we ended up over with the Tories in the political establishment, in the capitalist establishment, and the church social teaching we were brought up on wasn't on about that.'[19]

The Catholic Social Studies Movement that Bartholomew Augustine Santamaria founded under direct church control in the 1940s—precisely to protect and promote the church's social teachings—but renamed the National Civic Council in 1957, when he decided to defy that same church control, continued his work after he died in 1998. Outside the conservative, traditionalist Catholics who continue to look to it for guidance, it has little wider political influence. It persists with the same ideology and policies that saw Santamaria—King Canute-like—commanding the tide to reverse its inexorable flow.

Acknowledgements

Many people assisted this project in various ways—none more than John Grenville, who jointly conducted an extensive research endeavour with me in the early 1990s. His detailed knowledge and understanding of the history and internal workings of both the Catholic Church and The Movement have made it possible to tell this story. His own membership and eventual resignation from what was by then the National Civic Council forms an important element of the book's denouement. I am particularly grateful for his attention to detail in reading the many iterations through which the book has gone, and his numerous helpful suggestions that have improved the text in major aspects.

John and I are especially grateful to Armando Gardiman AM and Anna Katzmann, now a justice of the Federal Court. In 1992, Armando was a senior partner in the labour law firm Turner Freeman (where he is now the managing partner) when he readily agreed to take a case *pro bono* in the Administrative Appeals Tribunal to challenge the unnecessarily restrictive rules governing the release of ASIO records under the Commonwealth *Archives Act 1983*. His dogged persistence in pursuing the matter helped to shift the stubborn, conservative, and bureaucratic inertia within ASIO on the subject. Anna's appearance—also *pro bono*—as our barrister was a skilled and forensic performance in the face of impossible odds imposed by the tribunal's rules, which prohibit even the plaintiffs' counsel from examining the records at issue in such a case. This made cross-examining ASIO's expert witness almost impossible, but somehow her probing revealed layers that would otherwise have remained opaque.

We thank that witness—who cannot be named—for his good will in the face of our concerted attack on his organisation's reactionary policies governing access to its files. His open-mindedness was key to a positive result. The opposing barrister—Stephen Gageler, now a justice of the High Court—assisted greatly in providing a bridge between the two sides that eventually resulted in a compromise settlement that achieved a remarkable liberalisation of the access rules, bringing Australia more into line with international standards—especially the liberal framework operating in the United States—for the release of historical intelligence files.

Our own expert witness was an American citizen and my co-author of two books published in the 1990s. John Loftus was able to bring his expert knowledge of the US system to bear in a revelatory manner, and, despite at times extremely rugged questioning by Mr Gageler, he kept his composure and earned the respect of all present at the hearings. His contribution to the eventual settlement was considerable.

The outcome of that case is reflected in almost every phase of the story that unfolds in this book.

Professor John Warhurst made a very significant

contribution by preserving perhaps the only publicly available archive demonstrating The Movement's daily *modus operandi*. In 1977, when I first began my inquiries into this subject, I came across a paper that Professor Warhurst had written as a young academic, in which he told a very small part of the story of the archives of The Show's Adelaide branch. I visited him in Warrnambool, Victoria, to inspect those files, which were in his possession at that time. I copied a tiny selection of them, which he eventually lodged in the Australian National University, where John Grenville and I studied them in detail in the early 1990s. Several chapters in this book reflect the major importance of those papers in exposing the underside of the rock beneath which the details of The Movement's intelligence operations are otherwise still well hidden.

Father Edmund Campion — one of the finest historians of Catholic life in Australia — provided advice and practical assistance that is reflected in the text, especially covering the birth and early development of The Show. Former Western Australian Movement priest John Challis opened a valuable window into the history of The Movement's Perth branch, for which I am grateful.

Robert Manne and Bruce Duncan read the manuscript in earlier drafts, and provided generous and extremely useful comments that have improved the final product immeasurably. Lindsay Tanner also read an early draft and provided enthusiastic support.

The Australia Council provided me with a writer's grant in 1991 to write a parallel history of The Movement and the CPA, which assisted greatly with the research that is reflected in the text.

I also thank Henry Rosenbloom for taking on this project and for his attention to detail in editing the manuscript. I am also grateful to the professional team at Scribe, who turned it into this superb book.

Finally, I acknowledge the professional assistance that John Grenville and I received from numerous archivists and librarians right around the country, including in the National Archives of Australia and various university and church libraries and archives. I am especially thankful for the assistance of Father Stephen Hackett, the general secretary of the Australian Catholic Bishops' Conference and his archivist/librarian, Leonie Kennedy, for providing extracts of key minutes of the bishops' meetings of 1944 and 1945; Michael Taffe of the Ballarat diocesan archive; and former and current staff of the Mitchell Library in Sydney, also known as the State Library of NSW—in particular, Jim Andrighetti, Sally Hone, Ed Vesterberg, and Sarah Morley.

Santamaria's son, Paul, was both courteous and extremely helpful in arranging access to those of his father's papers in the publicly open date-range held in the State Library of Victoria, where Shona Dewar was professional in arranging for relevant material from this massive collection to be made available. Unfortunately, a significant part of these historically important papers is not yet available to researchers; only those files older than forty years are in the public domain. This has meant that I could not access much of the material I wished to consult, especially as it relates to the tumultuous events recounted in chapter twelve, dealing with the divisions and ultimate split in the NCC of the early 1980s.

John's and my work would never have been possible without the support—and forbearance—of my wife, Robyn Ravlich and John's, the late Mary Grenville, in whose memory I dedicate this book.

Select Bibliography

Aarons, Mark, *The Family File*, Black Inc, Melbourne, 2010.

Barnet, Richard J., *Intervention and Revolution: the United States in the Third World*, World Publishing, 1968.

Blaxland, John, *The Protest Years: the official history of ASIO, volume 2, 1963–1975*, Allen & Unwin, Sydney, 2015.

Blaxland, John and Crawley, Rhys, *The Secret Cold War: the official history of ASIO, volume 3, 1975–1989*, Allen & Unwin, Sydney, 2016

Calwell, Arthur, *Be Just and Fear Not*, Rigby, Melbourne, 1978.

Campion, Edmund, *Rockchoppers: growing up Catholic in Australia*, Penguin, Ringwood, 1982.

—, *Australian Catholics*, Penguin, Ringwood, 1987.

—, *The Santamaria Movement: a question of loyalties*, Working Paper No: 83, Working Papers in Australian Studies, Sir Robert Menzies Centre for Australian Studies, Institute of Commonwealth Studies, University of London, 1992–93.

Challis, John, 'Recollections of a Perth Movement Chaplain, 1952–1958', *Journal of the Australian Catholic Historical Society*, 35 (2014).

Cox, Robert W. (with Sinclair, Timothy J.), *Approaches to World Order*, Cambridge University Press, Cambridge, 1996.

Duffy, Paul, *Demons and democrats: 1950s Labor at the crossroads*, Freedom Publishing, North Melbourne, 2002.

Duncan, Bruce, *Crusade or Conspiracy? Catholics and the anti-communist struggle in Australia*, UNSW Press, Sydney, 2001.

Fitzgerald, Ross, *The Pope's Battalions: Santamaria, Catholicism and the Labor Split*, University of Queensland Press, St Lucia, 2003.

Franklin, James, *Catholic Values and Australian Realities*, Connor Court Publishing, Bacchus Marsh, 2006.

Gollan, Robin, *Revolutionaries and Reformists: Communism and the Australian Labour Movement, 1920–1955*, Australian National University Press, Canberra, 1975.

Henderson, Gerard, 'The Catholic Church and the Labor Split', in Jim Davidson (ed.), *The Sydney–Melbourne Book*, Allen & Unwin, Sydney, 1986.

—, *Mr Santamaria and the Bishops*, Studies in the Christian Movement, Sydney, 1982.

—, 'B.A. Santamaria, Santamariaism and the cult of personality', in *50 Years of the Santamaria Movement*, Eureka Street Papers Number 1, Melbourne, N.D.

—, *Santamaria: a most unusual man*, the Miegunyah Press, Carlton, 2015.

Hirsch, Fred and Richard Fletcher, *CIA and the Labour Movement*, Spokeman Books, London, 1977.

Horner, David, *The Spy Catchers: the official history of ASIO, volume I, 1949–1963*, Allen & Unwin, 2014.

Laffin, Josephine, *Matthew Beovich: a biography*, Wakefield Press, Kent Town, 2008.

Leopold, Les, *The Man Who Hated Work and Loved Labor: the life and times of Tony Mazzocchi*, Chelsea Green, White River Junction, 2007.

Lucas, Steve, *Freedom's War: the US crusade against the Soviet Union, 1945–56*, New York University Press, New York, 1999.

Macintyre, Stuart, *The Reds: The Communist Party of Australia from origins to illegality*, Allen & Unwin, Sydney, 1998.

McKnight, David, *Australia's Spies and their Secrets*, Allen & Unwin, Sydney, 1994.

—, *Espionage and the Roots of the Cold War: the conspiratorial heritage*, Frank Cass Publishers, London, 2002.

Morgan, Patrick (ed.), *B.A. Santamaria: Your Most Obedient Servant, selected letters: 1938–1996*, the Miegunyah Press, Melbourne, 2007.

— (ed.), *B.A. Santamaria: Running the Show, selected documents: 1939–1996*, the Miegunyah Press, Melbourne, 2008.

Murray, Robert, *The Split*, Cheshire, Melbourne, 1972.

Murray, Robert and White, Kate, *The Ironworkers: a history of The Federated Ironworkers' Association of Australia*, Hale & Iremonger, Sydney, 1982.

Ormonde, Paul, *The Movement*, Thomas Nelson, Melbourne, 1972.

Pybus, Cassandra, *The Devil and James McAuley*, University of Queensland Press, St Lucia, 2001.

Rabe, Stephen G., *U.S. Intervention in British Guyana: a Cold War story*, The University of North Carolina Press, Chapel Hill, 2005.

Radosh, Ronald, *American Labor and United States Foreign Policy*, Random House, New York, 1969.

Santamaria, B.A., *The Price of Freedom*, The Campion Press, Melbourne, 1964.

—, *Point of View*, the Hawthorn Press, Melbourne, 1969.

—, 'The Movement into the Eighties: A Study Paper', National Civic Council Extension Committee, ND.

—, *Against the Tide*, Oxford University Press, Melbourne, 1981.

Saunders, Malcolm, 'A Note on the Files of "The Movement" in South Australia', *Labour History* (99), November 2010.

Sheridan, Greg, *When We Were Young & Foolish: a memoir of my misguided youth with Tony Abbott, Bob Carr, Malcolm Turnbull, Kevin Rudd & other reprobates* ..., Allen & Unwin, Crows Nest, 2015.

Short, Susanna, *Laurie Short: a political life*, Sydney, Allen & Unwin, 1992.

Tanner, Lindsay, *The Last Battle*, Kokkino Press, Melbourne, 1996.

Trahair, Richard C. S. and Robert Lawrence Miller, *Encyclopedia of Cold War Espionage, Spies, and Secret Operations*, Enigma Books, New York, 2012.

Truman, Tom, *Catholic Action and Politics*, the Merlin Press, London, 1959.

Warhurst, John, 'United States' Government Assistance to the Catholic Social Studies Movement, 1953–54', *Labour History* (30), May 1976.

Weiner, Herbert E., 'The Reduction of Communist Power in the Australian Trade Unions', *Political Science Quarterly*, volume LXIX, number 3, September 1954.

Notes

Note on sources

The following abbreviations have been adopted in the notes:

B & L Archives: the former Archives of Business and Labour,
 now the Noel Butlin Archives Centre, ANU, Canberra
NAA: National Archives of Australia
NSW SL: State Library of NSW (Mitchell Library)
SLV: State Library of Victoria

Preface

1 For a view of a rank-and-file Movement member (and successful trade union operative), see interview with John Forrester, 1 December 1982, NSW SL MLOH 777.
2 Bruce Duncan, *Crusade or Conspiracy? Catholics and the anti-communist struggle in Australia*, UNSW Press, Sydney, 2001; Gerard Henderson, *Santamaria: a most unusual man*, the Miegunyah Press, Carlton, 2015.
3 David Horner, *The Spy Catchers: the official history of ASIO*, volume I, 1949–1963, Allen & Unwin, 2014; John Blaxland, *The Protest Years: the official history of ASIO*, volume 2, 1963–1975, Allen & Unwin, 2015. John Blaxland and Rhys Crawley, *The Secret Cold War: the official history of ASIO*, volume 3, 1975–1989, Allen & Unwin, Sydney, 2016.

Chapter 1 / Modelled completely on the Communist Party

1   This is the most reliable version of the genesis of the organisation, given by Santamaria's long-time colleague and first recruit to The Movement, Norm Lauritz, who was present at the inception. See Lauritz's speech to NCC members, 17 February 1959, in Patrick Morgan (ed.), *B.A. Santamaria: Running the Show, selected documents: 1939–1996*, the Miegunyah Press, Melbourne, 2008, pp. 456–57.

2   In his autobiography, Santamaria wrote that he was accompanied to his initial discussion with Mannix by H.M. (Bert) Cremean. B.A. Santamaria, *Against the Tide*, Oxford University Press, Melbourne, 1981, p. 73.

3   Morgan (ed.), *Running the Show*, pp. 456–57, and memo of 6 July 1944, from Richards to Mosely, NAA A6122, item 129.

4   Paul Ormonde, *The Movement*, Thomas Nelson, Melbourne, 1972, p. 17.

5   Robert Murray, *The Split*, Cheshire, Melbourne, 1972, p. 129; and Arthur Calwell, *Be Just and Fear Not*, Rigby, Melbourne, 1978, p. 166.

6   'Movement members were … required to take a pledge never to disclose "the existence or the activities of this Movement".' Duncan, *Crusade or Conspiracy?*, p. 103.

7   Murray, *The Split*, p. 129. Some details of Lalor are given in Ormonde, *The Movement*, pp. 17–19, 46, and I gratefully acknowledge the assistance of the late John Cowburn in providing other biographical information. See NSW SL ML MSS 9329, Box 33, John Cowburn file.

8   Duncan, *Crusade or Conspiracy?*, pp. 125–26.

9   Memo of 6 July 1944, from Richards to Mosely, NAA A6122, item 129.

10 Stuart Macintyre, *The Reds: The Communist Party of Australia from origins to illegality*, Allen & Unwin, Sydney, 1998, p. 398.

11 Memo from Deputy Director for W.A. to Director General, 6 July 1944, NAA A6122, item 129.

12 Memo from Richards to Deputy Director for W.A., 6 July 1944, NAA A6122, item 129.

13 Memo from Director General to Deputy Director for W.A., 18 July 1944, NAA A6122, item 129.

14 Memo from Mosely to Director General of Security, W.B. Simpson, 2 August 1944, NAA A6122, item 129.

15 Memos from Deputy Director for W.A. to Director General, 6 July 1944, and Mosely to Director General of Security, W.B. Simpson, 2 August 1944, and attached 'Report on Anti-Communist Campaign',

NAA A6122, item 129. Richards had actually reported that he had been informed that it was 'a special conference'. Memo from Deputy Director for W.A. to Director General, 6 July 1944, NAA A6122, item 129.

16 On 24 April 1944, the Australian bishops met in Sydney for their biennial conference. The official minutes of that meeting make no mention of the meeting of Victorian bishops in late 1943, nor was Santamaria's report of early 1944 officially considered at this meeting, but there is no doubt that it was what Santamaria labelled as his 'first annual report' when he presented his second annual report to the bishops' September 1945 extraordinary national conference. Indeed, there was no discussion at all of the formation of The Show at the 1944 bishops' conference, as disclosed by the extract of its minutes supplied to me by Father Stephen Hackett, the general secretary of the Australian Catholic Bishops' Conference via its archivist/librarian, Leonie Kennedy.

17 Lauritz speech to NCC members, 17 February 1959, in Morgan (ed.), *Running the Show*, p. 456.

18 Memo from Mosely to Director General of Security, W.B. Simpson 2 August 1944, and attached 'Report on Anti-Communist Campaign', NAA A6122, item 129.

19 Ibid.

20 Ibid. It is of interest to note that at the end of this report Santamaria included a section headed 'THE ASSISTANCE OF WHICH THE ORGANISATION STANDS IN NEED.' The second point was an appeal to the bishops for the 'Development of a Factory Y.C.W.' to ensure that only trustworthy men were used in the fight and that opportunists would be excluded thereby. This referred to the Young Christian Workers' Movement, a section of Catholic Action that over the following years was a major thorn in Santamaria's side as he tried to utilise it for his own purposes. Its head, Father Frank Lombard, opposed both the authoritarian discipline and the increasing involvement of The Movement in ALP politics, advocating that individual Catholics should be free to pursue the anti-communist struggle as they saw fit, not be conscripted and directed by Santamaria. This dispute was raised repeatedly with the bishops by Santamaria, but the YCW never bent to his dictates. For a good account of this, see Duncan, *Crusade or Conspiracy?*, pp. 71, 80–81, 100–101, 131–32, 155, 184, 198–200, 239.

21 Memo from Mosely to Director General of Security, W.B. Simpson, 2 August 1944, and attached 'Report on Anti-Communist Campaign', NAA A6122, item 129. The Movement's National Conference held on 20 September 1945 in Sydney agreed 'to the principle of a National Movement rather than a Federation of State Movements'. Minutes of 1945 National Conference, SLV MS 13492, series IX, box 1, folder 2.

22 Memo from Mosely to Director General of Security, W.B. Simpson, 2 August 1944, and attached 'Report on Anti-Communist Campaign', NAA A6122, item 129. I have used the Reserve Bank of Australia's pre-decimal currency inflation calculator to estimate the value of pre-February 1966 Australian pounds in 2015 dollars. See the bank's website at http://www.rba.gov.au/calculator/annualPreDecimal.html.

23 Santamaria's alleged unease has been given credence by a document he presented to the January 1947 Movement National Conference headed 'The Problem of Secrecy'. Morgan (ed.), *Running the Show*, pp. 160–64. This was never acted upon, and throughout his leadership (1942–98) secrecy was an essential characteristic of the organisation, even after it became widely known as a major force in politics in the mid-1950s.

24 Santamaria's control of The Movement's personnel was established from the very beginning. Prior to the bishops extending their formal imprimatur to the organisation in September 1945, Santamaria had already put key people on the payroll, including Norm Lauritz, William Crowe, and Frank McManus. At the first National Conference of the organisation in 1944, Lauritz was elected as national secretary, 'unopposed', and McManus's status was reflected in the decision to distribute his speech made at the previous National Committee meeting; Lauritz was re-elected at the National Conference held in Sydney on 20 September 1945, the day after the bishops had endorsed The Movement; there is no mention of this historic event in the minutes of The Show's National Conference. Minutes of 1944 and 1945 National Conferences, SLV MS 13492, series IX, box 1, folders 1 and 2.

Following the bishops' decision to formally endorse The Show, Santamaria wrote to Bishop O'Collins of Ballarat (who was effectively the treasurer of the bishops' committee supervising the organisation), requesting that these three be now formally appointed to 'the National headquarters of the Movement'. O'Collins and the other bishops on the committee approved his recommendation, establishing a pattern that dominated for over five decades: Santamaria selected loyalists for all key executive and administrative positions, thereby ensuring that at all times he effectively had the 'numbers' on the key policy committees to squash any dissent and assert his own personal authority and control of The Movement. See letters from Santamaria to O'Collins of 8 December 1945, O'Collins and Sydney's Archbishop Gilroy to Santamaria of 19 December 1945, and Santamaria's to O'Collins and Gilroy of 24 December 1945. Copies in author's possession.

25 Memo from Mosely to Director General of Security, W.B. Simpson, 2 August 1944, and attached 'Report on Anti-Communist Campaign', NAA 6122, item 129.

26 Ibid.

27 *Catholic Action at Work*, CPA publication, Sydney, December 1945, p. 3.

28 B.A. Santamaria, *Against the Tide*, p. 87. There is no mention in the minutes of the conference of the decision to provide this £10,000 to The Movement, but Santamaria's account would be correct. There is no doubt that such a sum was agreed and that each diocese was given a quota to fulfil; John Grenville read correspondence in the Ballarat diocese archives between Bishop O'Collins (the treasurer of the bishops' committee controlling and financing The Movement) and various bishops conveying to them their individual quotas and their responses in paying them. Bruce Duncan deals extensively with The Movement's funding by the bishops, *Crusade or Conspiracy?*, pp. 82–3. One example he gives notes that in fifteen months in 1954–55 the bishops had provided £15,427, 8 shillings, and 2 pence [$516,146] for wages alone. Ibid., p. 438, endnote 46.

29 Memo from Mosely to Director General of Security, W.B. Simpson, 2 August 1944, and attached 'Report on Anti-Communist Campaign', NAA 6122, item 129.

30 Edmund Campion, *The Santamaria Movement: a question of loyalties*, Working Paper No: 83, Working Papers in Australian Studies, Sir Robert Menzies Centre for Australian Studies, Institute of Commonwealth Studies, University of London, 1992–93, pp. 4–5.

31 This bishop was James Carroll of Sydney; Duncan, *Crusade or Conspiracy?*, p. 288.

32 Some of the original church documents are reproduced as Appendix C in Ormonde, *The Movement*, pp. 179–86.

33 In *Crusade or Conspiracy?*, Duncan deals forensically with Santamaria's systematic dishonesty on this issue. See Parts III and IV.

Chapter 2 / Truth will out

1. *News Weekly*, special supplement, 'National Civic Council Fortieth Anniversary Dinner Souvenir', 13 January 1982, speech by NCC President B.A. Santamaria.

2   Official records of the CPA's congress, in author's possession.

3   Ibid.

4   Robin Gollan, *Revolutionaries and Reformists: Communism and the Australian Labour Movement, 1920–1955*, Australian National University Press, Canberra, 1975, p. 130.

5   At the time the bishops' meeting occurred, Santamaria was the assistant director of the Australian National Secretariat of Catholic Action, and a few months later he engineered himself into the director's position. Duncan, *Crusade or Conspiracy?*, pp. 90–92. Santamaria had drafted a resolution for the bishops' consideration, proposing that The Movement should 'be recognised as being in principle a Movement of [Catholic Action] entitled as such to the full and unwavering support of all Catholics and to the full co-operation of other recognised Movements of [Catholic Action].' Morgan (ed.), *Running the Show*, p. 148.

His proposal was rejected by the bishops, however. The official minutes of the 'Extraordinary Meeting of the Hierarchy held in St Mary's Cathedral Presbytery, Sydney, 19 and 20 September 1945', record at item 9, 'Approval of the recently formed Industrial Movement':

> Before discussion on the motion for the formal approval of the Industrial Movement, as outlined in the General [Santamaria] Report sent to all the Bishops, Archbishop Simonds asked the meeting to decide whether or not this Movement should be given a Mandate within the scope of the approved movements of Specialised Catholic Action. He pointed out that its aim, scope and methods are not in harmony with the Popes' teachings on Catholic Action. He moved a motion that the Movement be not given a Mandate by the Bishops as Catholic Action, and the motion was seconded by Bishop Roper. Bishop Gleeson spoke against the motion, but it was eventually carried by the meeting. Bishop H. Ryan then moved, and Bishop Henschke seconded that the Bishops give their approval and support to the General Principles of the Movement, as set out in the Memorandum, with such amendments as this Meeting may determine. The discussion on this motion had not concluded when the conference adjourned for tea. In the evening session, at 7:30 pm, Mr. B.A. Santamaria was invited to be present, in order to answer

questions about the Movement proposed by various Bishops. On his departure, it was moved by the Bishop of Wagga Wagga and seconded by the Archbishop of Adelaide that the Movement be controlled, both in policy and finance, by a Special Committee of Bishops, consisting of the Archbishop of Melbourne (President), the Archbishop of Sydney (Secretary) and the Bishop of Ballarat (Treasurer). With this amendment to the Constitution, the motion to approve the Movement was carried. A further amendment to the draft Constitution was moved by Archbishop Beovich and seconded by Bishop O'Collins that a clause be inserted in the Memorandum empowering each Bishop to appoint a priest to assist groups in his diocese wherever it is deemed necessary. The motion was carried unanimously.

This extract of the minutes was supplied to me by Father Stephen Hackett, the general secretary of the Australian Catholic Bishops' Conference via its archivist/librarian, Leonie Kennedy. The minutes provide the founding mandate of the organisation, clearly indicating that The Movement was an *industrial*, not a *political*, body, which Santamaria later came to contest when he explicitly used the bishops' resolution as the rationale to take over the ALP.

6   This pamphlet appeared in its first edition in December 1945.

7   Santamaria, *Against the Tide*, p. 86.

8   Long-time Show member John Grenville heard the story directly from Santamaria in the late 1960s or early 1970s. Grenville always thought this account did not ring true, and when we jointly began the research for this book in 1991 he was adamant we should get to the bottom of Santamaria's allegation. As a result, I unravelled the mystery by interviewing key CPA members involved in the story, as detailed in the following pages. Interview with Grenville, 20 March 2016.

9   Gerard Henderson, 'The Catholic Church and the Labor Split', in Jim Davidson (ed.), *The Sydney–Melbourne Book*, Allen & Unwin, Sydney, 1986, p. 222. Murray in *The Split* also gives a version of how the CPA came into possession of the Movement's report to the 1945 bishops' conference, which supports Henderson's in some respects. Murray does not name Duhig as the culprit, and states that it was lost by a 'Bishop returning by train *from* Sydney after the historic 1945 conference'. [Emphasis added.] This is in conflict with both Santamaria's and Henderson's version that Duhig left it on the train on his arrival *in* Sydney.

10 In this version, Henderson wrote: 'when travelling overnight from Brisbane to Sydney, he placed the document under his pillow. It seemed like a good idea at the time. Except that when disembarking at Sydney's Central Railway Station, the Archbishop of Brisbane forgot to check his bed. The top-secret document was discovered, presumably by a unionist with connections to the Communist Party, and handed over to the CPA.' Gerard Henderson, *Santamaria*. Kindle file, Location 3638. On 24 May 2011, I—together with Bob Carr—addressed the Sydney Institute, of which Henderson is the executive director, on the topic 'Communism and the Labour Movement during the Cold War'. In my formal address, the version which is contained in this book was outlined, and in the final, published version the following appears:

> Communists had gained an invaluable insight into the forces that were marshalling against them in late 1945. In something of a cloak-and-dagger scene, a man quietly entered the Melbourne CPA office and leaked to them a printed copy of Bob Santamaria's ultra-secret report to the September 1945 Bishops' conference. There is still mystery surrounding this leak but according to the senior CPA official who received it, the original source was a dissident Catholic who was probably opposed to the Church's direct involvement in politics. Santamaria's explanation for the leak was that Brisbane's Archbishop Duhig had left his copy of the report under his pillow after reading it on the overnight train to Sydney. According to this account, it was discovered by a CPA supporter in the Australian Railways Union who handed it over. None of the CPA officials involved in the affair believed this to be true, although the possibility exists that a printer sympathetic to the CPA was the source, as for some inexplicable reason the report had been professionally printed.

See the Sydney Institute's *Sydney Papers Online*, Issue 12. During general discussion, Henderson rejected this version, repeating Santamaria's version. I corrected this by reference to interviews conducted with the relevant CPA officials, as cited below.

11 Duncan, *Crusade or Conspiracy?*, endnote 62, p. 419. Ross Fitzgerald also recounts a version of the Duhig story in *The Pope's Battalions: Santamaria, Catholicism and the Labor Split*, University of Queensland Press, St Lucia, 2003, p. 73.

12 The first mention of this important revision of Santamaria's defamation

of Duhig came during an interview with John (Jack) Hughes on 4 April 1991 when he highlighted Blake's role in obtaining the document. The exact words quoted in the text at this point are from a tape-recorded interview on 10 November 1991. Other interviews with Hughes were recorded on 13 August and 3 October 1991.

13 Macintyre, *The Reds*, p. 176.

14 Interview with Jack Blake, 3 May 1991.

15 Santamaria, *Against the Tide*, p. 86.

16 Interview with Jack Blake, 3 May 1991.

17 Ibid.

18 See, for example, Louis Nowra, 'The Whirling Dervish', *The Monthly*, February 2010.

19 Murray, *The Split*, p. 49.

20 Edmund Campion, in his paper *The Santamaria Movement: a question of loyalties*, p. 1, thanks Sister Margaret M. Press RSJ for providing his copy, which he generously allowed me to copy. Sister Margaret obtained her copy while working in Adelaide on the history of the South Australian church.

21 *Catholic Action at Work*, p. 18.

22 Ibid., pp. 1, 10–11.

23 The official minutes of the meeting record that Santamaria answered the bishops' questions about The Movement during the evening session on 19 September. In a typical example of Santamaria's false modesty, he described his presentation to the bishops as 'abysmal'. Santamaria, *Against the Tide*, p. 87. Santamaria's own papers, lodged in the State Library of Victoria, shed no light on this issue. The folder concerning The Movement's National Conference held in Sydney the following day (20 September 1945) are strangely silent about this momentous event and Santamaria's important role in making a presentation direct to the bishops. The minutes of this conference do not even mention the bishops' meeting, nor Santamaria; there is nothing in this file indicating that Santamaria even reported the event to his colleagues, merely a mysterious reference to the fact that the Melbourne delegate 'was requested to open the discussion.. The file contains a lengthy report on the work of The Movement's Sydney region, but nothing at all on the activities of the Melbourne or wider Victorian organisations. It is as though someone has been through the file and extracted key elements to expunge Santamaria's role from history. Minutes of 1945 National Conference, SLV MS 13492, series IX, box 1, folder 2.

Chapter 3 / An intelligence agency

1. See, for example, the article by former US labour attaché in Australia, Herbert E. Weiner, 'The Reduction of Communist Power in the Australian Trade Unions', *Political Science Quarterly*, volume LXIX, number 3, September 1954; Murray, *The Split*; Susanna Short, *Laurie Short: a political life*, Sydney, Allen & Unwin, 1992; Robert Murray and Kate White, *The Ironworkers: a history of The Federated Ironworkers' Association of Australia*, Hale & Iremonger, Sydney, 1982; Paul Duffy, *Demons and democrats: 1950s Labor at the crossroads*, Freedom Publishing, North Melbourne, 2002; Bruce Duncan, *Crusade or Conspiracy?*; and Ross Fitzgerald, *The Pope's Battalions*.

2. In his autobiography, Santamaria made it abundantly clear that The Movement was a guiding force in the ALP's decision to establish the Industrial Groups: Santamaria, *Against the Tide*, pp. 97–102.

3. Henderson, *Santamaria*. Kindle file, Location 1094.

4. Op. cit., Location 1521.

5. During the war, Franco claimed that 20,000 priests had been killed by the Republican side; then, after the war, this was revised down to 7,937 religious. According to Antony Beevor, however, in *The Battle for Spain: the Spanish Civil War 1936–1939*, Weidenfeld & Nicolson, London, 2006, pp. 82–3, that was still too high: Beevor wrote that thirteen bishops, 4,184 priests, 2,365 members of other orders, and 283 nuns were killed, most of them in the summer of 1936. He also wrote that there were many false claims of nuns being raped. As is well established, most of the atrocities happened in the period of the breakdown of law and order in the Republican-controlled areas during the early months of the war, and, as Beevor observed, mostly consisted of spontaneous revenge taken by ordinary Spaniards who saw the clergy as class enemies. This does not diminish the brutality used in the killings, but it was a brutal war on both sides.

6. Henderson, Santamaria. Kindle file, Location 1371.

7. For example, see Duncan, *Crusade or Conspiracy?*, pp. 168, 213. For a somewhat peculiar account of Santamaria's relationship with Evatt, see speech of Norm Lauritz to NCC members, 17 February 1959, in Morgan (ed.), *B.A. Santamaria: Running The Show*, pp. 480–83.

8. See Ormonde, *The Movement*, pp. 59–61 for an account of Evatt's statement.

9. See, for example, Duncan *Crusade or Conspiracy?*, p. 267.

10. Morgan (ed.), *Running the Show*, p. 156.

11 Duncan *Crusade or Conspiracy?*, pp. 156, 176.

12 Reproduced in Patrick Morgan (ed.), *B.A. Santamaria: Your Most Obedient Servant, selected letters: 1938–1996*, the Miegunyah Press, Melbourne, 2007, pp. 73–74.

13 Op. cit., p. 74.

14 Op. cit., p. 75.

15 John Challis, 'Recollections of a Perth Movement Chaplain, 1952–1958', *Journal of the Australian Catholic Historical Society*, 35 (2014), p. 81.

16 Josephine Laffin, *Matthew Beovich: a biography*, Wakefield Press, Kent Town, 2008, p. 193.

17 Morgan (ed.), *Running the Show*, p. 194. Morgan has speculated that it was the treasurer of the bishops' committee in charge of The Movement (James O'Collins of Ballarat) who was responsible for 'informally approving each expansion of the Movement's mandate as it happened, and that the other bishops may not have been aware of this.' Op. cit., p. 144. O'Collins was extremely close to both Santamaria and Mannix, and it is more likely that this triumvirate coordinated this process, if Santamaria ever requested permission of anyone—other than himself. The text of the resolution carried at the bishops' 1945 meeting is set out in full at endnote 5 of chapter two. In *Against the Tide*, p. 89, Santamaria wrote that he had first been informed of the details of the resolution a few months after the meeting, so he had been in possession of the facts since at least late 1945–early 1946.

18 Challis, 'Recollections of a Perth Movement Chaplain, 1952–1958', p. 80.

19 Duncan, *Crusade or Conspiracy?*, pp. 146, 218.

20 Duncan cites many internal Movement documents demonstrating the intention to 'control the ALP Executive and Conferences and eventually Caucuses by force of number of its own representatives and CONTROL of those representatives by their obedience to the authority of the organisation [The Movement], that is, ultimately by religious authority'. The Sydney bishops came to disagree strongly with this objective, especially as The Movement used the name of the hierarchy to promote it. *Crusade or Conspiracy?*, pp. 219, 314–15.

21 See David McKnight, *Espionage and the Roots of the Cold War*, pp. 153–171 for an account of this situation; and also Duncan, *Crusade or Conspiracy?*, p. 29. The CPA's organisation inside the NSW ALP

was confirmed to me by its chief architect, John Hughes. Interview of 13 August 1991.

22 An account of Ryan's life—and the debate with Ross—is given in James Franklin, *Catholic Values and Australian Realities*, Connor Court Publishing, Bacchus Marsh, 2006, chapter two.

23 Gerard Henderson, *Mr Santamaria and the Bishops*, Studies in the Christian Movement, Sydney, 1982, p. 103; Murray, *The Split*, pp. 128–29; Duncan, *Crusade or Conspiracy?*, pp. 308, 316.

24 Gilroy's abdication of his responsibility for the Sydney Movement began in late 1945, soon after it received the bishops' official imprimatur. See letter from Gilroy to Santamaria of 19 December 1945 in which he conveys *Ryan's* views on Santamaria's proposals for The Show's full-time national personnel as though they were his own. ('I delayed answering your letter ... to go thoroughly into the matter with Dr. Ryan ... One feature that Dr. Ryan wishes to have stressed at the outset...'.) Copy in author's possession. On Gilroy's non-attendance at meetings of the Episcopal Committee on the Catholic Social Studies Movement, see Duncan, *Crusade or Conspiracy?*, p. 83.

25 Henderson, *Mr Santamaria and the Bishops*, p. 26.

26 Ormonde, *The Movement*, pp. 34, 42–3; Murray, *The Split*, pp. 62, 129; and Duncan, *Crusade or Conspiracy?*, pp. 181, 208–09.

27 See, for example, memo of 19 September 1952 to Acting Director NSW, NAA A6122, item 1198. There is a limited account of Ryan's relationship with ASIO and its predecessors in Franklin, *Catholic Values and Australian Realities*, pp. 33–5. Franklin's assertion that The Movement and such intelligence agencies did not share a close relationship is, however, not supported by the evidence.

28 'LIAISON WITH CATHOLIC ACTION', memo of 27 October 1953, NAA A6122, item 1198.

29 Document J.25, NAA A6283, item 18.

30 Memos of 7, 9 and 30 November 1951 and 6 December 1951, and memo of 19 September 1952, NAA A6122, item 1198.

31 Memo of 15 October 1953 from Senior Section Officer to Director NSW, NAA A6122, item 1198.

32 Report of 19 September 1952 to Acting Director NSW, NAA A6122, item 1198. Santamaria described the functions of Movement 'groups' in very similar terms: 'the accumulation of real up-to-date intelligence'. Santamaria's opening address to the NCC National Conference, June 1966. Minutes of 1966 National Conference, SLV MS 13492, series

IX, box 5, folder 2. The focus on intelligence-gathering is reinforced in another Movement document: 'It is necessary firstly to train the individual as an intelligence agent'. Morgan (ed.), *Running the Show*, p. 145.

33 Report of 19 September 1952 to Acting Director NSW, NAA A6122, item 1198.

34 Ibid. The stenographer was June Mills, née Amelia Aarons, my great aunt.

35 Horner, *The Spy Catchers*, p. 197.

36 We spoke with one of the Movement liaison agents, who confirmed much of the information in the ASIO files, including that the £2 was deducted from his Movement salary; he insisted, however, that some of ASIO's information was inaccurate. Interview of 13 September 1994.

37 All the above quotes come from report of 19 September 1952 to Acting Director NSW, NAA A6122, item 1198.

38 Memo of 23 October 1952, NAA A6122, item 1198.

39 Memo of 13 November 1952, NAA A6122, item 1198.

Chapter 4 / The Show and ASIO

1 Memo of 15 October 1953, NAA A6122, item 1198.

2 Ibid.

3 Memo of 11 December 1953, NAA A6122, item 1198.

4 Ibid.

5 Report of 14 December 1953, NAA A6122, item 1198.

6 Memo of 6 January 1954, NAA A6122, item 1198.

7 Memo of 8 January 1954, NAA A6122, item 1198.

8 Report of 10 February 1954, NAA A6122, item 1198.

9 Ibid.

10 Report of 10 March 1954, NAA A6122 item 1198.

11 Handwritten note on memo of 24 March 1954, NAA A6122, item 1198.

12 Duncan, *Crusade or Conspiracy?*, p. 209.

13 Murray, *The Split*, p. 62.

14 Memo of 22 April 1954, NAA A6122, item 1198.

15 Memo of 27 April 1954, NAA A6122, item 1198.

16 Memo of 5 May 1954, NAA A6122, item 1198.

17 See 'Note for File' of 10 December 1956, undated memo (number 168) of circa 7 December 1956, 'Note for File' of 10 December 1956 and memo of 14 December 1956, NAA A6122, item 1198.

18 See David McKnight, *Australia's Spies and their Secrets*, Allen & Unwin, Sydney, 1994, pp. 200–01 and 204–08 for an account. The Movement liaison agent who we spoke to stated that Jack Clowes was the ASIO officer most involved in this relationship, confirming McKnight's research. He also told us that Clowes often proffered ASIO intelligence and was the only ASIO officer in his experience to engage in a genuine two-way traffic of information. Interview of 13 September 1994.

19 Memo of 25 November 1957, NAA A6122, item 1198.

20 Cassandra Pybus, *The Devil and James McAuley*, University of Queensland Press, St Lucia, 2001, p. 126 and endnote 20, p. 293.

21 Horner, *The Spy Catchers*, p. 198.

22 Blaxland, *The Protest Years*. Gerard Henderson took issue with Blaxland over his historical errors concerning The Movement/NCC in his 'Media Watch Dog', Issue number 301, 29 January 2016. See also Blaxland and Crawley, *The Secret Cold War*.

23 John Lyons, 'Santamaria admits links to ASIO in 1960s', *Sydney Morning Herald*, 17 March 1990. On this point, see also Blaxland and Crawley, *The Secret Cold War*, Kindle edition, locations 2593–2619.

24 John Lyons, 'Santamaria admits links to ASIO in 1960s', *Sydney Morning Herald*, 17 March 1990.

25 Ibid. and John Lyons, 'Against the Tide', *Good Weekend*, 17–18 March 1990.

26 On the RSL, see Blaxland and Crawley, *The Secret Cold War*, Kindle file, location 2593.

27 Royal Commission on Intelligence and Security Fourth Report [re Australian Security Intelligence Organization] Volume 1, NAA A8908, 4A, p. 101.

28 Op. cit., p. 262.

29 ASIO covering note to 'Extract from Appendix W to part IV of the unpublished history of ASIO', in my possession.

30 'Extract from Appendix W to part IV of the unpublished history of ASIO', in my possession.

31 This will be discussed in chapter 9, but is an analysis of the splits in the CPA dated 9 November 1970, NAA A6122, item 1522.

32 Interview with a former Movement member who wishes to remain anonymous, 13 September 1994. On Clowes's two-way exchange of intelligence with The Show and the ALP right, see also McKnight, *Australia's Spies and their Secrets*, pp. 22–23, and on Clowes's activities in the unions more generally, pp. 205–08.

Chapter 5 / The conspiratorial method

1   Memo of 11 September 1952 and copies of vertically cut letters, NAA A6122, item 1222.

2   B & L Archives, Farrell Collection, Z197. According to Patrick Morgan, The Show 'had suspicions of Communist supporters on the postmaster general's department, who might intercept letters.' Morgan (ed.), *Running the Show*, p. 145.

3   I am grateful to former Movement priest in Perth, John Challis, for this information.

4   Memo of 11 September 1952, NAA A6122, item 1222.

5   An excellent account of the development of the Movement's Perth branch is contained in John Challis's memoir of his time as a Movement parish chaplain, 'Recollections of a Perth Movement Chaplain, 1952–1958', pp. 73–84.

6   Interviews with John Grenville, circa August 1977, and John Forrester, circa July–August 1977, NSW SL MLOH 777.

7   Interview with John Grenville, circa August 1977, NSW SL MLOH 777. A vast collection of the NCC's Victorian membership index cards can be found in NSW SL, ML MSS 9329, Box 17, NCC membership lists and cards file.

8   Letter from Adelaide to Sydney, 17 October 1956, B & L Archives, Farrell Collection, Z197, box 2.

9   Ibid. The Adelaide delegate to The Movement's 1944 National Conference reported that it was run by a five-member directorate, each having responsibility for one of the organisation's sections, which were defined as industrial issues, propaganda, finance, the census and the ALP, which members were instructed to join. Minutes of 1944 National Conference, SLV MS 13492, series IX, box 1, folder 1.

10 Letter (in two parts, taped back together) from Sydney to Adelaide, 28 November 1956, B & L Archives, Farrell Collection, Z197, box 2.

11 Santamaria, *Against the Tide*, p. 76.

12 The collection of the South Australian Movement branch—known as the Farrell papers—is replete with examples of these codenames, as is a file of James Normington Rawling's papers dealing with the Adelaide Movement. Farrell wrote to Boylan specifically giving his codenames: see letter from Adelaide to Sydney, 17 October 1956, B & L Archives, Farrell Collection, Z197, box 2. The Farrell papers are found in the B & L Archives under items Z197 and N119. These records are listed according to the title of the institution at the time

John Grenville and I examined them in the early 1990s (the Archives of Business and Labour, or B &L Archives), not by the title it is now known as (the Noel Butlin Archives Centre). Farrell's use of the name J. Edwards is also recorded in his letter to Lauritz of 10 July 1945, in the Rawling's papers dealing with Adelaide, B & L Archives, N57/547. David Shinnick, a member of the Adelaide Movement from 1952, when shown correspondence addressed to L. Norman, immediately identified the recipient as Norm Lauritz. He also was surprised at Farrell's lapse of security in addressing him as 'Dear Norm' in one letter. Interview with Shinnick, 3 December 1991.

13 See Mark Aarons, *The Family File*, Black Inc, Melbourne, 2010, p. 112.

14 Malcolm Saunders, 'A Note on the Files of "The Movement" in South Australia', *Labour History* (99), November 2010, pp. 181, 182 and endnote 17; and Laffin, *Matthew Beovich*, p. 172.

15 Interview with John Warhurst, circa June–July 1977, SL NSW MLOH 777.

16 I first studied these files after reading Professor Warhurst's article 'United States' Government Assistance to the Catholic Social Studies Movement, 1953–54', *Labour History* (30), May 1976, pp. 38–41, in mid-1977. The papers were then in Warhurst's possession, and I visited him in Warrnambool, where he was teaching at that time, and he kindly provided access to them. The priest who obtained these files was John Hepworth, who received them from his colleagues around 1971–72 after Gleeson replaced Archbishop Matthew Beovich upon his retirement in May 1971. See Malcolm Saunders, 'A Note on the Files of "The Movement" in South Australia', p. 183.

17 Saunders, 'A Note on the Files of "The Movement" in South Australia', p. 184.

18 I am grateful to Bruce Duncan for drawing this aspect to my attention. He wrote extensively about the YCW's disagreements with Santamaria in *Crusade or Conspiracy?*. See p. 269 for his account of Farrell's role in convincing Archbishop Beovich to reject the formation of a breakaway party during the Labor Split.

19 Printed document, signed Ted, B & L Archives, Farrell Collection, Z197, Box 2.

20 Ibid

21 Ibid.

22 Ibid.

23 Letter from Farrell to Lauritz, 11 April 1944, Rawling's papers, B & L

Archives, N57/547.

24 Letter from Farrell to Lauritz, 7 August 1944, and attachment, Rawling's papers, B & L Archives, N57/547.

25 Letters from Farrell to Lauritz, 19 November 1944 and 3 December 1944, Rawling's papers, B & L Archives, N57/547.

26 See handwritten copies of internal FIA correspondence of 26 May 1944 and 5 September 1944, and letter from Farrell to Lauritz, 14 January 1945, Rawling's papers, B & L Archives, N57/547.

27 Letter from Sydney to Adelaide, signed F. Kayes, 3 July 1948, B & L Archives, Farrell Collection, Z197, box 2. 'Ferguson' was Jack Ferguson, later NSW deputy premier under Neville Wran and father of the Ferguson clan of trade union leaders and politicians, including Martin, Laurie, and Andrew.

28 Handwritten notes, undated, B & L Archives, Farrell Collection, Z197, box 2.

29 Note of 13 January 1953, B & L Archives, Farrell Collection, N119/16 S, Concertina File, box 1.

30 Series of handwritten notes, first and third undated, second of 3 August 1955, B & L Archives, Farrell Collection, Z197, box 2.

31 Handwritten notes, 1954, B & L Archives, Farrell Collection, Z197, box 2.

32 Handwritten notes, August 1954, B & L Archives, Farrell Collection, Z197, box 3.

33 Interview with Jim Moss, 2 December 1991.

34 Handwritten notes, 20 December 1954, B & L Archives, Farrell Collection, Z197, box 3, and interview with Jim Moss, 2 December 1991.

35 Handwritten notes, undated, B & L Archives, Farrell Collection, Z197, box 3.

36 Typed notes, 14 May 1955, B & L Archives, Farrell Collection, Z197, box 3.

37 Handwritten notes, June 1955, B & L Archives, Farrell Collection, Z197, box 3.

38 Handwritten and typed reports, B & L Archives, Farrell Collection, Z197, box 2.

39 Letter from Sydney to Adelaide, 18 December 1952, B & L Archives, Farrell Collection, Z197, box 2. ASIO did compile a hefty file on Bandler, recording that he had first come under 'adverse notice' in 1941 (two years after arriving in Australia), had been dismissed by the Tasmanian Hydro-Electric Commission in August 1951 for his

communist activities, and had admitted his CPA membership but stated
he had left the party in 1948. There is no mention of the Adelaide job
in his publicly available ASIO file. See report of 27 September 1951
and Minute Paper of 4 August 1975, NAA A6119, items 1594 and
1595.

40 I discussed this with Hans Bandler soon after I had seen this document
when I visited John Warhurst in Warrnambool to inspect the Farrell
papers in 1977. Bandler confirmed his application for this position.

Chapter 6 / The jewel in Ted's Crown

1 The first report on the incident was dispatched to ASIO headquarters
on 15 September 1952, as mentioned in memos from Regional Director
South Australia to Headquarters, 14 November 1952 and to Regional
Director NSW, 29 September 1952, NAA A6119, item 764.

2 Memo from Regional Director South Australia to Regional Director
NSW, copied to ASIO headquarters, 29 September 1952, NAA A6119,
item 764.

3 Memo from Security Officer to Chief Security Officer (probably of the
Department of Supply), 9 September 1952, NAA A6119, item 764.

4 This version was given by Maynes to John Grenville who, as federal
secretary of the Federated Clerks' Union in the 1970s, had asked
Maynes (federal president of the union) how he had obtained proof
that the South Australian union secretary Harry Krantz was a secret
CPA member. Maynes replied that Krantz's name appeared in many
places in Moss's papers. Interview with Grenville, 9 March 2016.

5 ASIO 'pen-picture', attached to Minute to Director B1 of 1 July 1954,
NAA A6119, item 765.

6 Interview with Jim Moss, 2 December 1991.

7 Speech to Movement school by Ted Farrell, June 1947, Rawling's papers,
B & L Archives, N57/547.

8 Interview with David Shinnick, 3 December 1991.

9 Memo to ASIO Headquarters from Regional Director South Australia,
14 January 1953; memo to Regional Director South Australia
from ASIO Director General, 19 January 1953; and memo to ASIO
Headquarters from Acting Regional Director South Australia, 5 July
1954, NAA A6119, items 764 and 765.

10 Memo to Chief Security Officer, Department of Supply, from ASIO
Director General, 10 December 1952, NAA A6119, item 764.

11 B & L Archives, Farrell Collection, Z197, box 3. When interviewed, Moss identified with precision 54 items of his papers. Interview with Jim Moss, 2 December 1991.

12 Interview with Jim Moss, 2 December 1991.

13 Memo to ASIO Headquarters from Regional Director South Australia, 14 January 1953, NAA A6119, item 764.

14 Interview with Jim Moss, 2 December 1991.

15 Memo to ASIO Headquarters from Regional Director South Australia, 24 November 1952, NAA A6119, item 764.

16 Memo to ASIO Headquarters from Regional Director South Australia, 14 January 1953, NAA A6119, item 764.

17 Memo to ASIO Headquarters from Regional Director South Australia, 14 October 1954, NAA A6119, item 765.

18 Report to ASIO Headquarters, 23 October 1952, NAA A6119, item 764.

19 B & L Archives, Farrell Collection, Z197, box 3 and interview with Jim Moss, 2 December 1991.

20 Krantz's ASIO file is replete with evidence of his secret CPA membership and his denials of such membership. See, for example, memo from South Australian Regional Director to headquarters, 1 December 1955; report of the CPA's 19th Annual South Australian State Conference, 20 October 1953, at which Krantz was a prominent participant; Commonwealth Investigation Service report, 6 June 1949, for an example of Krantz's public denial of his CPA membership; and numerous Army reports and Krantz's letters, subjected to wartime censorship, which demonstrate his membership began in the early 1940s. NAA A6119, item 203. Moss was not the only senior CPA leader to confirm his membership; others included my father, Laurie Aarons, who was an official of the South Australian CPA in the 1940s, and later CPA national secretary.

21 Handwritten notes, undated, B & L Archives, Farrell Collection, Z197, box 3.

22 Handwritten lists, undated, B & L Archives, Farrell Collection, Z197, box 2.

23 Handwritten notes, undated, B & L Archives, Farrell Collection, Z197, box 2.

24 Memo to Chief Security Officer, Department of Supply, from ASIO Director General, 10 December 1952, NAA A6119, item 764.

25 Memo to ASIO Headquarters from Regional Director South Australia, 14 January 1953, NAA A6119, item 764.

26 Interview with Jim Moss, 2 December 1991.

27 Ibid.

28 Ibid.

29 Letter from Santamaria to O'Collins of 8 December 1945. Copy in my possession.

30 Interview with Jim Moss, 2 December 1991.

31 Speech to Movement school by Ted Farrell, June 1947, Rawling's papers, B & L Archives, N57/547. Sydney had introduced the concept of a Gospel Discussion as a part of every Movement meeting in 1945. See report of the Sydney delegate to the National Conference of 20 September 1945, covering the period 31 March–20 September 1945. Minutes of 1945 National Conference, SLV MS 13492, series IX, box 1, folder 2.

32 Speech to Movement school by Ted Farrell, June 1947, Rawling's papers, B & L Archives, N57/547.

33 Morgan (ed.), *B.A. Santamaria: Running The Show*, p. 140. The pledge evolved over time, a more modern version being: 'As I have freely entered this Movement I acknowledge my duty to accept its policies and its discipline. I undertake to work for all its objectives and I promise to perform the tasks allotted to me under its authority, particularly those tasks given to me at this meeting. I undertake to respect at all times the trust reposed in me, even if I cease to be a member.' See *Background Briefing*, ABC Radio National, 12 December 1982.

34 In the transcript of his speech, he is noted simply as 'Father Kelly', but David Shinnick identified him as Father Paddy Kelly. Interview with David Shinnick, 3 December 1991. Malcolm Saunders cites him as the editor of *Southern Cross*, 'A Note on the Files of "The Movement" in South Australia', p. 183.

35 Speech to Movement school by Father Paddy Kelly, June 1947, Rawling's papers, B & L Archives, N57/547.

36 Ibid.

37 Speech to Movement school by Norm Lauritz, June 1947, Rawling's papers, B & L Archives, N57/547.

38 Ibid.

39 Letter from Sydney to Adelaide, 26 March 1953, B & L Archives, Farrell Collection, Z197, box 2.

40 Letter from Sydney to Adelaide, 8 July 1953, and letter from Adelaide to Sydney, 22 July 1953, B & L Archives, Farrell Collection, Z197, box 2.

41 Letters from Adelaide to Sydney, 9 April 1954 and 10 June 1954, and letter from Sydney to Adelaide, 8 September 1954, B & L Archives, Farrell Collection, Z197, box 2.

42 Interview with John Warhurst, circa June–July 1977, NSW SL MLOH 777. Warhurst first wrote about this relationship in his article 'United States' Government Assistance to the Catholic Social Studies Movement, 1953–54', pp. 38–41.

43 On aspects of the relationship between the AFL–CIO and US labour attachés, see Robert W. Cox (with Timothy J. Sinclair), *Approaches to World Order*, Cambridge University Press, Cambridge, 1996, note 32, p. 465. This relationship was first exposed by Senator J. William Fulbright in congressional hearings examining the American Institute of Free Labor Development in 1969.

44 Warhurst, 'United States' Government Assistance to the Catholic Social Studies Movement, 1953–54', p. 38.

45 Duncan, *Crusade or Conspiracy?*, p. 209.

46 For an account of the CPA's dire financial situation, see Aarons, *The Family File*, chapter fifteen.

Chapter 7 / Spy versus Spy: part one

1 ASIO report of 5 May 1958, NAA A6126, Item 625.

2 Ibid.

3 History of Vic Campbell (Victor GORE), circa 1950, and Second '[Hartley] Eighth Report' of 13 March 1958, CPA CDC files, C17, copies in author's possession. These files were handed to me by former CPA union official and senior party functionary John Hughes in 1991. They were subsequently lodged in the Mitchell Library (State Library of NSW) by the SEARCH Foundation, but they remain inaccessible to researchers as of 2017. The documents from these files cited in this book were copied by me and are held in my possession.

4 History of Vic Campbell (Victor GORE), circa 1950, CPA CDC files, C17; undated circular to all branches from section executive, NAA A6122, item 596; and interview with CPA wharfie Ric Divers, 2 August 1994.

5 Interview with Eric Parker, 2 August 1994.

6 Ibid.

7 ASIO report of 19 October 1951, NAA A6119, item 304. When shown this document in 1994, McPhillips denied that this event

had happened: 'That's wrong', he stated, claiming he 'wouldn't have known him then, not until around 1954 ... When I was an FIA official I was not particularly acquainted with Campbell ... That statement about Campbell in 1951 is rubbish, it's not true.' Interview with Jack McPhillips, 21 September 1994. How ASIO's agent attending the meeting could have inserted that into his report is mysterious, but then McPhillips and the truth on such matters were often strangers.

8   For an account of these events, see Short, *Laurie Short*, chapters ten and eleven.

9   ASIO reports of 4 April 1952, NAA A6122, item 335; and 16 April 1952, 19 May 1952, 13 June 1952, NAA A6119, item 1213; and 18 June 1953, NAA A6119, item 304.

10 ASIO index card of details from report Number 2746, 12 September 1952, NAA A6119, item 124; interview with CPA wharfie Ric Divers, 2 August 1994; and undated report on the CPA WWF National Fraction meeting of 22–23 November 1952, NAA A6119, item 1213.

11 ASIO index card of details from report Number 2746, 12 September 1952, NAA A6119, item 124; and undated report on the CPA WWF National Fraction meeting of 22–23 November 1952, NAA A6119, item 1213.

12 ASIO report of 25 August 1954, NAA A6119, item 213.

13 There are numerous such incidents dealt with in Campbell's CDC file. See, for example, note of 18 September 1951 'Re V. K. Cambell [sic],' from Queensland State Committee, and from E.B. (Ted Bacon) per JRH (Jack Hughes); Report of 7 January 1953, 'Interview Vic Campbell, re assault charges,' in front of HBC (Herbert Bovyll Chandler), JG (Jess Grant) and JAG (unknown); Report of 11 December 1957, 'Re Vic Campbell, from Don Morcom'; Report of 3 December 1954, 'From Tom Nelson, re Vic Campbell'; Report of 20 January 1955, 'From Vic Campbell'; Note from Wally Stubbings sent through the Queensland State Executive, January 1955; Letters and notes of 8 February, 4, 5 April, 8, 9, 10 May 1956; note of 15 January 1957, 'matter of Vic Campbell', CPA CDC files, C17. For an example of Campbell's clashes with Nelson see ASIO report of 27 September 1957, NAA A6119, item 1214.

14 Interview with Bill Brooks, 29 August 1994.

15 Report of 11 December 1957, 'Re Vic Campbell, from Don Morcom,' CPA CDC files, C17.

16 Notes of 17 April 1956, CPA CDC files, C17. Hughes scrawled some

initial notes on the incident: 'Bad—should be severely reprimanded and decision that he give up the drink—as offerred [sic] by him and to extent we discussed with him any further lapses will lead to much greater penalty. Before whole membership.'

17 Letter of 15 June 1956 from District Executive to City Section Committee, CPA CDC files, C17.

18 ASIO report of 24 July 1956, NAA A6119, Item 306.

19 Report of 11 December 1957, 'Re Vic Campbell, from Don Morcom,' CPA CDC files, C17.

Chapter 8 / Spy versus Spy: part two

1 Duncan, *Crusade or Conspiracy?*, p. 129; interview with a former Movement member who wishes to remain anonymous, 13 September 1994.

2 Interview with a former Movement member who wishes to remain anonymous, 13 September 1994.

3 Interview with Bill Brooks, 29 August 1994.

4 Interview with Ron Maxwell, 5 August 1994.

5 Those present included Ted Ross, Glen Fingleton, Norm Woodley, and Sippy Davis, with Neville Isaksen sending an apology. Ross, Woodley, Davis, and Isaksen were ALP supporters who had previously stood on unity tickets with the CPA for the Sydney branch executive, while Fingleton was a leading Grouper and secretary of the Sydney WWF Mechanical Branch. Undated '[Hartley] Third Report,' CPA CDC files, C17.

6 CPA CDC files, C17.

7 'Healy, Nelson and some of the other CPA functionaries would've been involved ... probably Don Morcom ... and they kept it pretty close to their chests until they were ready to blow it.' Interview with former CPA WWF member, who wishes to remain anonymous, 4 August 1994.

8 Interview with former CPA WWF member, who wishes to remain anonymous, 4 August 1994.

9 It was a propitious moment for Hartley to challenge Campbell, because he had just attended a meeting of the Groupers' Sydney inner sanctum—Brooks, Macken, and Fingleton—at a local waterfront watering hole, the Dumbarton Castle hotel. Apparently now desperate to demonstrate his preparedness to co-operate with his old comrades, Campbell produced a copy of the Groupers' leaflet supporting John (Paddy) Kenneally for the position of returning officer in the union

national election. Nine-page statutory declaration of Vic Campbell, 8 April 1958; and anonymous report of 20 February 1958 (written by Jack Hartley), CPA CDC files, C17. Bill Brooks confirmed the basic accuracy of most of Campbell's statutory declarations, although he maintained that there were some exaggerations on some points. Interview with Bill Brooks, 29 August 1994.

10 'Last Sunday 16th February, I was in the Trade Union Club and got into a discussion with C[ampbell]'. After the confrontation, Campbell 'took me to the phone and invited me to listen whilst he called Fingleton ... I listened in on the phone. He spoke to Fingleton about a meeting that was to take place in Melbourne of opponents of the existing Federation officials.' Hartley then listened in to Campbell and Macken's phone conversation. 'Mains (sic) was going through to Brisbane to try and convince the Assistant Secretary, Wilkinson to run against Roach. Bill Brooks, and G. Fingleton are in on this and are the leading lights in it in Sydney. The suggestion is that F. Ellis will oppose Nelson, but he will not get the support of the Groupers. The Groupers are trying to set C. in for the [Sydney] Secretaryship.' Anonymous report of 20 February 1958, (written by Jack Hartley), CPA CDC files, C17.

11 Nine-page statutory declaration of Vic Campbell, 8 April 1958; anonymous report of 20 February 1958, (written by Jack Hartley); and undated '[Hartley] Report No. 2', CPA CDC files, C17.

12 Anonymous report of 20 February 1958, (written by Jack Hartley); undated '[Hartley] Report No. 2'; and nine-page Statutory Declaration of Vic Campbell, 8 April 1958, CPA CDC files, C17.

13 Op.Cit. Hartley's life now became hectic. He met Campbell again on 23 February, obtaining 'some notes from him which were handed over to the General Secretary.' Undated '[Hartley] Third Report,' CPA CDC files, C17.

14 '[Hartley] Seventh Report' of 6 March 1958, CPA CDC files, C17.

15 Interview with John Burraston, 18 August 1994.

16 Second '[Hartley] Eighth Report' of 13 March 1958, and Statutory Declaration by Vic Campbell of 8 April 1958, CPA CDC files, C17.

17 Second '[Hartley] Eighth Report' of 13 March 1958, CPA CDC files, C17.

18 Interview with John Burraston, 18 August 1994.

19 Second '[Hartley] Eighth Report' of 13 March 1958, CPA CDC files, C17.

20 '[Hartley] Seventh Report' of 6 March 1958, and Second '[Hartley]

Eighth Report' of 13 March 1958, CPA CDC files, C17. Hartley had reported that Shortell was to arrange for accommodation at the Quay for them so that they would have an office. Hartley had listened to Campbell's phone call to Fingleton about Shortell getting them an office at the Quay. Fingleton told Campbell 'they would have to see' Macken about this. Undated '[Hartley] Fifth Report,' CPA CDC files, C17. But when approached, Macken was adamant that Campbell 'raise that in Melbourne with Maynes', who later confirmed that it would be in Customs House. Anonymous report of 20 February 1958, (written by Jack Hartley), CPA CDC files, C17. On The Movement's support for Shortell, see Duncan, *Crusade or Conspiracy?*, p. 187.

21 Undated '[Hartley] Report No. 2.', CPA CDC files, C17.

22 '[Hartley] Sixth Report' of 4 March 1958, and '[Hartley] Seventh Report' of 6 March 1958, CPA CDC files, C17.

23 Leaflet of 13 March 1958 issued by Tom Nelson, Jim Young, and Sid Barrett, copy in my possession.

24 *Wharfie*, 13 March 1958, copy in my possession. The CPA press followed up with major front-page feature length articles on the affair. See, for example, *The Guardian*, 17 April 1958.

25 A few days later, Campbell informed his CPA handler, Jack Hartley, that Macken had told him that they intended to sue the union over the leaflet's contents. Macken 'had made arrangements for a person to be at the meeting to take shorthand notes'. This did not concern the CPA, which knew it had the goods on its enemy. '[Hartley] Ninth Report' of 17 March 1958, CPA CDC files, C17.

26 '[Hartley] Tenth Report' of 18 March 1958 and '[Hartley] Report' of 20 March 1958, CPA CDC files, C17.

27 Hartley reported on 25 March that Campbell 'says ... it does not look like, we can continue, or go much further over this week.. O'Brien, Burraston, and Brooks were also present at the meeting with Alford and Macken. '[Hartley] Report' of 25 March 1958 and '[Hartley] Report' of 28 March 1958, CPA CDC files, C17.

28 '[Hartley] Reports' of 28 March and 1 April 1958, CPA CDC files, C17.

29 '[Hartley] Report' of 31 March 1958, CPA CDC files, C17.

30 Campbell's 'wife answered each time and stated that C was not home'. '[Hartley] Report' of 31 March 1958, CPA CDC files, C17.

31 '[Hartley] Report' of 1 April 1958, CPA CDC files, C17.

32 Interview with a former Movement member who wishes to remain anonymous, 13 September 1994.

33 Interview with Bill Brooks, 29 August 1994.

34 For examples of this propaganda, see All Branches and Federal Councillors national office circular, 17 April 1958, and Rank and File Committee leaflet, late June 1958, B & L Archives, Z248, box 63 and box 68A, WWF records.

35 General Secretary's Report, Seventh All Ports Biennial Conference, 22 September 1958, B & L Archives, Z248, box 56, WWF records.

36 Conversations between the author and Norm Docker, late 1970s and early 1980s.

37 See ASIO Index Card summarising agent's report of 5 June 1959, report from ASIO WA Regional Director to NSW Regional Director, 8 June 1960, and ASIO index cards summarising reports of 7 December 1961, 5 and 15 November 1962, 1 February 1963, 26 November 1963, 4 and 6 December 1963, 25 July 1964, NAA A6126, Item 625.

38 Interview with Sydney wharfie Paddy Kenneally, 19 September 1994.

Chapter 9 / The ghost of Stalinism

1   Memo to ASIO headquarters from Regional Director NSW, 8 December 1970, NAA A6122, item 1522.

2   Report of 9 November 1970, NAA A6122, item 1522.

3   Interview with John Grenville, circa August 1977, NSW SL MLOH 777. Maynes also received an honorarium as Victorian president.

4   Interview with John Grenville, 15 November 2014.

5   Interview with John Grenville, circa August 1977, NSW SL MLOH 777.

6   Interview with John Grenville, 15 November 2014. Maynes was supremely confident that Jordan would deliver on this undertaking, as he reported to the June 1966 NCC National Conference on the situation at the Trades Hall: 'Position gradually improving. (Expect appointment of favourable Research Officer.)' Industrial notes presented to 1966 National Conference, SLV MS 13492, series IX, box 5, folder 2.

7   Interview with John Grenville, circa August 1977, NSW SL MLOH 777.

8   Ibid.

9   Interview with John Grenville, 15 November 2014.

10 Interview with John Grenville, circa August 1977, NSW SL MLOH 777.

11 Interview with John Grenville, 15 November 2014.

12 Interview with John Grenville, circa August 1977, NSW SL MLOH 777.

13 David McKnight, Age, 20 February 2003. On Lindahl, see Richard

C. S. Trahair and Robert Lawrence Miller, *Encyclopedia of Cold War Espionage, Spies, and Secret Operations*, Enigma Books, New York, 2012, p. 211.

14 Letter of 13 September 1971 to Duncan Cameron, Victorian Secretary clerks' union, NSW SL ML MSS 9329, box 26, Allegations about Grenville's membership of the Federated Clerks' Union file.

15 Interview with John Grenville, circa August 1977, NSW SL MLOH 777.

16 Ibid.

17 NSW SL ML MSS 9329, box 26, Allegations about Grenville's membership of the Federated Clerks' Union file.

18 Interview with John Grenville, circa August 1977, NSW SL MLOH 777.

19 Ibid.

20 Ibid.

21 Ibid.

22 Ibid.

23 Ibid.

24 See 'Union head from the other side', *Business Age*, 18 September 1975 for an account of Egan's union career. For his own account, see Barry Egan interview transcript, 25 January 1980, NSW SL ML MSS 9329, box 30, Barry Egan Interview file.

25 Interview with John Grenville, circa August 1977, NSW SL MLOH 777.

26 Interview with Barry Egan, 25 January 1980, NSW SL ML MSS 9329, box 30, Barry Egan Interview file.

27 Interview with John Grenville, circa August 1977, NSW SL MLOH 777.

Chapter 10 / The Show, the CIA, and international unionism

1 There is a rich amount of source material dealing with this issue. See, for example, Fred Hirsch and Richard Fletcher, *CIA and the Labour Movement*, Spokeman Books, London, 1977; Lenny Siegel, 'AFL–CIA' in *Pacific Research & World Empire Telegram*, volume VI, number 1, November–December, East Palo Alto, 1974; Lenny Siegel, 'Asian Labor: The American Connection', in *Pacific Research & World Empire Telegram*, volume VI, number 5, July–August, East Palo Alto, 1975. On US congressional inquiries, the report of the House Permanent Select Committee on Intelligence conducted in 1975–76 and chaired

by Otis Pike was never officially released; however, the final draft report was leaked to the media and published in Britain as *CIA: the Pike Report*, Spokesman Books, London, 1977. The United States Senate Select Committee to Study Governmental Operations with Respect to Intelligence Activities, chaired by Senator Frank Church, published fourteen damning reports on a number of US intelligence agencies, particularly the CIA.

2   For example, Ronald Radosh published an influential book in 1969 exposing many aspects of US-directed operations in the international trade union movement, *American Labor and United States Foreign Policy*, Random House, New York, 1969.

3   On the origins of IFPCW, see Steve Lucas, *Freedom's War: the US Crusade Against the Soviet Union, 1945–56*, New York University Press, New York, 1999, p. 113. On Haskins, see Les Leopold, *The Man Who Hated Work and Loved Labor: the life and times of Tony Mazzocchi*, Chelsea Green, White River Junction, 2007.

4   On the British Guyana operation, see Stephen G. Rabe, *U.S. Intervention in British Guyana: a Cold War Story*, The University of North Carolina Press, Chapel Hill, 2005.

5   Interview with John Grenville, circa August 1977, NSW SL MLOH 777.

6   Letter of 19 September 1973 from Maynes to O'Keefe, NSW SL ML MSS 9329, box 26, International file. O'Keefe's role on behalf of the CIA was the subject of hearings before the Church Committee (the United States Senate Select Committee to Study Governmental Operations with Respect to Intelligence Activities), chaired by Frank Church. O'Keefe was also one of the CIA–Labor operatives involved in the British Guyana covert operation to destabilise the Cheddi Jagan government, see Richard J. Barnet, *Intervention and Revolution: the United States in the Third World*, World Publishing, 1968 and Rabe, *U.S. Intervention in British Guyana*. Grenville stated that at the February 1973 meeting of the clerks' union's federal executive committee, Maynes arranged that he would have sole preserve in the international arena. Interview with John Grenville, circa August 1977, NSW SL MLOH 777.

7   Interview with Barry Egan, 23 July 1977, NSW SL MLOH 777.

8   Interview with John Grenville, circa August 1977, NSW SL MLOH 777.

9   Interview with Barry Egan, 23 July 1977, NSW SL MLOH 777.

10 Interview with John Grenville, circa August 1977, NSW SL MLOH 777.
11 Ibid.
12 Ibid.
13 Ibid. Santamaria had been building a base in Asia for the previous twenty years. See Duncan, *Crusade or Conspiracy?*, p. 275.
14 Interview with John Forrester, 1 December 1982, NSW SL MLOH 777; and *Background Briefing*, ABC Radio National, 12 December 1982.
15 Interview with John Grenville, circa August 1977, NSW SL MLOH 777.
16 Op. cit.
17 Op. cit.
18 Report by J. P. Maynes, clerks' union federal president, 'Where I Went and Why', 14 May 1974, NSW SL ML MSS 9329, box 26, International file.
19 Interview with John Grenville, circa August 1977, NSW SL MLOH 777.
20 See series of four articles by Goldberg in the AFL's *Free Trade Union News*, 1952.
21 Report by J. P. Maynes, clerks' union federal president, 'Where I Went and Why', 14 May 1974, NSW SL ML MSS 9329, box 26, International file. On Lee's role in the British Guyana operation see Rabe, *U.S. Intervention in British Guyana*.
22 Goldberg's reports were supplied to me by David Ransom, commencing with two reports from the beginning of February 1966, then 21 February, 1 May, 18 July, 23, 28, and 29 November 1966.
23 *Sydney Morning Herald*, 28 March 1960.
24 As described to me by my father, Laurie Aarons.
25 Harry Goldberg, report on his Australian visit, Honolulu, 9 April 1960, published in *Underground Tribune*, 1961; republished *Tribune*, 11 May 1977.
26 Ibid.
27 Ibid.
28 Ibid.
29 Ibid.

Chapter II / The NCC schism

1 Interview with John Grenville, circa August 1977, NSW SL MLOH 777.
2 Interviews with John Grenville, circa August 1977, NSW SL MLOH

777 and 24 April 2016.

3   Interview with John Grenville, circa August 1977, NSW SL MLOH 777. John Forrester was also adamant that Maynes and Harry Hurrell (of the ironworkers' union) were the two principal 'bagmen' for the NCC in collecting funds from large employers, especially from the aluminium, oil, and chemical industries. Interview, circa July–August 1977, NSW SL MLOH 777. Greg Sheridan gives an insider's account of the NCC's fundraising among big business in *When We Were Young & Foolish: a memoir of my misguided youth with Tony Abbott, Bob Carr, Malcolm Turnbull, Kevin Rudd & other reprobates ...*, Allen & Unwin, Crows Nest, 2015. He especially credits NSW DLP Senator Jack Kane with being the source of much of this finance, a great deal coming from the Packer family, Frank and Kerry, but also from a wide range of business contacts. See, for example, Kindle edition, Locations 2951, 2969, 2970, and 2980. Sheridan also gives a lively account of the NSW ALP right wing's fundraising with big business, especially by union and party powerbroker John Ducker.

4   Interview with John Grenville, 24 April 2016.

5   Interview with John Grenville, circa August 1977, NSW SL MLOH 777. The letter Grenville quoted is dated 9 April 1975. See NSW SL ML MSS 9329, box 27, Health Funds Exposure file.

6   Interview with John Grenville, 24 April 2016.

7   Interview with John Grenville, circa August 1977, NSW SL MLOH 777.

8   Ibid.; letter from John Forrester to Bob Santamaria, 21 May 1975; letter from John Grenville to Bob Santamaria, 15 May 1975, NSW SL ML MSS 9329, box 27, Appeals of Grenville and Forrester to B.A. Santamaria and related papers file.

9   Interview with John Grenville, circa August 1977, NSW SL MLOH 777.

10   Letter from John Forrester to Bob Santamaria, 21 May 1975; letter from John Grenville to Bob Santamaria, 15 May 1975, NSW SL ML MSS 9329, box 27, Appeals of Grenville and Forrester to B.A. Santamaria and related papers file.

11   Letter from John Grenville to Bob Santamaria, 15 May 1975, NSW SL ML MSS 9329, box 27, Appeals of Grenville and Forrester to B.A. Santamaria and related papers file.

12   Letter from John Forrester to Bob Santamaria, 21 May 1975, NSW SL ML MSS 9329, box 27, Appeals of Grenville and Forrester to B.A. Santamaria and related papers file.

13 Interview with John Grenville, 24 April 2016.

14 Interview with John Grenville, circa August 1977, NSW SL MLOH 777.

15 Ibid.

16 Two letters from John Forrester to Bob Santamaria, 21 May 1975; letter from John Grenville to Bob Santamaria, 15 May 1975, NSW SL ML MSS 9329, box 27, Appeals of Grenville and Forrester to B.A. Santamaria and related papers file.

17 Letter from John Grenville to Bob Santamaria, 15 May 1975, NSW SL ML MSS 9329, box 27, Appeals of Grenville and Forrester to B.A. Santamaria and related papers file.

18 Interview with John Grenville, circa August 1977, NSW SL MLOH 777.

19 Interview with John Grenville, 24 April 2016.

20 Interviews with John Grenville, circa August 1977, NSW SL MLOH 777 and 24 April 2016.

21 Interview with John Grenville, circa August 1977, NSW SL MLOH 777.

22 Ibid.

23 Forrester letter to Santamaria, 12 August 1975, NSW SL ML MSS 9329, box 27, Appeals of Grenville and Forrester to B.A. Santamaria and related papers file.

24 Interview with John Grenville, 24 April 2016.

25 Ibid.

26 Interview with John Grenville, 3 December 1982, NSW SL MLOH 777.

27 Interview with John Grenville, circa August 1977, NSW SL MLOH 777.

28 Ibid.; letter by Brian Mullins to 'Dear Pat', NSW SL ML MSS 9329.

29 Interview with John Grenville, circa August 1977, NSW SL MLOH 777; letter by Brian Mullins, NSW SL ML MSS 9329.

30 Letter of 18 August 1976 to T W Sullivan, NSW SL ML MSS 9329, box 33, NCC and FCU file. Forrester also discussed this conversation with Santamaria in a recorded interview conducted circa July–August 1977, NSW SL MLOH 777. John Grenville corroborated Forrester's account, reporting he had a similar conversation with Santamaria in May 1975, in which he was informed that Santamaria had had to cancel a planned trip to visit Lausanne, Switzerland, because of embarrassment caused by Maynes's globe-trotting. Interview, 30 June 2016.

31 Interview with John Grenville, circa August 1977, NSW SL MLOH 777.
32 Ibid.
33 For an excellent account of these events see Duncan, *Crusade or Conspiracy?*, especially chapters 16 to 22.
34 Lindsay Tanner, *The Last Battle*, p. 41.
35 Op. cit., p. 67.
36 Op. cit., p. 82.
37 Op. cit., p. 94.
38 Op. cit., pp. 145–46.
39 *News Weekly*, 17 August 1991.

Chapter 12 – The cult of personality

1   Gerard Henderson, 'B.A. Santamaria, Santamariaism and the cult of personality', in *50 Years of the Santamaria Movement*, Eureka Street Papers Number 1, Melbourne, N.D., pp. 43–44.
2   In his 2015 biography, *Santamaria: a most unusual man*, Henderson altered this—without explanation—to: 'The original agenda, as circulated, lists a total of eight papers to be delivered over two days—all but two are to be by Santamaria.' Kindle file, Location 6954.
3   Henderson, 'B.A. Santamaria, Santamariaism and the cult of personality', p. 44.
4   Op. cit., pp. 44–45.
5   Louis Nowra, "The Whirling Dervish", *The Monthly*, February 2010.
6   *National Civic Council: Fortieth Anniversary Dinner Souvenir*, NSW SL ML MSS 9329, box 27, Fortieth Anniversary Dinner file.
7   Letter written by John Cotter, 3 August 1981, NSW SL ML MSS 9329, box 27, Fortieth Anniversary Dinner file.
8   Ibid.
9   B.A. Santamaria, *The Price of Freedom*, The Campion Press, Melbourne, 1964, p. 28.
10 B.A. Santamaria, *Against the Tide*, p. 76.
11 Mosely to Director General of Security, W.B. Simpson, 2 August 1944, and attached 'Report on Anti-Communist Campaign', NAA A6122, item 129.
12 Santamaria, *Against the Tide*, p. 76, and minutes of The Show's 1944 National Conference, SLV MS 13492, series IX, box 1, folder 1.
13 Morgan (ed.), *B.A. Santamaria: Running The Show*, pp. 456–57. Santamaria's account of these events makes no mention of Lauritz's

involvement, instead giving prominence to H.M. (Bert) Cremean's role. *Against the Tide*, p. 73.

14 Morgan (ed.), B.A. *Santamaria: Running The Show*, p. 458.

15 Laffin, *Matthew Beovich*, p. 170.

16 Memo from Mosely to Director General of Security, W.B. Simpson, 2 August 1944, and attached 'Report on Anti-Communist Campaign', NAA A6122, item 129.

17 Annual Report presented by Santamaria to the bishops' conference, 19 September 1945. My copy was obtained from Ed Campion.

18 Memos from Richards to Deputy Director for W.A., 6 July 1944, Deputy Director for W.A. to Director General, 6 July 1944, and Mosely to Director General of Security, W.B. Simpson, 2 August 1944, and attached 'Report on Anti-Communist Campaign', NAA A6122, item 129.

19 The official minutes of the meeting record the following: 'In the evening session, at 7:30 pm, Mr. B.A. Santamaria was invited to be present, in order to answer questions about the Movement proposed by various Bishops.' This information was provided by Father Stephen Hackett, the general secretary of the Australian Catholic Bishops' Conference via its archivist/librarian, Leonie Kennedy.

20 Henderson, 'B.A. Santamaria, Santamariaism and the cult of personality', p. 46.

21 Writ issued on the 8th day of October 1982, In the Supreme Court of Victoria, No. 8038 of 1982, NSW SL ML MSS 9329, box 27, Supreme Court file.

22 Affidavit of Gerald Mercer, In the Supreme Court of Victoria, No. 8038 of 1982, 14 October 1982, p. 7, NSW SL ML MSS 9329, box 27, Supreme Court file. John Forrester traced the divisions between Santamaria and Maynes back to at least the early 1970s. One issue he highlighted was Maynes's failure to visit South Vietnam regularly in the late 1960s and early 1970s, which Santamaria was critical of, especially as he visited the country regularly himself and travelled widely throughout the countryside. Forrester interview, circa July–August 1977, NSW SL MLOH 777. For another account of the divisions and ultimate split in the NCC, see Henderson, *Santamaria*, chapter seventeen. See also Morgan (ed.), *Running the Show*, chapter twelve, which confirms the Maynes group's account of the immediate causes of the split.

23 Morgan (ed.), *Running the Show*, p. 386.

24 Statement by the NCC national executive, *Newsweekly*, 27 October 1982.

25 Industrial Action Fund brochure, 'Keep the fight going', NSW SL ML MSS 9329, box 27, IAF file.

26 Bob Carr, 'Split reported in the NCC', *The Bulletin*, 15 July 1980.

27 Affidavit of Gerald Mercer, In the Supreme Court of Victoria, No. 8038 of 1982, 14 October 1982, p. 7, NSW SL ML MSS 9329, box 27, Supreme Court file.

28 Writ issued on the 8th day of October 1982 (Statement of Claim), In the Supreme Court of Victoria, No. 8038 of 1982, p. 6, NSW SL ML MSS 9329, box 27, Supreme Court file.

29 Carr, 'Split reported in the NCC', *The Bulletin*, 15 July 1980.

30 Writ issued on the 8th day of October 1982 (Statement of Claim), In the Supreme Court of Victoria, No. 8038 of 1982, p. 6; Industrial Action Fund brochure, 'Keep the fight going', NSW SL ML MSS 9329, box 27, Supreme Court and IAF files; Henderson, *Santamaria*, Kindle file, Location 7721; and Morgan (ed.), *Running the Show*, p. 379.

31 Industrial Action Fund brochure, 'Keep the fight going', NSW SL ML MSS 9329, box 27, IAF file.

32 Santamaria letter of 20 May 1983, NSW SL ML MSS 9329, box 27, IAF file.

33 Affidavit of Gerald Mercer, In the Supreme Court of Victoria, No. 8038 of 1982, 14 October 1982, p. 9, NSW SL ML MSS 9329, box 27, Supreme Court file.

34 Affidavit of Peter Westmore, In the Supreme Court of Victoria, No. 8038 of 1982, 19 October 1982, p. 3, NSW SL ML MSS 9329, box 27, Supreme Court file.

35 Affidavit of Gerald Mercer, In the Supreme Court of Victoria, No. 8038 of 1982, 14 October 1982, p. 13, NSW SL ML MSS 9329, box 27, Supreme Court file.

36 Op. cit., p. 14.

37 Santamaria letter of 20 May 1983, NSW SL ML MSS 9329, box 27, IAF file.

38 Quoted in Henderson, *Santamaria*, Kindle file, Location 7819. In fact, Santamaria had first issued this edict many weeks earlier, in July 1982; in replying to Maynes's proposal for a phased reunification of the organisation, Santamaria had written that then current full-time officers 'would be offered re-employment on the basis' that they 'accept direct responsibility to the N.P. [National President—that is, Santamaria] as chief executive officer (according to the 1966 Resolution) and to no other person'. He also made it clear in his reply to Mercer (although in

a somewhat more muted form), writing that he and the other dissidents must be 'subject to accountability to whoever may be the superior officer'. Morgan (ed.), *Running the Show*, pp. 388–89.

39 Santamaria letter of 20 May 1983, NSW SL ML MSS 9329, box 27, IAF file.

40 Judgement of Justice Beach, In the Supreme Court of Victoria, No. 8038 of 1982, 14 October 1982, pp. 6–7, NSW SL ML MSS 9329, box 27, Supreme Court file.

41 Op. cit., p. 8.

42 Letter from Rennick & Gaynor (Santamaria's solicitors) acting on behalf of both parties, 9 May 1983, NSW SL ML MSS 9329, box 27, Supreme Court file.

43 Henderson, *Santamaria*, Kindle file, Location 7763.

44 IAF letter by Appeal Chairman John Fox, 13 May 1983, NSW SL ML MSS 9329, box 27, IAF file.

45 See Industrial Action Fund brochure, 'Keep the fight going' and Santamaria's Statement of Claim, In the Supreme Court of Victoria, ND, pp. 2–3, NSW SL ML MSS 9329, box 27, IAF and Supreme Court files; Henderson, *Santamaria*, Kindle file, Location 7771.

46 Santamaria statement, 24 June 1980, quoted in Industrial Action Fund brochure, 'Keep the fight going', NSW SL ML MSS 9329, box 27, IAF file.

47 Santamaria statement, 25 June 1980, quoted in Industrial Action Fund brochure, 'Keep the fight going', NSW SL ML MSS 9329, box 27, IAF file.

48 Santamaria letter of 20 May 1983, NSW SL ML MSS 9329, box 27, IAF file.

49 Ibid. In a somewhat caustic phrase, after the split was finalised Santamaria ironically referred to the 'purged group … as "our separated brethren".' Morgan (ed.), *Running the Show*, p. 380.

Postscript

1 Interview with Frank Knopfelmacher, 6 December 1982, NSW SL MLOH 777. His reference to Hans Kuhn was in error. The book he mentions was *The Politics of Cultural Despair: a study in the rise of the Germanic ideology* by Fritz Stern.

2 Morgan (ed.), *B.A. Santamaria: Your most obedient servant*, pp. 73–74.

3 Industrial Action Fund brochure, 'Keep the fight going', NSW SL ML

MSS 9329, box 27, IAF file.

4 For an account of such matters, see Ben Schneiders and Royce Millar, 'Shopped Out', in the Fairfax magazine *The Good Weekend*, 3–4 September 2016.

5 *Sydney Morning Herald*, 28 May 1983.

6 See David Hirst's article, 'Santamaria and the deeply divided NCC', *The Australian*, 27 May 1983, and Santamaria's letter published in *The Australian Financial Review*, October 1982.

7 B.A. Santamaria, 'The Movement into the Eighties: A Study Paper', National Civic Council Extension Committee, ND, NSW SL ML MSS 9329, box 27, Fortieth Anniversary Dinner file.

8 Interview with John Grenville, 3 December 1982, NSW SL MLOH 777.

9 B.A. Santamaria, 'The Movement into the Eighties: A Study Paper', National Civic Council Extension Committee, ND, NSW SL ML MSS 9329, box 27, Fortieth Anniversary Dinner file.

10 Ibid.

11 Ibid.

12 Ibid.

13 Ibid.

14 Ibid.

15 Geoffrey Barker, 'Cold Warriors', *The Australian Financial Review Magazine*, 29 November 1996.

16 Ibid.

17 Ibid.

18 Interview with John Forrester, 1 December 1982, NSW SL MLOH 777.

19 Ibid.

Index

118; disciplined organisation,
11, 21, 32; leadership, 11,
20, 25, 31, 99, 199, (central
committee), 21–2, 95, 117,
(dishonesty), 18
Sydney branch, 110–11; as
headquarters, 48, 95
see also Show, The
Cremean, Bert, 218, 248
Crowe, William, 220

Darroch, Harry, 173
Davis, Kevin, 51
Democratic Labor Party (DLP), 32,
135, 138, 146, 181
Dezman, Franz, 85
Dixon, Richard (Dick), 21,25,113,178
Docker, Norm, 131, 132
Dowling, Frank, 138
Dubček, Alexander
and the Prague Spring, 133–4
Duhig, Archbishop James, 24, 25, 26,
27–8, 223–4
Duncan, Bruce
Crusade or Conspiracy?, xv, 25, 39,
221, 227, 232

Egan, Barry, 143, 146, 148, 149, 157,
170, 172
Evatt, H.V. (Bert)
and BAS, 38, 226
and The Movement, 38;
denounces it, 35, 38–9, 42–3
precipitates Labor Split, 35

Farrell, Ted, 77, 78, 79
and intelligence-gathering, 80,
81–3, 84, 85–90, 92, 93, 98–9,
100, 231, 232
liaising with ASIO, 85, 94
runs school for Show members,
100, 101–3

Ferguson, Jack, 84, 233
Finger, Alan, 20
Fingleton, Glen, 239
Fitzgibbon, Charlie, 131, 132
Forrester, John, 208, 249
supporters of, 168–9, 171
unionist and NCC member, 151,
152, 157, 159, 208, 246; and
conflict, 162, 163–5, 166–7, 169–
71, 188; defeat, 171, 172, 173
Franco, Francisco, 37, 226
Franklin, James, 228
Fraser, Malcolm
and BAS, 180–1

Galleghan, Frederick, 46
Gay, Michael, 174
Gilroy, Cardinal Norman, 45, 52, 53,
228
Gleeson, Archbishop James, 79
Goldberg, Harry, 153, 154–6
Goodman, Hector, 87
Grenville, John, i, 167–8, 171–2,
204, 221, 223, 234
as an industrial advocate, 136;
on staff at Trades Hall, 136–7,
(assistant secretary), 137–8, 139
and Maynes, 138, 146, 147, 160,
171; disenchantment, conflict,
149, 150–1, 152, 153, 157–9,
161–6, 167, 188
as member of clerks' union, 139,
140, (expelled), 167, (reinstated),
175; dummy employer, 140–1;
as federal secretary, 141–3, 146,
147, 149, 151–2, 157–9, 160,
174, 244, (resigns), 167
as NCC member, 135, 223, 138,
139–40, 141–2, 148, 149, 161,
163–5, 176, (pressure), 138;
employed by, 140; resigns, 166
Grenville, Mary, 167

intelligence agencies, 147, 243–4
embassy in Australia, 105, 127, 139

Wake, Bob, 51
Warhurst, John, 78–9, 232
Weiner, Herbert, 105, 106

Westmore, Peter, 187, 191
Whitlam, Gough, 32, 140
Whitlam government
 and ASIO, 61
World War II, 3, 19
Wright, Tom, 20, 117